ALSO BY RUBY TANDOH

Eat Up!

Cook
As
You
Are

RUBY TANDOH

Cook As You Are

RECIPES FOR REAL LIFE, HUNGRY COOKS, AND MESSY KITCHENS

Alfred A. Knopf   New York   2022

Library of Congress Cataloging-in-Publication Data
Names: Tandoh, Ruby, author. | Park, Sinae, illustrator.
Title: Cook as you are : recipes for real life, hungry cooks, and messy kitchens / Ruby Tandoh ; illustrations by Sinae Park.
Description: First American edition. | New York : Alfred A. Knopf, [2022] | Includes index.
Identifiers: LCCN 2022001815 (print) | LCCN 2022001816 (ebook) | ISBN 9780593321546 (hardcover) | ISBN 9780593321553 (ebook)
Subjects: LCSH: International cooking. | LCGFT: Cookbooks.
Classification: LCC TX725.A1 T323 2022 (print) | LCC TX725.A1 (ebook) | DDC 641.59—dc23/eng/20220419
LC record available at https://lccn.loc.gov/2022001815
LC ebook record available at https://lccn.loc.gov/2022001816

Some of the recipes in this book include raw eggs, meat, or fish. When these foods are consumed raw, there is always the risk that bacteria, which is killed by proper cooking, may be present. For this reason, when serving these foods raw, always buy certified salmonella-free eggs and the freshest meat and fish available from a reliable grocer, storing them in the refrigerator until they are served. Because of the health risks associated with the consumption of bacteria that can be present in raw eggs, meat, and fish, these foods should not be consumed by infants, small children, pregnant women, the elderly, or any persons who may be immunocompromised. The author and publisher expressly disclaim responsibility for any adverse effects that may result from the use or application of the recipes and information contained in this book.

Illustrations by Sinae Park
Jacket illustration by Sinae Park
Jacket design by Linda Huang
Book design: Evelin Kasikov and M. Kristen Bearse
Manufactured in China
First American Edition

Contents

Introduction

No two people cook alike. Some of you might fry plantain at 2 a.m. while your roommate is asleep. Others will spend languorous hours making stew for the family on a Sunday afternoon. You might be a master of microwave cooking, or assemble towering, legendary birthday cakes, or stand anxious watch over the jollof rice while it cooks. Maybe you cook with curiosity, plucking ingredients from outside your comfort zone to get a taste of something good and new. Or perhaps you cook in a fugue state, just getting some easy nutrition in before your shift starts. Some cooks move with their appetite; others work methodically through the basics. There are cooks in gleaming kitchens and those toiling over a hot plate. Some of you will hardly cook at all, perhaps preferring to immerse yourself in cookbook daydreams while eating a frozen dinner. That's fine too. Our ways of cooking are as diverse as we are, reflecting every conceivable taste, talent, culture, body, ability (or disability), kitchen, mindset and skill set. I think that's something to be grateful for.

Too often when we cook, we turn the old cliché inside out: instead of *you are what you eat*, it becomes *you eat what you want to be*—how you think you should be, what you believe you deserve. We cook and eat as a way of traveling up or down in society, in the esteem of our friends and in our own self-worth. We try to cook ourselves better somehow—maybe into a different body or a bigger kitchen or a more accomplished persona—instead of meeting our hungers here and now, as we are. Sometimes these aspirations can push us outside our comfort zones and lead us towards new experiences. But much of the time, we're so stuck in striving that we lose sight of the good stuff already right here in front of us: the way onions cook in butter, the fun of a corner-store snack haul, the guidance of our own gut feelings.

So, when I ask you to cook as you are, it's a vague direction, and one that could lead you along any of countless different paths. The aim of this book—with six chapters, from everyday dinners in **Feed me now** to low-effort cooking in **More food, less work** and immersive cooking projects in **For the love of it**—is to afford you the space to discover what kind of cooking works for you. You'll find that a lot of the recipes here (especially in **Hidden in plain sight**) repurpose pantry staples, showing familiar and inexpensive ingredients in a new light. There's a focus on flexible daily cooking, with variation and substitution ideas giving you the freedom to adapt recipes to your needs. There are special-occasion meals in **Wild appetites**, or cooking ideas to furnish the everyday in **Normal perfect moments**. At every step, it's about encouraging you to see the goodness—in your kitchen, your food and yourself—that might ordinarily go unnoticed.

To be clear, I'm not claiming that this cookbook will accurately capture every aspect of every reader's life. I'm a cook like you, with my own likes and dislikes, cultural reference points, strengths and weaknesses. Everything that I am and that I have been through informs, in one way or another, how I cook and eat. So, in this book, you'll see my heritage come through in the West African recipes. My Britishness comes out when I linger on the merits of custard powder or Yorkshire puddings, or sing the praises of the corner store (or bodega, convenience store, 7-Eleven—whatever you want to call the little miracle store near you). Between the lines of "junk" food recipes, you'll read a little of my upbringing. You'll probably gather from the number of vegetarian and vegan recipes that I don't eat much meat. No matter what some may claim, a cookbook can never be an objective thing: at best, it is an act of curation, spinning together many food stories into one instructive document. But as you cook from this book, I really hope you'll see enough of yourself and your life in it to be inspired. My dream is that instead of taking these recipes as gospel, you'll rehash them to suit you and create your own kitchen folklore.

In case you haven't already realized, this cookbook doesn't have photos. I know how useful photos can be, especially if you're a visual learner or if you're not a confident reader. Photos can give us something to aim for, or a standard to hold our cooking attempts up against to judge how well we've done. If you absolutely need photos, I'd encourage you to find a cookbook that will deliver on that front—there are many to choose from. But for most cooks I don't believe things are that black and white.

When we look through cookbooks at the photos (and believe me, I love doing this as much as you do), we're not just gleaning clues about what the food is and how to prepare it. We're also absorbing cues about lifestyle, class and background, from everything from the silverware on the table to the (usually) white hands stirring the pot. This can be a beautiful thing, allowing author, photographer, stylist and home economist to evoke a sense of place and time, setting the dishes in an appropriate cultural context or simply showing the food in the best possible light. But it can also be limiting: by photographing a cookbook in one kitchen, with one cook, I'd be capturing only one very narrow vision of what cooking looks like and who these recipes are for. Such photos can also end up feeling aspirational, drawing us towards the often-unattainable shiny and new.

With *Cook As You Are*, I knew the focus had to be different. I wanted a book that would show food being made in many different kitchens, by many different people—some of whom may remind you of yourself as you already are. The focus of the imagery here is less on the food itself than on the places, hungers and cultures from which that food is born. Food needs cooks and eaters: without those human elements, it's just *stuff*.

I know that this may be daunting if you're used to the gloss and promise of photography, but I won't leave you in the lurch. Sinae Park, the illustrator of this book, has created dozens of beautiful images that capture particularly important parts of the cooking process, from how to fold flatbreads to the easiest way to fill pierogi. And from me you can expect extra help with sensory cues so you know what to look out for when cooking, as well as descriptions of what kind of dish something is and how it might look. I've been deliberately thorough in my instructions in the hope that you'll find comfort in my words. A photo might speak a thousand words, but it can't tell you what something should smell like, or explain the texture of kneaded bread dough, or reassure you that it's all going to work out fine.

My hope is that you'll start to judge your success by whether the food tastes, smells and looks good to you—not by whether it matches up with a photo of a meal staged by a food stylist for a cookbook photo shoot. Think hard about what you consider to be good cooking. Sometimes this is just whatever fills you up: you can put those dreams of perfectly hosted dinners for friends to one side and settle comfortably in the realm of the everyday.

Turning your kitchen into a tiny dictatorship doesn't help anyone. The more upset you get at yourself for your real or imagined mistakes, the more likely it is that your cooking will be shaped by that fear, and you'll end up with burnt onions and split custards.

A lot of the time, cooking is just functional: we cook to live, not the other way round. But if you're reading this book, I'm guessing that there are at least moments in your life when food rises beyond mere sustenance, when you want to enjoy yourself as you cook and eat. And there is so much to be enjoyed. There is noticing an appetite—for fries, or hot chocolate, or soothing pea soup—at the exact moment it awakens, and knowing that you have the resources and the ability to satisfy that craving. There is the pride you have when you can feed yourself or someone you love. There is the freedom to cook by numbers or to take creative license, to respect or disrespect the recipe in front of you. There is the multisensory fantasia that home cooking can become, when you draw on every one of your senses to guide you towards a good meal. And—most important of all—at the center of all of this there is you: in your ordinary kitchen, with your likes and dislikes, your tastes and aversions and your washing-up piled in the sink, cooking as you are.

THE BASICS

- **Olive oil**: When I specify olive oil, I mean everyday olive oil—not extra-virgin. If you need delicious, peppery extra-virgin olive oil, I'll make that clear.
- **Vegetable oil**: Often, the oil is just a cooking medium and flavor isn't too important. When this is the case, I call for vegetable oil, though any neutral-flavored cooking oil can be used, including sunflower oil, corn oil and peanut oil.
- **Salt**: Most of the time, I'll instruct you to add salt to taste. People have incredibly different salt tastes and tolerances, and different salts—sea salt flakes, table salt, fine sea salt, chunky rock salt pieces—vary in their saltiness. In some recipes, especially baking recipes where precision is paramount, I've specified how much salt you need: when I do this, I'm referring to basic table salt. If you use flaky sea salt, you'll want roughly double the volume (so up to 2 teaspoons instead of 1 teaspoon) to get the same weight.

- **Black pepper**: I use a lot of black pepper to add heat and pep to my cooking. It's best not to use the powdery ready-ground stuff if you can avoid it—it doesn't have the same warmth as the freshly ground stuff, and it can taste a little musty. I understand that's not always an option though, so do use what you have. I'll specify in cases where ready-ground pepper is an absolute no.

- **Canned tomatoes**: Ordinarily I specify chopped canned tomatoes, because they're cheaper and easier to use than canned whole plum tomatoes. If you have whole plum tomatoes, you can of course use them instead, breaking up the tomatoes gently with a fork before adding them to the dish.

- **Soy sauce and tamari**: I'll let you know if you need dark or light soy sauce for a recipe. When it's light soy sauce, you can swap for gluten-free tamari if necessary.

- **Onions**: When I call for onion in a recipe, it will be a medium yellow onion. If you need red onion, I'll make this clear.

- **Garlic**: I buy big garlic bulbs, so the cloves I use tend to be large. Depending on the size of your garlic cloves, you may want to add an extra one or two.

- **Fresh herbs**: These can really bring a meal to life—from the peppery fragrance of basil to bright, grassy parsley—but I understand they're a luxury you might not always be able to afford. When cheaper dried herbs can be used instead of fresh ones, I'll let you know.

- **Butter and milk**: I'll ordinarily tell you what kind—salted or unsalted butter, or whole, reduced-fat or nonfat milk—but if it's not specified you should feel free to use whatever you have. When dairy and non-dairy milk can be used interchangeably, I'll let you know.

- **Eggs**: If I specify egg size, that's because it's important for the taste and texture of a dish. Where it's not specified, you can use any size and trust that the recipe will work well.

MAKING THIS BOOK WORK FOR YOU

You'll notice that the recipes in this book usually have a **Variations and substitutions** section, with easy ingredient or method changes to help you adapt a recipe to your needs and tastes. Often, this is about convenience or budget: if you can't get hold of dried mushrooms, for instance, here's how the recipe can be made without them. Sometimes it's about allergies, intolerances or dietary requirements, with easy swaps given for meat, fish or wheat when that swap won't have a detrimental impact on how the recipe turns out. Sometimes it's just about keeping things flexible and fresh, so that you can give new life to old favorites or make them work with whatever you happen to have in the fridge. These variations are self-explanatory, and I hope you'll make good use of them. Here are a few further notes though, in case you need extra guidance.

Vegetarian and vegan cooking

Thanks to the key at the top of each recipe, helpfully created by designer and artist Evelin Kasikov, you can see at a glance whether a dish is vegetarian or vegan (or can be easily altered to become so). In recipes where the adaptation is slightly more involved, the vegan version is outlined separately with its own ingredients and method for you to follow.

Working around allergies or intolerances

Where a swap to gluten-free flour can be made, I have listed this in the recipe introduction, ingredient list or variations and substitutions section. For pasta, gnocchi or bread-based dishes, or ones with ingredients that may contain gluten, such as oats, you can of course swap in a gluten-free product to make the recipe work for you. For other common allergens, I've given substitution ideas where applicable, but it's important to note that not every recipe will be adaptable.

Bottled, canned and frozen food swaps

Wherever possible, I've specified if an ingredient can be swapped for a pantry version. This may be helpful if you're shopping on a budget, cooking for one, have little or no fridge space or rely on foodbanks for some or all of your food. It might also help you to minimize food waste. You can find a list of the cheaper recipes in this book on page 334, but you can adapt many of the recipes to your needs. Here are some swaps that you should feel free to make:

- **Bottled lemon or lime juice** in place of fresh. I've listed both the volume (e.g., 1 tablespoon lemon juice) and the real lemon equivalent (e.g., juice from ½ lemon) in these recipes so that you can make this swap easily.
- **Frozen or canned vegetables** can sometimes be used instead of fresh, but it depends on whether they're in the recipe to provide bulk, color, flavor or texture. If they are one of several vegetables in a stew, using

canned veg in place of fresh generally works fine. In stews, soups, curries and pies, frozen spinach, peas, carrots, broccoli, sweet corn and more can be used with good results. But in dishes where a vegetable plays some structural or textural role—maybe it needs to be grated to make fritters or to add bite in a noodle stir-fry—canned and frozen veg don't do so well.

- **Evaporated milk and milk powder** can be used in some recipes that require milk. You'll want to dilute the evaporated milk, or make up the milk powder, according to the package instructions. This substitution works well when creaminess isn't a massive priority—in a bread dough, for instance—but is less effective in something like a creamy potato gratin.

Cooking with limited energy or mobility

For lots of people, whether because of temporary illness, chronic illness or disability, cooking can be exhausting. If you struggle with this, you may want to skip to the More food, less work chapter, which focuses on dishes that don't need too much chopping, stirring or tending to. If you have a chronic illness, you may find a slow cooker helpful, as it could save you the hassle of standing at the stove. While I don't have a slow cooker myself, and know it's an expense that many cooks can't justify, there are lots of specialist slow-cooker cookbooks that might help you to adapt the recipes here.

Even if you have a hard time with chopping, grating, slicing or other complex kitchen tasks, you can still make great food. In More food, less work, you'll find recipes with a special focus on minimizing cutting and chopping (or that give easy alternatives). If you turn to pages 332–33, you can find lists of the low-prep, speedy and more hands-off recipes in the book.

Here are a few other things you can do to make life as easy as possible as you cook:

- Wherever I specify diced onions, you can use frozen diced onions (¼–⅓ pound/100–150g per onion), unless the onions are to be used raw as a garnish or in a salad (they'll go mushy as they defrost). In soups, stews and sauces, frozen diced onions will work perfectly well and save you a lot of chopping.

- Instead of crushing or finely grating garlic, you can use 1 teaspoon of garlic paste per 1 garlic clove. Another option is garlic powder—use about

¼ teaspoon per garlic clove. Ginger can be swapped for chopped ginger or ginger purée.

- If you have the means to buy one, a food processor will help you massively with food prep. You can use it to roughly chop onions, tomatoes and other veg (wherever veg needs to be cut into little pieces), to grate things (whether that's cheese or zucchini) or to thinly slice stuff (like potatoes for a gratin, or onions to garnish a dish).

- Things like butternut squash (which is a nightmare to peel and cut) can often be bought pre-chopped from larger supermarkets.

- Take a seat: if you struggle with prolonged periods of standing, have a seat at your kitchen table or on a tall stool near the kitchen counter. I know it might sound obvious, but sitting while you prepare and cook your ingredients can make a massive difference.

- Look into tools that could make cooking easier for you, whether that's a wall-mounted mechanical can opener or a chopping board with little spikes on it to hold the food in place as you cut.

Cooking with sensory impairments or differences

If you're blind, Deaf or have any sensory impairment or difference (this can include some autistic people, or anyone who experiences sensory sensitivity or overload), cooking can require a diverse range of approaches, and you might need to rely more heavily on other senses or on cooking aids. I've tried in this book to give you lots of different sensory cues rather than relying on just one sense. These sensory cues are paired with details about temperature and timings so that you can cook however suits you. The ebook version of this book is compatible with screen readers.

Serving sizes

One of the most difficult parts of the recipe testing and writing process has been the matter of serving sizes. It's impossible: sometimes I cook a dish and it makes four portions; other times I make the same dish in the exact same way and it serves me only twice, as my appetite waxes and wanes. Appetite—and so serving size—is a hugely subjective thing. So, when I write "Serves 4," please consider it a rough guide rather than a gold standard. Once you've cooked a couple of these recipes, you should get a feel for what my idea of a serving looks like, and you'll be able to adapt recipes however you please.

Scaling up and down

When I was developing these recipes, I wanted to minimize waste and fuss wherever possible. That meant that recipes that used half a can of chopped tomatoes were to be avoided at all costs. I found that four servings seemed to be a sweet spot in this regard, usually needing a nice round number of onions, a whole can of something or other, an entire pack of this or that. What's more, lots of dishes cook differently when made in small quantities: water might evaporate more from sauces, and consistency can vary dramatically depending on the size of the pan you use. And for a lot of the roasting-pan dishes, a four-serving quantity fits perfectly in a 13 x 9 inch (22 x 33cm) roasting pan, which seems to be one of the easiest-to-find (and affordable) sizes. I know four servings won't work for everyone, but that's my rationale. You can scale the recipes up or down if you need to using the sensory cues in the recipe to help guide you towards the correct color and consistency as you cook. Alternatively, check out the make-ahead storing and freezing suggestions on pages 322–331 to help deal with leftovers.

A NOTE ON EATING

Eating isn't always easy, especially if you (or people around you) have a difficult relationship with your body. Our appetites can sometimes feel like an alien force: weird rumblings, cravings that seem to arise from nowhere and bodily hungers at odds with the priorities of our minds. You can trust that there won't be any moralizing language in this book about "good" or "bad" foods or "good" or "bad" bodies. However, I understand that, if you're struggling in your relationship with food, it's going to take more than this neutrality to get you back on track. Here are a few books that address disordered eating, body image and fatphobia, for if you want to feel less alone and maybe even come to terms with your own hunger.

Eating with My Mouth Open by Sam van Zweden
Just Eat It by Laura Thomas
Not All Black Girls Know How to Eat by Stephanie Covington Armstrong
Fearing the Black Body by Sabrina Strings
What We Don't Talk About When We Talk About Fat by Aubrey Gordon
Health at Every Size by Lindo Bacon
The Body Is Not an Apology by Sonya Renee Taylor
and my previous book, **Eat Up!**

THE RECIPE TREE

Recipes don't grow on trees. They don't spring fully formed from people's minds, either. Read between the lines of any recipe in this book and you'll find the work of hundreds of cooks whose craft, teaching, words and recipes have woven together over time, to create not just one dish but a whole cooking culture. So although it's my name on the spine of this book, I want to be clear that I'm not a creator but a curator: collecting, untangling, building upon and reinterpreting the food knowledge that is our precious shared domain. Part of the challenge of writing a cookbook is figuring out how to balance the demands of authorship ("I should be an authority! I need to innovate!") with the reality of these collective, collaborative food cultures.

When I draw from other cultures, these questions become even thornier. Especially considering the colonial history of both the UK and the U.S., it feels important not to steamroll a culturally important recipe in the name of novelty, or claim ownership of a dish that's really not mine to claim. Brits will spend a lifetime arguing about the correct condiments to have with fries, and then make some dismal culinary mashup that breaks every rule of someone else's food culture. These missteps are understandable day to day: if you're not immersed in a culture, you won't be wise to the nuances of its cuisine, of what ingredient defines a dish or makes it come to life, of exactly how something should taste. But when we step out of the domestic kitchen and start writing and sharing recipes—creating and reshaping the food world around us—we have to take more care.

Many of the recipes in this book draw from the diverse foods to be easily found on shelves today: They mix Italian techniques with flavors from East Asia, or add Middle Eastern spices to simple root vegetables. Lots are recognizably British in a more old-fashioned kind of way, while some take inspiration from West Africa, specifically Ghana, where one branch of my family tree has its roots. There are a few that draw heavily on cultures that are not my own, like a Korean soft tofu stew or a red lentil dal. When I have written such recipes, I've taken great care to highlight the people who helped me to understand the dish, and to make clear that these recipes aren't my inventions. You'll find reading lists at the beginning of each chapter so that you can consult and enjoy the work of the writers and cooks whose work I've drawn upon. I'd encourage you to buy or borrow their books if at all possible.

Finally, because I know that there's only so much that one cookbook can achieve: as well as donating copies of this book to charities and projects around the UK, I have donated copies of several of the books mentioned in the reading lists. These books will find their way into libraries, community projects, schools and prisons, and it's my hope that the diversity of the books and their authors will reflect the wonderful diversity of the communities we live in. We need as many food makers, sharers, teachers and writers as we can get. Whatever anyone might say, there's no such thing as too many cooks.

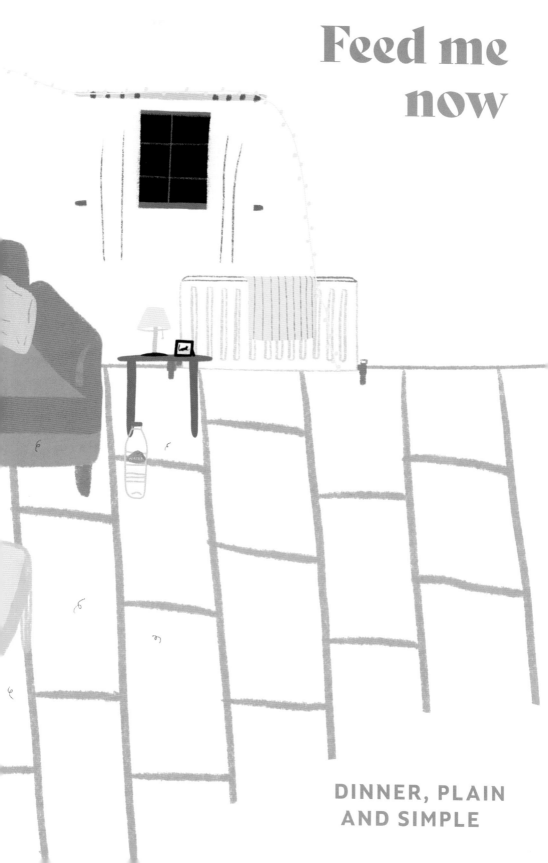

Feed me now

DINNER, PLAIN AND SIMPLE

Recipe list

Introduction

The recipes in this chapter are exactly what you'd expect: simple dinners for days when your motivation stretches beyond just a can of soup, but when you don't necessarily have the headspace (or kitchen space) to tackle multiple courses and elaborate side dishes. Lots of these dinners are self-contained: a risotto-like pearl couscous with anchovies and olives, a plate of chunky fries with tangy chaat masala seasoning, pearl barley bowls with sautéed zucchini and fresh dill. Others just need something carby to complete them, and I've given suggestions for how to pad them out into a whole meal. If you've slogged through another day of dreary work, these are dinners to enliven and nourish—something to look forward to.

Further reading

East by Meera Sodha
Made in India by Meera Sodha
Fresh India by Meera Sodha
Carpathia by Irina Georgescu
Hibiscus by Lopè Ariyo
Longthroat Memoirs by Yemisí Aríbisálà
I Am a Filipino by Nicole Ponseca
7000 Islands by Yasmin Newman
Tikim by Doreen Fernandez
A Girl Called Jack by Jack Monroe
Heartburn by Nora Ephron
The Kitchen Diaries by Nigel Slater
Korean Home Cooking by Sohui Kim and Rachel Wharton
Maangchi's Big Book of Korean Cooking by Maangchi
Cook Korean! by Robin Ha
Home Cookery Year by Claire Thomson

PEARL COUSCOUS WITH ANCHOVIES, TOMATOES AND OLIVES

This is just like a traditional puttanesca but with bouncy pearl couscous in place of the usual pasta. I love the chewiness of pearl couscous and how it releases starch into the sauce, creating something between pasta and risotto in its carby creaminess. Pearl couscous is also sold as giant or Israeli couscous. You can get it from lots of Middle Eastern stores and most larger supermarkets. Don't be tempted to swap it for regular couscous, or the dish will end up thick and oatmeal-like. There are better alternatives listed below.

The toppings here—crunchy breadcrumbs and bright parsley—are optional, but I think they provide a welcome textural and flavor contrast to the salty, silky pearl couscous underneath.

Serves: 4
Ready in: less than 30 minutes

Vegan option

2–2⅔ cups (300–400g) pearl couscous
4 cups (1 liter) water, freshly boiled
2 tablespoons olive oil
4 garlic cloves, crushed or finely grated
6–8 anchovy fillets (from 1 small can)
1 tablespoon tomato paste
14 ounces (400g) cherry tomatoes, halved
½ cup (60g) black olives, pitted (Kalamata olives are particularly good)
3 tablespoons (25g) capers

½–1 teaspoon chili flakes, to taste

To finish:
1 tablespoon olive oil
¼ cup (20g) dried breadcrumbs or fresh breadcrumbs from 1 slice of white bread
Handful of parsley leaves (roughly ½ ounce/10–15g), roughly chopped

1. If you're planning on topping the dish with breadcrumbs, it's best to get these out of the way first. Heat 1 tablespoon of olive oil in a small frying pan over a medium-low heat and add the breadcrumbs. Toast them for a few minutes, stirring very often, until they're golden brown and crispy, then tip them into a small bowl and leave to cool.

2. Pour the pearl couscous into a large mixing bowl and cover with the freshly boiled water. Give it a good stir, then cover with a large plate and leave to sit for 12 minutes.

3. Meanwhile, set a medium saucepan over a medium-low heat, and add the olive oil, garlic and anchovy fillets. Sauté gently for a couple of minutes, stirring all the time, until the garlic is cooked and the anchovies have dissolved into the fragrant oil. Add the tomato paste and sauté for 30 seconds more, then add the cherry tomatoes, olives, capers and chili flakes. Cook the mixture over a medium heat for 6–8 minutes, or until the tomatoes are collapsed and pulpy.

4. By now, the couscous should be ready: the grains should have the slightest bite in the middle, but be almost cooked through. Drain it and stir to break up any lumps, then add to the tomato sauce. Mix to combine, then simmer for 2–3 minutes more so that the grains finish cooking and absorb some of the flavor. Once the couscous is springy—neither chewy nor mushily soft—it's done. The sauce should generously engulf the couscous, creating a risotto-like consistency. Serve straightaway, sprinkled with the toasted breadcrumbs and chopped parsley, if using.

Variations and substitutions:

As I mentioned above, the traditional accompaniment for this sauce is pasta. Just cook your pasta—roughly 4 ounces (100g) per person—according to the instructions on the package and mix with the sauce before serving. Orzo—a pasta shape that looks like little grains of rice (although confusingly it means "barley" in Italian)—is also an option: soak 1⅓–1¾ cups (300–400g) orzo in plenty of freshly boiled water for 8–10 minutes, until it's cooked but al dente, then proceed with the recipe.

If you don't like olives or capers, you can leave these out, though I really love the tangy pop of caper in the midst of what is quite a rich, flavorful sauce. You can make this dish vegan by leaving out the anchovies, but it'll have a completely different energy. Make sure you add a pinch of salt if you do so.

A can of chopped tomatoes is a good swap for the fresh cherry tomatoes if you struggle with chopping things; just leave out the tomato paste if you make this change. You could also swap the cherry tomatoes for diced larger tomatoes if that's what you have.

COCONUT, PLANTAIN AND SPINACH CURRY WITH TOASTED CASHEWS

This is the first of a few plantain recipes in this book, testament to the versatility of this wonderful fruit. You'll find it in the **eden rice with black beans and plantain** (page 58), spiced and fried as **kelewele** (page 238), sugared and wrapped in spring roll pastry (**turon**, page 312) and shaped into crunchy, savory fritters (**green plantain, coconut and chili rösti**, page 169). Writer and photographer Yvonne Maxwell discussed the magic of plantain in the online food magazine *Vittles*. "Its skin is perfectly blemished and, at its finest, darkened with black lines," she wrote. "Even bruised, its beauty shines through and sweetness prevails." It has a place in the hearts—and bellies—of people from so many different culinary cultures.

In this recipe, medium-ripe plantain provides bulk to a creamy coconut curry, loosely similar to South Indian kache kele ki sabzi. You should use yellow plantain, which are sweet enough to complement the creamy coconut sauce, but firm enough to hold their shape as they simmer. This won't be the last time I say this in this book, but I need to be very clear: banana isn't a good substitute for plantain here. Its flavor is stronger, and it will collapse into mush when cooked.

Serves: 4
Ready in: less than 1 hour
Make-ahead and storage tips: page 322

Vegan

---

1 cup (100g) unsalted cashews
1⅔ cups (400ml) water, freshly boiled
2 tablespoons coconut or vegetable oil
1 medium onion, finely diced
5 tablespoons (75g) tomato paste
1½-inch (4cm) piece of ginger, peeled and grated
4 garlic cloves, crushed or finely grated
1½ teaspoons black or brown mustard seeds
1 teaspoon garam masala
1 teaspoon cumin
½–1 teaspoon chili powder, to taste
½ teaspoon turmeric

1 x 14 ounce (400ml) can coconut milk, full-fat or "light"
2 yellow plantain
7 ounces (200g) fresh or frozen whole leaf spinach
1 tablespoon lemon or lime juice (from roughly ½ lemon or 1 lime)
Salt, to taste

Serve with: steamed rice
Special equipment: stick blender, food processor or blender (check the variations and substitutions below if you don't have one)

1. Start by soaking ¾ cup (75g) cashews in 1⅔ cups (400ml) freshly boiled water. Leave to sit for 10 minutes or so, then blitz the cashews and water together using a blender or food processor.

2. Heat the oil in a large saucepan over a medium-low heat. Add the diced onion and sauté for 10–12 minutes, stirring often, until it begins to lightly brown in parts. Add the tomato paste, ginger and garlic and sauté for a couple more minutes, stirring, then add the mustard seeds, garam masala, cumin, chili powder and turmeric and cook for 30 seconds or so, until fragrant. Stir in the coconut milk and blitzed cashew mixture, making sure you scrape the brown bits (known as the fond) off the bottom of the pan from when you fried the onions—this sticky stuff adds a lot of flavor.

3. Bring the sauce to a simmer, then turn down the heat and cook gently for 10 minutes. While it simmers, peel the plantain (cut off each end, slit the skin lengthways and peel it all around—not down—the fruit) and cut into ½–¾ inch (1.5–2cm) slices.

4. Add the sliced plantain and spinach to the curry. Simmer for a further 15 minutes, stirring often and adding a little extra water if the sauce catches or browns on the bottom of the pan. It's ready when the spinach has collapsed and the plantain is tender.

5. Roughly chop the remaining ¼ cup (25g) cashews and toast for a few minutes in a dry frying pan, until just beginning to brown. When the curry is ready, add the lemon or lime juice, then check the seasoning and salt generously to taste—I start with about ½ teaspoon table salt and work from there. Serve with lots of steamed rice, with the toasted cashews sprinkled on top.

Variations and substitutions:

In place of the spinach, you could use Tuscan kale, chard or spring greens (slice across the leaf into ⅜ inch [1cm] ribbons). Frozen peas also work really well!

Brown or black mustard seeds can be found in any large supermarket or in a South Asian grocery, but if you can't get hold of them you can use 1 tablespoon wholegrain mustard instead—add it at the same time as the coconut milk.

Butternut squash—peeled and cut into 1¼ inch (3cm) chunks—is a good alternative to plantain. It takes longer to cook, though, so add it to the curry at the same time as the coconut milk.

If you don't have a blender or food processor (and so can't blitz the cashews), use ¼ cup (60g) cashew or peanut butter instead. Add the nut butter to the pan just after you've fried the spices, stir to combine, then slowly mix in the coconut milk and the 1⅔ cups (400ml) boiling water.

EARTHY, SMOKY LENTIL AND BEET STEW

I'm pretty confident that, even if you think you're not a beet fan, you'll enjoy it in this smoky, comforting stew. In the absence of meat, the root vegetable contributes an earthy depth and also has the benefit of dyeing this dish an amazingly vibrant fuchsia color.

Serves: 4
Ready in: less than 1 hour
Make-ahead and storage tips: page 322

Vegan

2 tablespoons olive or vegetable oil
2 medium onions, finely diced
Salt, to taste
9 ounces (250g) cooked or fresh beets
4 garlic cloves, crushed or finely grated
1½ teaspoons smoked paprika
1½ teaspoons cumin
1 teaspoon dried oregano
½–1 teaspoon chili powder, to taste
⅔ cup (125g) dried French green lentils
(you might see them sold as
Puy lentils or lentilles vertes)

1 x 14 ounce (400g) can chopped
tomatoes
1 x 14 ounce (400g) can red kidney
beans, drained
2 tablespoons light soy sauce or tamari
2 teaspoons cocoa powder
2½ cups (600ml) water

Serve with: steamed rice, tortillas
or baked potatoes, along with a dollop
of sour cream or yogurt (dairy or non-
dairy)

1. Heat the oil in a large, deep pot over a medium-low heat. Add the diced onion and a pinch of salt and cook for 10 minutes, stirring occasionally to make sure the onion doesn't stick and burn. The onion should soften and become translucent.

2. Meanwhile, prepare the beets. If you're using cooked beets—the ones that come in a vacuum-sealed pack—just drain them and coarsely grate them. If you're using fresh beets, wash and trim off the roots and stems before grating. (If the fresh beets have their leaves still attached, you can use these! Wash them well, then roughly chop and add to the stew 5 minutes before the end of the cooking time.)

3. Add the grated beets to the onions, stir to combine, then put a lid on the pan. Let the veg sweat for 10 minutes, stirring every so often.

4. Add the garlic, smoked paprika, cumin, oregano and chili powder. Stir well and cook for 1–2 minutes, until the garlic loses its raw pungency and the smell of the spices begins to waft up from the pan.

5. Into the pot, add the lentils, chopped tomatoes, red kidney beans, soy sauce and cocoa powder, and stir to combine. Add the water (2½ cups/ 600ml is the same as filling the empty chopped tomato can 1½ times), then bring the mixture to a simmer and cook for 25 minutes partially covered by a lid. Stir regularly to make sure the lentils don't stick to the bottom of the pan—if it starts to dry out (it will sputter and puff rather

than quietly bubbling), add a splash more water. When it's ready, the lentils and beets should be tender. Add plenty of salt to taste, and check whether you want to add more chili powder. Serve straightaway.

Variations and substitutions:

Swap the ground cumin for cumin seeds (toasted for a minute or so in a hot dry frying pan) if that's what you've got, or leave it out if you must. Chili, in some form or other, is vital: swap in chili flakes, hot sauce or chopped fresh red chilies if that's all you have. Marjoram or dried mixed herbs can take the place of the oregano.

You can use green or brown lentils in place of the French green lentils if that's what you have available. I wouldn't recommend using red lentils as they tend to break down and lose their shape during cooking. If you want to use canned green lentils, or the cooked French lentils that come in pouches, go ahead. You'll need roughly 9 ounces (250g) of cooked lentils, and should use much less water to start off with, adding more only if needed. Because these lentils are pre-cooked, they don't technically need a long cook. However, I think the stew tastes better with extra simmering time—the flavors get a chance to mingle and soften—so I'd cook it for at least 20 minutes regardless of the type of lentil you use.

As for the beets, I really would encourage you beet-skeptics to give it a try. You can leave them out or replace with grated carrot if you're absolutely adamant that you won't like it. I won't be angry, just disappointed.

FRIES WITH CHAAT MASALA, PICKLED ONIONS AND POMEGRANATE

Chaat, in case you're not already familiar with it, is a broad term for many related Indian snack foods that usually involve hot, crisp, fresh, tangy, herbal and fruity elements combining to create a dish that is different with every mouthful. Sometimes this includes potatoes, like in aloo chaat—potatoes fried with spices and served with onion. Aloo tikki chaat combines sizzling mashed potato patties with yogurt and green chutney. Often sev (dried chickpea noodles, like in Bombay mix, an Indian snack mix), yogurt, chickpeas and tamarind are involved, but there are countless ways to spin these recipes and no one true way. Meera Sodha, always a reliable guide, has a wonderful recipe that uses samphire and chickpeas, and another very different version that makes use of leftover roast vegetables. In her book, *East*, she restyles the dish with Jerusalem artichoke.

Although there's more than one way to skin a chaat (I'm sorry), I'm gonna hold off officially calling this recipe chaat. It's really not my place to decide that, especially considering how off-piste I've gone with the inclusion of oven fries. What I can say is that this recipe is heavily influenced by aloo chaat, with a jumble of different flavors and textures on the plate. Vital to this recipe is chaat masala—a spice mix of amchur (dried sour mango powder), cumin, chili, sugar, salt and pepper—to give it that moreish tang. I like to mix my own (I make three or four times the quantity used below, and then keep the leftovers in a jar in the spice drawer), but you can buy ready-mixed chaat masala instead if that's easier for you. Both amchur (for the homemade version) and ready-mixed chaat masala can be found in Indian stores and supermarkets (the chaat masala will ordinarily be in a smallish box near the biryani masala and other spice blends).

Serves: 4
Ready in: 35 minutes

Vegan

For the fries and garnishes:
½ medium red onion, thinly sliced
¼ cup (60ml) white vinegar, optional
1 pomegranate
2¼ pounds (1kg) chunky oven fries
Handful of cilantro leaves
   (roughly ½ ounce/10–15g)
1–2 tablespoons lemon juice
   (from roughly ½–1 lemon)

For the chaat masala:
2 teaspoons amchur
1 teaspoon cumin
1 teaspoon white sugar
½ teaspoon chili powder
½ teaspoon salt
Lots of freshly ground black pepper

1. Preheat the oven to 425°F (220°C) and get out a couple of large baking sheets.

2. Next, get your garnishes ready. Soak the sliced onion in the vinegar for 20 minutes to take the acrid edge off. (This soaking stage isn't vital—if you want to, you can leave the onion as it is.) Halve the pomegranate across its belly, then give it a thwack with a rolling pin to dislodge the seeds.

3. Spread your fries out on the baking sheets and place in the preheated oven. Cook for 10 minutes while you prepare the spice blend (they'll have more time in the oven later).

4. To make the chaat masala spice blend, simply stir all ingredients together in a small bowl. If you're using ready-mixed chaat masala, just have it ready.

5. After the fries have cooked for their initial 10 minutes, remove them from the oven and sprinkle over all the homemade spice blend and toss to coat. Ready-mixed chaat masala is slightly saltier than the homemade blend, so you won't need quite as much by volume—I use 3–4 teaspoons.

6. Return the chaat-coated fries to the oven for a further 15 minutes or so, depending on the thickness of your fries. I like to make sure that the total cooking time is about 5 minutes longer than the time specified on the package: the fries need to be crisp-edged and golden for this dish.

7. Divide the fries between your plates or put on a large serving dish. Scatter over the red onion slices (drained, if you soaked them in vinegar), cilantro leaves and pomegranate seeds, then squeeze over some lemon until the salt–tang balance is perfect and serve right away.

CARROT, LEMON AND TAHINI SOUP

I don't know what it is about soup that inspires so much uncertainty among my otherwise kitchen-savvy friends. I know people who can make a lasagna from scratch, but ask them to make soup and they freeze. I guess it must be something about the simplicity of soup: there's nothing to hide behind, no bells and whistles to draw attention away from blandness or lumpiness or oatmeal-y thickness. But if a thirteenth-century cook could make "gourdes in potage" flavored with saffron and enriched with egg yolks, or a "caboche" (cabbage) soup cooked with broth, leek whites and onions, then you can make a vegetable soup no problem in the luxury of the modern kitchen.

You can mess around with a vegetable soup all day if you want, but I don't see the point in complicating what should be a very simple—and, crucially, a one-pot, low-washing-up—process. All you need is: 1) A vegetable, whether it's leafy like spinach or lumpy like celery root. In this soup, I've used carrots. 2) Water (or stock). 3) Flavorings, which could be alliums like onion, leek, shallot or garlic, to add savoriness and depth; herbs (dried herbs like thyme and rosemary are best for soup, as they're fragrant enough to hold their own); or spices, like cinnamon, cloves or cumin seeds. Spice and curry pastes are also a good bet. 4) Salt, whether bouillon cubes, table salt or flaky sea salt.

Once you've nailed these four basics, you can try adding a touch of acidity in the form of lemon juice, or richness from cream, coconut milk, yogurt or nut butters. But, at its heart, soup is just a vegetable, cooked with water, flavorings and salt. If you can do this well, and particularly if you can then blend it to silky smoothness, you really can't lose.

Serves: 4

Ready in: 45 minutes (over half of this is downtime while the soup simmers)

Make-ahead and storage tips: page 322

Vegan

---

2 tablespoons olive or vegetable oil
1 large onion, thickly sliced
4 garlic cloves, crushed or finely grated
1⅓ pounds (600g) carrots, thickly sliced
2 celery sticks, thickly sliced
2 teaspoons dried thyme
½–1 teaspoon chili flakes, to taste
Salt, to taste
5 cups (1.2 liters) water, freshly boiled
3 tablespoons tahini

1 tablespoon honey or light brown sugar, plus extra to taste
3 tablespoons lemon juice (from roughly 1½ lemons), plus extra to taste

Serve with: bread and butter; yogurt or crème fraîche, optional; extra-virgin olive oil

Special equipment: stick blender, food processor or blender

1. Heat the oil in a large, deep pan set over a medium heat, then add the onion, garlic, carrots, celery, thyme, chili flakes and a pinch of salt. Once the veg starts to sizzle, put a lid on the pan and let sweat for 10 minutes, stirring often, until the carrots have started to soften and the flavors have mingled. Add the water and bring to a boil. Once the mixture is simmering, turn the heat down slightly and cook for 25 minutes, or until the carrots are really tender.

2. When the soup is cooked, remove from the heat and add the tahini, honey or sugar, lemon juice and a couple of good pinches of salt. Blend using a stick blender. (You can use a blender or the jar attachment of a food processor if that's what you have, but not all models are suitable for blending hot liquids.) Once the mixture is silky, taste the soup and add more lemon juice, honey (or sugar) or salt as necessary. The amount of salt that you need to add to make it taste like soup (rather than vegetable water) will look remarkable, but remember that any store-bought soup will have somewhere between ¼ teaspoon and ½ teaspoon salt per portion—a tiny little pinch of salt isn't gonna cut it. Add little by little, tasting as you go, until the soup is moreish. That's the best benchmark I have. Serve straightaway with a dollop of crème fraîche or yogurt if you fancy it, or a drizzle of extra-virgin olive oil if you don't eat dairy. Bread on the side is non-negotiable.

Variations and substitutions:

You can swap the carrot for butternut squash or sweet potato if you want. You do need a sweet vegetable here to balance the bitterness of the tahini. If you don't have celery in the fridge and can't be bothered to buy any, that's fine—just leave it out. You could also swap it for 4–5 ounces (100–150g) diced celery root, as I have done in the past. The onion can be replaced with leeks or shallots, if that's what you have. If you can't eat alliums, replace the onion and garlic with a pinch of asafoetida.

You can find tahini in most supermarkets, but you could use peanut or almond butter instead. If you do so, leave out the honey or sugar, as you'll no longer need to counterbalance the bitterness of tahini.

As ever, feel free to swap in pre-chopped carrots—whether fresh or frozen—if you struggle with chopping. I find canned carrots don't blend very well for soup. Celery is harder to find prepped, but bear in mind that it only needs to be cut into rough chunks, as the soup will be blended, so no need to spend too much time or energy on this.

PASTA WITH SAUERKRAUT, CARAMELIZED ONIONS AND SOUR CREAM

There are lots of variations on this basic premise—pasta plus cabbage and onion—from across central and eastern Europe, from Germany to Ukraine, Poland and Slovakia. This particular version owes its existence to a tweet by Romanian food writer Irina Georgescu, whose cookbook *Carpathia* is all about the diverse and underknown food of her home country. Irina tweeted a photo of a bowl of homemade tagliatelle with onions and sauerkraut, suggesting you could also stir through some sour cream, and I knew I had to make it straightaway.

Some people swear by eating sauerkraut raw: When fermented properly, the cabbage that sauerkraut is made from becomes a food source for countless bacteria, which are supposedly beneficial for gut health. When you cook the sauerkraut, of course those bacteria die, and you may lose out on some of those health benefits. But cooking is as much about culture as nature, as much about enjoyment, meaning and connection as survival. So, if cooking sauerkraut makes a dish taste good—which in this case it absolutely does—that's just what we do, and we do it with pleasure.

You can find sauerkraut in most supermarkets—often with the central and eastern European foods in the pantry aisle—or in any Polish store. You can also get gentrified sauerkraut in health food stores and delis, if that's your jam.

Serves: 4
Ready in: 30 minutes

Vegetarian

Vegan option

¼ cup (60g) salted or unsalted butter *or* 3 tablespoons (45ml) olive oil

2 medium onions, thinly sliced

Salt, to taste

11 ounces (300g) pasta (tagliatelle works well, but use whatever you have)

1 cup (200g) sauerkraut, drained and well rinsed

scant ½ cup (100ml) sour cream or crème fraîche
 or ⅓ cup (75g) vegan cream cheese

Lots of freshly ground black pepper

Handful of fresh parsley leaves or dill fronds (roughly ½ ounce/ 10–15g), roughly chopped

1. Add the butter (or oil, if you want a vegan version), onions and a pinch of salt to a medium saucepan, cover with a lid and cook over a medium-low heat, stirring often, for 10 minutes, or until the onions are softened and fragrant. Next, remove the lid and cook for a further 8–10 minutes, uncovered, still stirring regularly. You want the onions to color—that browning will add so much flavor to the dish—but not to burn. If you sample a ribbon of onion now, it will taste sweet and very slightly bitter.

2. While the onions cook, bring a large pan of well-salted water to a boil, then add the pasta and cook according to the instructions on the package. Drain the pasta once cooked, but reserve a couple of tablespoons of the cooking water just in case.

3. Once the onions are ready, add the sauerkraut (make sure you've rinsed it really well, or it will be too salty) and continue to heat for 2–3 minutes, or until everything's hot. Turn off the heat, add the cooked pasta and the sour cream (or alternative). Mix everything well, then check the seasoning and add plenty of black pepper and a pinch of salt if necessary. If it's slightly dry or gummy (this may be the case if you used vegan cream cheese), add some of the reserved pasta cooking water. Serve straightaway, sprinkling the chopped parsley or dill on top of each bowl.

Variations and substitutions:

Caraway seeds work very nicely here—I'm pretty sure I can see a few scattered on top in the photo in Irina's tempting tweet. Just add ½ teaspoon to the onions as they cook.

Use a gluten-free pasta if preferred.

MEATBALLS WITH BASIL, CREAM AND MUSTARD

I spent hours perusing Nigel Slater's *Real Food* as a kid. Unlike the usual starters, mains, sides and desserts, it was divided into chapters addressing life's best things, from garlic to potatoes, sausages and ice cream. Straightaway, I was drawn to this greedy way of seeing the world. One of my favorite recipes from that book is for pasta with sausages, basil and mustard: the vibrant, almost aniseed fragrance of the basil works to offset the rich cream, while grainy mustard adds warmth and bite. The recipe that follows is heavily influenced by that old favorite, channeling the basil-mustard pepperiness into a creamy sauce with meatballs. You'll want to have boiled or mashed potatoes and some greens ready to serve this with.

Serves: 4
Ready in: less than 45 minutes

Vegetarian option

---

1 pound (450g) meatballs (vegetarian, pork or beef)
1 tablespoon olive or vegetable oil
1 medium onion, thinly sliced
⅔ cup (160ml) heavy cream
Scant 1 cup (200ml) water
Small bunch of fresh basil (roughly 1 ounce/30g), stalks discarded and leaves sliced into thin ribbons

1½ tablespoons wholegrain mustard
1 teaspoon instant chicken gravy *or* vegetarian gravy, optional
Salt, optional
¼–½ teaspoon chili flakes, to taste
Freshly ground black pepper

Serve with: mashed or boiled potatoes and boiled or steamed greens

1. Check the instructions on your meatball package and set the oven to the correct temperature. Once the oven is hot, cook according to the instructions. Depending on whether they're fresh or frozen, they should take roughly 25–30 minutes in an oven at 400°F (200°C).

2. While the meatballs cook, heat the oil in a medium saucepan or large frying pan. Add the onion and cook over a medium heat, stirring often, for 12–14 minutes, or until the onion is collapsed and beginning to brown. Adjust the heat if necessary to prevent it burning.

3. Take the pan off the heat and add the cream, stirring well to scrape up any onion scraps (and color) from the bottom of the pan. Next, pour in the

water and add the basil, mustard, instant gravy (or a small pinch of salt, if you don't want to use), chili flakes and pepper. Return the pan to the heat, setting the heat as low as it'll go, until the cream sauce is warmed through. Don't let it boil, or the sauce might split.

4. By the time the sauce is done, the meatballs should be cooked. Serve with potato and steamed or boiled greens, pouring the mustard-seed-flecked sauce over the meatballs on the plate.

TINOLANG MANOK

Soothing chicken, ginger and chayote soup

My friend Leah has slowly trained me in the ways of tinolang manok, or chicken tinola—a Filipino chicken and chayote soup fortified with ginger and greens—so I have her to thank for this recipe, but really the threads trace back to Leah's mum, Candy. Like so many overseas Filipino workers, Candy left the Philippines as a teenager to make money to send back home and ended up creating a whole life for herself halfway across the world—first in the UK, then in the Netherlands, before settling in the UK once more. Wherever she went, she took her masterful Filipino cooking with her. Her tinola is one of Leah's favorites and has become one of mine, too. It's a perfect, soothing chicken soup.

Chayote adds a freshness that works so well alongside the salty depth of the fish sauce. It's a smallish, pear-shaped kind of squash, with apple-green skin and a mellow freshness a little like zucchini or bok choy stems. It's also sold as choko, chuchu or mirliton, depending on where you're from. You should be able to find it in Afro-Caribbean, South Asian, Filipino and some East Asian grocery stores. If you can't find it, check the variations and substitutions on page 32, but it's worth getting acquainted with if you aren't already. It's also really good as a side dish, sautéed in butter or oil and garlic, then drizzled with lemon juice.

If you're after more Filipino recipes, check out *I Am a Filipino* by Nicola Ponseca. In *7000 Islands*, Yasmin Newman's recipes capture the diversity of the country's cooking, while the writing of Doreen Fernandez is a wonderful primer if you want to know more about Filipino food culture.

Serves: 4 generously
Ready in: less than 1 hour 15 minutes
  (of which 30 minutes is hands-off cooking time)
Make-ahead and storage tips: page 322

1½ cups (300g) long-grain rice, such as
  basmati
3 tablespoons vegetable oil
1 medium onion, cut into wedges
6 chicken thighs, skins removed but
  bone in*
6 garlic cloves, crushed or finely
  grated

2¼-inch (6cm) piece of ginger, peeled
  and grated
3 tablespoons fish sauce, plus extra to
  taste
2 chayote
3½ ounces (100g) fresh or frozen whole
  leaf spinach
Salt, to taste

*To remove the chicken skins, it's easiest to use a piece of paper towel to help you grip it as you peel it away from the chicken flesh. You don't have to throw away these skins! If you want to, you can make crispy chicken skin to crumble over the finished soup. Preheat the oven to 400°F (200°C) and lay the chicken skin on a baking sheet lined with parchment paper. Sprinkle with salt, then lay another piece of parchment on top and compress using a second baking sheet. Bake for 15–25 minutes, checking regularly, until the skins are crisp and lightly browned. The timing will depend on the weight of your trays—keep an eye on the skins as they'll become bitter if cooked too long.

1. Start off by preparing your rice washings—this is the starchy water left when you wash rice, and will add smoothness and body to the soup. Wash the rice briefly in a large bowl or pan, and tip the first washings away. Then add lots more water and swirl the rice gently around. Strain the rice, collecting the cloudy washings in a separate bowl or jug. Repeat until you have 8 cups (2 liters) of rice washings. Set aside the rice and, while the soup is cooking, steam it for serving with the dish.

2. Heat the oil in a large, deep saucepan over a medium-low heat. Add the onion and cook gently, stirring every couple of minutes, until it's lightly browned and collapsing—this should take 12–15 minutes. Add the chicken thighs (on the bone) and increase the heat slightly. Let the meat brown for a few minutes, then add the garlic and ginger and cook for a further 2 minutes. When it's ready, the smell of the browning chicken and aromatics should rise temptingly from the pan.

3. Pour in the 8 cups (2 liters) of rice washings you prepared earlier and add the fish sauce. Bring the soup to a simmer, then lower the heat and cook for 30 minutes, skimming any foam off the surface if necessary. While it cooks, prepare the chayote. Peel the fruits and cut out the fibrous cores, much like you would for an apple or pear, then slice into thick wedges. (Sometimes chayote gives off a sap that can make the skin on your hands feel weird—a bit like if you slightly covered your hands in Elmer's glue and left it to dry! If you're worried about this, just wear gloves when chopping.)

4. After the soup has simmered for 30 minutes, remove the chicken pieces and shred the meat from the bone. Return the meat to the pan, then add the chayote and spinach and cook for a further 5 minutes or so, or until the chayote is tender. Season to taste with salt, or add extra fish sauce if you prefer. Serve straightaway with your steamed rice.

Variations and substitutions:

Malunggay or moringa leaves are more traditional than spinach, so do use them if you can get hold of them. Watercress leaves also work really nicely, adding a peppery bite.

If you can't get hold of chayote, add a couple of bunches of bok choy cut into thick slices. Green papaya is also an option. In a pinch, you could add thickly sliced zucchini (like in Melissa Hemsley's recipe for her mum's tinola), but I can't promise it'd get Candy's approval.

CRISP BROWN BUTTER LIMA BEANS WITH GARLIC YOGURT AND SPICED TOMATO SAUCE

This triple-threat lima bean dish is a joy: the beans are fried with nutty brown butter until they're crisp and blistered, then dotted with garlicky yogurt and a chili-spiked, sweet and sour tomato sauce. These three kind-of-sauces are loosely based on those sometimes served with Turkish manti—little lamb dumplings. (Özlem Warren has a very good recipe on her website, Özlem's Turkish Table.) You can also use the sauces with pasta or with parboiled and crisply fried gnocchi.

This dish is ideal with bread and salad, or as part of a vegetarian mezze spread.

Serves: 4 as a main with bread and salad,
   or 8 as a vegetarian mezze
Ready in: 30 minutes

Vegetarian   Vegan option

For the garlic yogurt:
1 cup (200g) full-fat Greek-style yogurt
½ garlic clove, crushed or finely grated
Salt, to taste

For the tomato sauce:
4 tablespoons tomato paste
5–7 tablespoons (75–100ml) water
2 tablespoons olive oil
2 teaspoons paprika
1–2 teaspoons chili flakes, to taste
1 teaspoon dried mint
Salt, to taste

For the brown butter lima beans:
3 tablespoons salted or unsalted butter
Salt, to taste
3 x 14 ounce (400g) cans lima beans,
   drained and rinsed (roughly
   1½–1¾ pounds/650–750g cooked
   lima beans total)

To garnish:
Handful of mint leaves (½ ounce/
   10–15g), finely chopped, or leaves from
   8 fresh thyme sprigs

Serve with: crusty bread and salad

1. Start by mixing the yogurt, garlic and a pinch of salt together in a small bowl, then set aside for the garlic to infuse.

2. Combine the tomato sauce ingredients in a small pan, starting with just 5 tablespoons (75ml) of the water. Set the pan over a medium-low heat and cook for a couple of minutes, until the sauce is deep red and the

oil begins to separate. Add a splash more water if it's very thick. Once ready, set aside.

3. In a large frying pan, melt the butter over a medium-low heat, adding a pinch of salt if your butter is unsalted. Once the butter is melted, it will start to bubble and sputter: let it cook like this for 3–5 minutes, stirring often, until the milk solids are brown (they'll start as puddles of milky white, before turning golden and then toasty brown) and the butter is nutty and fragrant. Transfer half of the brown butter to a small dish and leave the remaining half in the pan.

4. Turn up the heat under the frying pan to medium, then add half of the lima beans. Sauté for about 1½ minutes on each side, noticing as they blister, brown and pop. Once cooked, transfer to a large serving dish, then return the other half of the brown butter to the pan and cook the remaining beans. Add the second batch of beans to the serving dish when ready.

5. Dot little spoonfuls of the garlic yogurt over the dish, then drizzle over the tomato sauce: the sea of buttery beans should be broken up with puddles of white and vivid red. Sprinkle over the herbs, then enjoy either warm or at room temperature.

Variations and substitutions:

To make a vegan version of this dish, swap the dairy yogurt for a non-dairy version, and use 2 tablespoons olive oil instead of the butter to sauté the beans: you won't be able to brown the olive oil, of course, so you'll lose that nutty richness, but the beans will blister and brown all the same.

SOBA NOODLES WITH FERMENTED BLACK SOYBEANS AND BROCCOLI

Nutty soba noodles—usually made from a mixture of wheat and buckwheat—are a perfect match for the broccoli in this easy noodle dish. I also use douchi—fermented black soybeans—here: a Chinese ingredient made from soybeans that are salted and fermented until sharp and deeply savory. It can be found in any Chinese supermarket.

Serves: 4
Ready in: less than 30 minutes

Vegan

Salt, to taste
1 large or 2 small broccoli heads
8 scallions, thinly sliced
2½-inch (6cm) piece of ginger, peeled and grated
4 garlic cloves, crushed or finely grated
3 tablespoons douchi (fermented black soybeans)
9 ounces (250g) soba noodles
2 tablespoons olive or vegetable oil

For the dressing:
2 tablespoons light soy sauce
1 tablespoon white wine vinegar, rice vinegar or cane vinegar
2 teaspoons superfine or granulated sugar
½–1 teaspoon chili flakes, to taste
Splash of sesame oil (this is the best option) or vegetable oil

1. Bring a large pot of lightly salted water to a boil. While the water heats, cut the broccoli into bite-size florets—small enough that they'll mix well with the cooked noodles. It'll seem like a lot of veg, but it'll shrink slightly as it cooks. (Save the broccoli stalk for use in soups; you could also finely chop it and add to a base for stews and casseroles.)

2. Make sure you've got your scallions, ginger and garlic all prepared and ready to go. In a sieve, rinse the douchi really well to remove excess salt, then drain and finely chop.

3. Combine all the ingredients for the dressing in a small bowl.

4. By now, your pot of water should be boiling. Simmer the broccoli florets for 2 minutes, then remove from the water using a slotted spoon. Leave the water on the stovetop—we're going to use this to cook the noodles in a moment.

5. Now cook the noodles: boil them in the pot of water for a minute less than the time suggested on the package, or until they're cooked but still retain some bounce. (If you overcook them, they'll become flabby and sticky.) Drain the cooked noodles into a sieve, rinse with cold water and toss with half of the oil—this helps to stop the noodles clumping.

6. While the noodles cook, you can start pulling everything together. In a large frying pan or preferably a wok, heat the other half of the oil. Sauté the parboiled broccoli over a medium-high heat for 3–5 minutes, or until lightly browned in parts. Add the scallions, ginger, garlic and douchi, and sauté for a minute or two, or until the garlic no longer smells raw. Add the noodles and the dressing and cook over a high flame for a further couple of minutes, or until everything's well combined and steaming hot. Serve straightaway.

Variations and substitutions:

If you can't find the douchi (fermented black soybeans), you can use black bean paste, sold in some larger supermarkets. I wouldn't recommend using black bean sauce. Fermented black beans are most definitely not to be confused with black beans, which are a different kind of bean and an entirely different preparation.

You can swap in different noodles depending on what you happen to have in the pantry. Vermicelli rice noodles are a good option if you can't eat gluten, though they can be more difficult to toss with the broccoli, and you'll have to take care not to overcook them— they'll need to be soaked for only a minute or two in freshly boiled water. (If you do want to make this dish gluten free, use tamari in place of the light soy sauce.) Whatever the case, make sure you check the cooking instructions on the package and adjust the cooking method and times to work with this recipe.

TOMATO AND FENNEL RISOTTO

I'm not sure whether tomato-based risottos are canon, but at this point I don't really care: as someone who'll happily eat stuffed-crust pizza, I think I've lost the right to take any interest in Italian authenticity. Whatever the case, this risotto is easy and works very well with the tomato sweetness alongside the freshness of fennel. I like it a lot.

Serves: 4
Ready in: less than 45 minutes

Vegan option

2 tablespoons olive oil
7 ounces (200g) shallots or 1 large onion, finely
   diced
Salt, to taste
2 fennel bulbs
1 x 14 ounce (400g) can chopped tomatoes
1½ cups (250g) risotto rice
4–5 cups (1–1.2 liters) vegetable stock, hot
Lots of freshly ground black pepper
2–3 tablespoons salted or unsalted butter,
   optional
Parmesan *or* vegetarian alternative, optional

1. Heat the olive oil in a medium, deep pan over a medium heat. Add the shallots or onion and a pinch of salt, and cook for 5–6 minutes, stirring often.

2. While the shallots (or onion) start to soften, prepare the fennel. No need to worry if you've never cooked with fennel bulbs before. Here's what you need to do: Start off by giving them a rinse. Next, peel off the outermost layer if it's looking grubby, bruised or blemished (fennel is a little like onion—and Shrek—in that it has layers). If the fennel you're using has the leafy, bright green fronds still attached—great! Chop these off and set aside for garnishing the risotto later. Now, halve each fennel bulb and set the cut edge facing down onto your chopping board, giving you a stable cutting surface. Chop the fennel bulb halves into ⅜-inch (1cm) cubes, just like you'd chop an onion, cutting in rows down and across. The fennel is now ready to use.

3. With the shallots or onions now slightly softened, sizzling and fragrant, add the chopped fennel and stir well to combine. Cook for 8–10 minutes over a medium heat, putting a lid on the pan between stirs. During this time, the veg should sweat and soften.

4. Add the chopped tomatoes and risotto rice and stir to mix well with the veg. Add a third of the stock. Now it's time to stake a claim to the bit of floor space in front of the stovetop: you'll be rooted here for the next 15 minutes or so, stirring pretty much constantly, as you add the remaining stock a ladle at a time. You'll know it's time to add some more once the rice has absorbed most of the stock already in the pan. Keep stirring throughout, as this helps to shift the rice's starch off the grain and into the sauce, giving the risotto its trademark creaminess. After around 15 minutes, at least 4 cups (1 liter) of the stock will have been added and the rice should be cooked but not mushy. If the rice is too dry or not yet cooked, add the remaining stock and cook for an extra few minutes.

5. Add plenty of black pepper and check the salt, adding a pinch more if necessary. Beat in the butter, if you're using it—it adds creaminess, but it's not vital. If you set fennel fronds aside earlier, roughly chop these to sprinkle on each bowl of risotto, and add grated Parmesan (or similar) if you want to.

Variations and substitutions:

If you don't have risotto rice, you can use long-grain rice in a pinch. Food writer Jack Monroe first opened my eyes to this possibility, and it's a great tip if you don't have the budget or pantry space to have two kinds of rice in the house. If you do use long-grain rice, be aware that you might need slightly less stock and less time on the stovetop for the rice to cook.

You can make this as a straightforward tomato risotto without the fennel, but if you do so consider adding a couple of cloves of garlic with the sautéing shallots or onion to ramp up the flavor.

Fresh tomatoes work well in place of the canned tomatoes here, if you happen to have a glut of them. Add just under 1 pound (400g) roughly chopped cherry, salad or plum tomatoes to the pan along with the fennel, softening them for a while before adding the rice and stock.

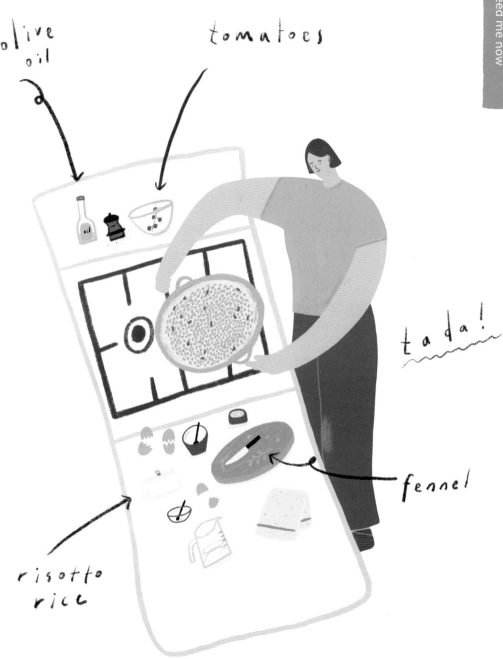

olive oil

tomatoes

ta da!

fennel

risotto rice

39

ZUCCHINI PEARL BARLEY BOWLS WITH SOUR CREAM AND DILL

"What I love about cooking," writes Nora Ephron in her 1983 novel, *Heartburn*, "is that after a hard day, there is something comforting about the fact that if you melt butter and add flour and then hot stock, it will get thick! It's a sure thing! It's a sure thing in a world where nothing is sure." I feel this way about zucchini: the way it will always change from pearly white to tender, sunny and mottled with bronze when cooked with olive oil in a hot pan. And also about pearl barley, knowing that when boiled and seasoned just right, it will swell to perfectly bouncy, nutty grains. And then there's another reliable truth, that sour cream added to more or less any dinner will make it sing. This recipe is unbelievably easy to make and easier still to eat: no messing around, no guesswork, no surprises—a sure thing.

If you want other uses for pearl barley, it works well in stews: there's a variation of the **smoky chicken, okra and chorizo casserole** on page 175.

Serves: 4
Ready in: less than 40 minutes

Vegetarian   Vegan option

---

5 cups (1.2 liters) vegetable or chicken stock, hot
1½ cups (300g) pearl barley
4 small or 2 large zucchini
2 tablespoons olive oil
Handful of dill fronds (roughly ⅓ ounce/10g), roughly chopped
Lots of freshly ground black pepper
Salt, to taste
⅔ cup (150ml) sour cream

1. Bring the stock to a boil, then reduce to a simmer, then add the pearl barley and cook for 20–30 minutes. The difference in cooking times between brands can be a lot, but you want to cook the barley until the grains are tender but still have some bounce to them. Once it's cooked, drain the pearl barley.

2. While the pearl barley cooks, cut the zucchini into ⅜–½ inch (1–1.5cm) cubes. Heat half of the oil in a large frying pan over a medium-high heat. Add the diced zucchini and sauté for 4–5 minutes, stirring often, until the zucchini is mottled with patches of brown and gold.

3. Mix the cooked and drained pearl barley with the fried zucchini, chopped dill and the remaining olive oil, then add black pepper and salt, to taste. Serve in bowls with a couple of spoonfuls of sour cream in each.

Variations and substitutions:

Swap the dill for parsley, basil or mint if you don't like its fennel-like aniseed flavor. You can use plain yogurt or crème fraîche in place of the sour cream. If you want to make this vegan, non-dairy versions are also fine.

SILKY, SMOKY
EGGPLANT STEW

Eggplant tends to need a bit of coaxing to really perform. Some vegetables are at their best when exposed to brief flashes of intense heat—in a griddle pan, in the wok, under the grill—but (with the exception of deep-frying) eggplant prefers to simmer, roast, stew, sweat and soften in its own good time. Rush it and it'll stay spongy, even squeaky. But, with a bit of love, eggplant will cook to perfect silky tenderness. It is also very partial to olive oil. I relate.

Serves: 4
Ready in: less than an hour
Make-ahead and storage tips: page 322

Vegan

2 large or 3 medium eggplant
3 tablespoons olive oil
Salt, to taste
1 medium onion, thinly sliced
1 cinnamon stick or ½ teaspoon
  ground cinnamon
3 bay leaves
5 garlic cloves, crushed or finely grated
2 tablespoons tomato paste
1 teaspoon dried oregano
1 teaspoon smoked paprika
½–1 teaspoon chili flakes, to taste
1 x 14 ounce (400g) can chopped
  tomatoes

Scant 1 cup (200ml) water
1 tablespoon balsamic vinegar

Serve with: steamed rice, couscous
  or bulgur wheat

1. Preheat the oven to 400°F (200°C). Cut the eggplant into 1¼ inch (3cm) cubes. Toss the chopped eggplant with 2 tablespoons of the oil and a sprinkle of salt on a large baking sheet, then roast in the preheated oven for 30 minutes.

2. While the eggplant roasts, you can get started on the stew's aromatic base. Heat the remaining tablespoon of olive oil in a medium to large pan. Add the onion, cinnamon stick (if you're using ground cinnamon, add it later with the garlic instead) and bay leaves along with a pinch of salt. Cook over a medium-low heat, stirring regularly, for 10–12 minutes, or until the onion is starting to soften and lightly brown in parts.

3. Add the garlic, tomato paste, dried oregano, smoked paprika and chili flakes. Stir everything together and sauté for a further minute or two. Add the chopped tomatoes and water (you could roughly half-fill the now-empty chopped tomato can to measure the water). Bring the stew to a simmer over a medium heat and cook for roughly 15 minutes, stirring every so often, while the eggplant finishes roasting.

4. Once the eggplant is ready, add it to the stew, stir to coat with the sauce and add a splash of water if the sauce is very thick. Cook for a further 12–15 minutes, stirring occasionally, until the eggplant has collapsed to silky softness and the sauce is rich and thick. Add the balsamic vinegar. Pluck out the cinnamon stick and bay leaves, add extra salt to taste, and serve with steamed rice, couscous or bulgur wheat.

Variations and substitutions:

As ever, please adapt this to suit what you've got in the cupboard. If you don't have smoked paprika, just leave it out or swap for unsmoked paprika (usually just sold as "paprika")—you won't get that same mellow smokiness in the stew, but it'll be delicious nonetheless. In place of oregano, you can use thyme, rosemary, marjoram, basil or even a dried herb mix, or omit the herbs altogether if you must.

If you have fresh, ripe tomatoes, use these in place of the canned tomatoes, but also add an extra 1 tablespoon of tomato paste. Leeks are a great substitute for the onion if that's what you've got. Just trim one or two, halve them along their length and cut into ⅜-inch (1cm) slices. You can sauté them just as you would the onion, but I'd recommend using an extra tablespoon of olive oil (or, better still, some butter), because leeks taste best if cooked slowly with plenty of fat. Don't even try to substitute the eggplant, you cheeky bastards. It's an eggplant stew.

RED LENTIL DAL WITH LIME

This easy dal is *very* loosely based on Meera Sodha's recipe for her mother's masoor (red lentil) Daily Dal, published in her book *Made in India*. I like the pop of whole seeds so I've added cumin and black mustard seeds, and I'm partial to a sprightly squeeze of lime so that's in there too. But let's be perfectly clear: this is not an improvement on Meera's recipe—just an adaptation to suit my tastes, made in the full knowledge that mum (Meera's or otherwise) will always know best. If you're keen to expand your dal repertoire, I'd highly recommend Meera's vegetarian Indian cookbook *Fresh India*, which contains a number of dal recipes and showcases just how much varied, enlivening cooking can be done with a load of lentils.

Serves: 4
Ready in: 50 minutes
Make-ahead and storage tips: page 322

Vegan

---

2 tablespoons ghee *or* vegetable or coconut oil
1 teaspoon cumin seeds
1 teaspoon brown or black mustard seeds
1 teaspoon chili flakes
1 medium onion, finely diced
1½ tablespoons tomato paste
1½-inch (4cm) piece of ginger, peeled and grated
4 garlic cloves, crushed or finely grated
2 cups (275g) split red lentils (also sold as masoor dal)

1 x 14 ounce (400g) can chopped tomatoes
1 teaspoon garam masala
½ teaspoon turmeric
5½–6 cups (1.3–1.5 liters) water
½ teaspoon salt, plus more to taste
2–4 tablespoons lime or lemon juice (from 2–4 limes or 1–2 lemons), to taste

Serve with: rice or flatbreads (the **roti canai** on page 290 works well), optional

1. In a large pan over a medium heat, heat the ghee or oil and add the cumin seeds, mustard seeds and chili flakes. Let the seeds sizzle for 30–45 seconds or so, then add the onion and stir well to mix everything together. Turn down the heat slightly, then sauté the onion for 10–12 minutes, until lightly golden and soft.

2. Add the tomato paste, ginger and garlic. Sauté for a further few minutes, until the tomato paste has deepened in color and the garlic has lost its sharp, raw edge.

3. Add the red lentils, chopped tomatoes, garam masala, turmeric and most of the water. Increase the heat to bring the mixture to a simmer. Once it's briskly bubbling, turn down the heat and let it cook for 20–25 minutes, stirring often. The dal is ready when the lentils are soft and falling apart, creating a thick, soupy mixture. If you prefer a thicker consistency, cook the dal for longer; if you prefer a looser, soupier dal, add the remaining water.

4. Add the salt and lime juice, then taste the dal: if you feel it needs a bit more of either, add that now. Serve straightaway. A thicker dal can work well with flatbreads, while a thinner dal lends itself to being spooned over steamed white rice.

Variations and substitutions:

If you have fresh tomatoes, you can use these in place of the canned tomatoes specified above. Just cut 4–6 ripe tomatoes into small cubes and add to the pan along with the garlic and ginger. Give the tomatoes a few minutes to soften and collapse before adding the lentils and the remaining ingredients. If you do this, you may also want to double the amount of tomato paste to add extra sweetness and depth.

In place of the cumin seeds, you can use ground cumin: just add ½ teaspoon when you add the garam masala and turmeric. Black and brown mustard seeds are available in larger supermarkets and most South Asian grocery stores, but if you can't get hold of them, feel free to leave them out.

BACK-OF-THE-NET PASTA

Salmon pasta with crème fraîche, sun-dried tomatoes and spinach

I don't think there's much point in being a hobby cook—someone with the time, resources and inclination to cook for pleasure—if you're not able to have fun with it. We all know someone who's gone wrong on this count: the guy who gets so deep into the science of his morning coffee that he's forgotten what it means to relax into those first sips, or the person so hell-bent on throwing the perfect dinner party that they don't ever want to play around with flavors or bend a recipe to their tastes. This kind of cooking—by science, to the letter, of the moment—is fair enough if your job is to cook or if you're so pressed for time or money that failure just isn't an option. But if you cook for fun, I beg of you to remember the fun part of the pie, and not take it all too seriously.

With that in mind, I'd ask that you serious food nerds reserve your judgment of this recipe. *Yes*, salmon is a bit obvious, and *yes*, sun-dried tomatoes are extremely passé. But just like the hosts of my favorite podcast, *You're Wrong About,* like to restore the reputations of unfairly maligned women of the nineties, I'm here to say that maybe sun-dried tomatoes aren't so bad after all. And, importantly, it's a riff on a meal that Arsenal soccer players Vivianne Miedema and Lisa Evans make and eat on a regular basis. If it's good enough for a record goal scorer and a Scottish women's national team player, it's good enough for me. (If you're a Tottenham fan, I'm sorry.)

To make enough to serve 4, you may find it easier to cook the salmon in the oven rather than crowding everything into the pan. Check the variations and substitutions below to see how to do this.

Serves: 2
Ready in: less than 30 minutes

Salt, to taste

2 tablespoons oil from the sun-dried tomato jar or olive oil

3 tablespoons fresh breadcrumbs or 1–2 tablespoons dried breadcrumbs

5 ounces (150g) pasta of your choice (Viv and Lisa use tagliatelle, but I find that the sauce and pasta mix easier with penne)

½ medium onion, finely diced

3 garlic cloves, crushed or finely grated

½ cup (60g) sun-dried tomatoes, roughly chopped

5 ounces (150g) fresh or frozen (and defrosted) whole leaf spinach

2 salmon fillets, skin cut off

Lots of freshly ground black pepper

5 tablespoons (75ml) crème fraîche

1. First, bring a large pot of salted water to a boil for the pasta. While the water heats, prepare the breadcrumbs, which are going to be fried to create a salty, crunchy topping for this pasta. Heat 1 tablespoon of oil in a large frying pan over a medium heat, and add the breadcrumbs. Sauté, stirring very often, until the breadcrumbs are a rich golden color and crisp. Scoop the crumbs into a small bowl or ramekin, and set to one side.

2. Add the pasta to the boiling water and set a timer, cooking it according to the instructions on the package. Once it's done, drain it well.

3. While the pasta cooks, pour the remaining tablespoon of oil into your frying pan and add the diced onion. Sauté for 6–8 minutes over a medium heat, or until the onion starts to soften. Add the garlic and sun-dried tomatoes and sauté for a minute or two more, until the garlic loses that acrid raw smell and becomes fragrant. Add the spinach and stir until it's wilted and well mixed with the other ingredients.

4. Next, move all the veg to one side of the pan and lay down the salmon fillets on the other side of the pan. Continue to cook for 3 minutes, then turn over the fillets and cook for a minute or two more. As soon as the salmon is just cooked enough that you can break it apart with a wooden spoon—it should be flaky, tender and rosy, not firm, deeply pink and jelly-like—gently flake it into big chunks and stir to mix with the veg. Turn off the heat.

5. Season the salmon and veg mix with salt and pepper, then add the cooked, drained pasta and the crème fraîche. Toss everything gently to combine, then serve straightaway. If you're an Arsenal fan, this kind of soothing, carby meal is exactly the remedy you'll need after the nail-biting trauma of a game.

Variations and substitutions:

If you really have something against sun-dried tomatoes, you can use cherry tomatoes instead. Halve 5 ounces (150g) cherry tomatoes and add them to the pan at the same time as the onion.

To make enough to serve 4, double all the ingredient quantities, and bake the salmon fillets at 350°F (180°C) for 10–15 minutes, or until flaking and rosy. While the salmon cooks, cook the pasta and prepare the veg in the frying pan as described above. Combine the salmon, veg, pasta and crème fraîche, flaking the salmon apart as you go.

Kitchen diaries

Much as I love him, I'm not sure I live under the same sun as Nigel Slater. Writing about the rhythms of his culinary year, he describes Jerusalem artichokes, Christmas wreaths and tender stalks of pink rhubarb as midwinter shifts into spring. There are blood oranges and plump shrimp and trips to the vegetable garden and the grocery store, always chancing upon some new seasonal bounty. This isn't the food world I recognize, though that's not to say I don't envy it.

I know that the seasons have shifted when the supermarket near me wheels out the mince pies (a British quirk) and candy canes, or when Mariah's crystal vocals begin to drift out across the store. There are some times of year when the plantain at the corner store are fat and mottled with black, and other times when they're wizened—crowned, at the stem, with the faintest halo of mold. These ebbs and flows aren't something I could mark out on the calendar, but I sense them in my gut. At some point, I notice Cadbury Creme Eggs in a box by the cash register: this is my reminder to buy my grandma a birthday present. When the morning sun streams in through the bedroom window but the cars haven't started roaring in the street below, I know it's midsummer and watermelon in the store across the road will be as heavy and sweet as ever. I can't see the stars in the London sky or the ground beneath my feet, but whenever I pick up some ghoulish novelty flavored chips, I know exactly when and where I am.

TOFU AND GREENS WITH
HOT AND SOUR CHILI SAUCE

This is a reassuringly easy dinner for days when nothing seems to be going quite right. What I most love about it, aside from how simple it is, is the contrast between the bright tofu and the deep emerald tangle of the greens. I know on sight that it'll do me good. When everything else is so unpredictable, tiny certainties like this count for something.

The sauce here is similar to a sweet and sour sauce that you might find in Chinese takeout. That sauce is in turn similar to Cantonese sweet and sour pork, or Korean Chinese tangsuyuk (battered meat with a tangy sauce), or any number of maasim (sour) Filipino sauces and accompaniments. You'll need firm tofu for this, which is the type ordinarily sold in a plastic pack in the refrigerated aisle of the supermarket, with all the other vegetarian and vegan stuff. It is not—and I can't stress this enough—the same as silken tofu, which is much softer and sold in a smaller pack in the pantry aisle. If you accidentally pick up silken tofu, you can use it in the **spicy soft tofu and mushroom stew** on page 52.

Serves: 4
Ready in: less than 45 minutes
Make-ahead and storage tips: page 323

Vegan

---

14 ounces (400g) firm tofu
1 tablespoon vegetable or olive oil
10 ounces (300g) greens,* sliced across
  the leaf into thick strips 1 inch
  (2.5cm) wide

For the sauce:
1 tablespoon vegetable or olive oil
4 scallions, thinly sliced
4 garlic cloves, crushed or finely grated
1¼-inch (3cm) piece of ginger, peeled
  and grated

2 tablespoons light soy sauce or tamari
2 tablespoons white vinegar
  (rice, white wine or cane vinegar
  are all good options)
2 tablespoons superfine or
  granulated sugar
2 teaspoons paprika
½–1 teaspoon chili flakes, to taste
1⅔ cups (400ml) water
1½ tablespoons cornstarch

Serve with: steamed white rice

*I use the cheap stuff, just labeled in the supermarket as "greens" or "spring greens," but Tuscan kale, kale or chard would also work really nicely here. Spinach would be too soft and slippery, though.

1. First of all, drain the tofu if it came in a container of liquid, then wrap the block in a few sheets of paper towel (or a perfectly clean tea towel). Place the wrapped tofu on top of one chopping board and underneath another. A heavy wooden chopping board is best for on top here, as we're aiming to gently press the water from the tofu, but if you only have lightweight boards, just balance a can or two on top, or perhaps a bag of flour. Let it sit like this while you prepare the rest of the dish.

2. Now heat the oil for the sauce in a medium saucepan over a medium heat. Add the scallions, garlic and ginger and fry for 1–2 minutes, or until the garlic stops smelling sharp and raw and takes on a mellower note, then add the soy sauce (or tamari), vinegar, sugar, paprika, chili flakes and all but 2 tablespoons of the water. In a small bowl, mix the reserved 2 tablespoons of water with the cornstarch to create a slurry, and set to one side. Now bring the sauce to a simmer, then cook over a low heat for 10 minutes to give the flavors a chance to get to know each other. If it's reducing very quickly, turn the heat down or add a splash more water.

3. While the sauce cooks, now would be a good time to cook some rice, if that's what you want to serve this with. It's also time to get on with the tofu and greens. Retrieve your tofu from its press and unwrap it, then slice into ½–¾ inch (1.5–2cm) cubes. Heat the oil in a large frying pan (preferably one you have a lid for, though this isn't vital) or a wok, if you have one. Over a medium-high heat, sauté the tofu cubes for 2–4 minutes, stirring often, until they're golden in parts and beginning to firm and crisp at the edges (this will be quicker in a wok than in a frying pan).

4. Once the tofu is mottled with gold, add the sliced greens and stir well. Cook for a further few minutes. Exactly how long this takes will depend on the size and type of your pan. If your greens are heaped high in the frying pan, you'll need to stir often until they collapse down into the pan—this is where a lid can come in handy, because you can add a splash of water to the pan, put the lid on and watch the greens wilt in just a minute or two. If you're using a wok, this will be a quicker process and it'll be easier to stir the greens as they cook. Either way, this shouldn't take longer than 5–6 minutes maximum. Once it's done, turn the heat down as low as it'll go.

5. The sauce should have simmered for 10 minutes by now. Give the cornstarch–water slurry a brisk stir, then add it to the sauce and turn

up the heat slightly. Very quickly, the sauce will thicken and the hissy, delicate simmer will turn to a happy bubbling noise. It won't be custard-thick, just slightly thickened and glossy. Mix with the tofu and greens in the frying pan, stirring to coat everything with that jewel-red sauce, and serve straightaway with lots of rice.

Variations and substitutions:

Tofu is honestly the best protein for the job here: it contrasts really nicely with the greens and the sweet, sour, sticky sauce. If you're a committed meat-eater though, you could use diced chicken pieces instead—just sauté them for slightly longer before adding the greens.

Finely chopped onion would work instead of the scallions. Sauté it by itself for 8–10 minutes before adding the ginger and garlic, so that it has a chance to soften. If you use frozen diced onion, along with pre-prepped ginger and garlic pieces or pastes, this is a good way to cut down (pun intended) on any chopping work involved in this dish, which might be particularly useful if you struggle with these kinds of fine movements—whether because of the way your body works or because you've got a baby on one hip.

SPICY SOFT TOFU AND MUSHROOM STEW

I've been cooking for a while, but I've only recently come to grips with the magic of contrast. I'm talking about hot fries and cool mayo, crunchy hazelnuts with tender asparagus or tangy Filipino sawsawan with sizzling barbecued meat. This Korean stew is a master class in this kind of contrast: the most delicate, ivory clouds of soft tofu nestle among the veg and the hot, spicy red broth. It's beautiful.

There are so many ways to make this stew, so I can't claim that this recipe is definitive: some recipes include pork; others feature seafood like clams, shrimp or scallops. I've gone heavy on the veg, using potato to bulk it out alongside the cabbage and mushrooms, and have adapted the cooking process so that it can be made in a large saucepan rather than the traditional small stoneware pots, or dolsot. If you're after a more traditional rendering of this wonderful dish, there's a recipe in *Korean Home Cooking* by Sohui Kim and Rachel Wharton, and another on the blog *My Korean Kitchen*. To learn more about Korean cooking, *Maangchi's Big Book of Korean Cooking* is a great primer, or Robin Ha's *Cook Korean!* is a fun comic-style riff on the classics.

The most vital part of this stew is the soft tofu, which is jiggly and tender—very different from firm tofu. If you go to a Korean food store, you'll be able to buy fresh soft tofu in a sausage-shaped package in the refrigerated section. This is my favorite kind. If you can't get that, just use the silken tofu that comes in a rectangular package and can be found in any large supermarket. It's not quite as quiveringly light, but it'll do the job just fine.

Gochugaru is a kind of Korean chili flake: spicy, bright red and robust. If you're going to the effort of making this beautiful stew, I'd recommend getting some from a Korean food store or a large supermarket. It's what's responsible for the beautiful scarlet color of the soup. I also use it in the **cheesy kimchi cornbread muffins** on page 224, so you don't need to worry about having nothing to do with the rest of the container.

Serves: 4
Ready in: less than 45 minutes
Make-ahead and storage tips: page 323

Vegan option

¼ medium green or Savoy cabbage (roughly ½ pound/200g)

1 large potato (roughly ½ pound/200g)

5–7 ounces (150–200g) shiitake mushrooms

4 scallions

4 tablespoons vegetable oil

1–2 tablespoons gochugaru (Korean red pepper flakes), to taste

4 garlic cloves, crushed or finely grated

1½ tablespoons fish sauce (Korean anchovy sauce if possible), plus extra to taste

1 tablespoon light soy sauce *or* tamari

4–5 cups (0.9–1.2 liters) water, freshly boiled

Salt, to taste

12 ounces (350g) very soft or silken tofu

Serve with: steamed white rice, optional

1. Start by preparing the veg: Very thinly slice the cabbage, then peel the potato and cut into ¾–1¼ inch (2–3cm) cubes. Remove the shiitake stalks (they're tough when cooked) and thickly slice the caps. Thinly slice the scallions.

2. In a large saucepan, heat the vegetable oil over a medium heat. Add the gochugaru and garlic. Sauté for 1–2 minutes, stirring all the time, until the garlic no longer smells raw. Make sure you don't let the gochugaru burn, or it'll become bitter.

3. Add the prepared cabbage, potato, mushrooms, scallions, fish sauce, soy sauce and 4 cups (900ml) of the freshly boiled water. Bring the mixture to a simmer, then put on a lid, reduce the heat to low and simmer gently for 15 minutes. During this time, you can wash and cook some rice to serve with this stew, if you want.

4. Check the seasoning of the stew, adding extra fish sauce and a pinch of salt if necessary. If it needs a little more water, add that now. Reduce the heat as low as it'll go—the stew needs to be kept hot but shouldn't be simmering, or the bubbles will break up the delicate tofu. If the stew is still bubbling even on the lowest heat, just turn off the heat altogether. Decant the quivering white tofu from its packaging, keeping it in one piece. Using a teaspoon, gently scoop heaped spoonfuls into the stew, dotting it throughout. Put a lid on the pot and let it sit on or off the heat, depending on how low your burner will go, for 3 minutes. Serve straightaway with rice or as it is.

Variations and substitutions:

To make a vegan version of this stew, you can leave out the fish sauce and increase the amount of soy sauce from 1 tablespoon to 2 tablespoons. As a replacement for the fish sauce flavor, you can also add a large sheet of nori, cut into 1¼ inch (3cm) squares. Add the squares to the stew when you add the vegetables, water and soy sauce.

You should be able to find shiitake mushrooms in East Asian food stores, but if you're struggling to find them you can use dried mushrooms and standard cremini mushrooms to similar effect: the dried mushrooms add loads of flavor, while the fresh mushrooms provide texture and bulk. Add 1 ounce (30g) dried shiitake or porcini mushrooms to the boiling water for the stew, letting them soak for 10 minutes. Once soaked, roughly chop the rehydrated mushrooms and add to the pan along with their mushroom-y soaking liquid. Add 5–7 ounces (150–200g) cremini mushrooms as well, putting them into the pan at the same time as the cabbage and potatoes.

If you happen to have cabbage kimchi in the fridge, you can use this in place of the cabbage! It adds loads of flavor as well. Another alternative is shredded Brussels sprouts.

If you really can't get hold of gochugaru, you can use 1 tablespoon paprika and 1 teaspoon chili flakes, but it won't be quite the same.

GNOCCHI WITH HARISSA BUTTER AND BROCCOLI

I love gnocchi. These chewy, portly little dumplings have saved me on many a lazy evening when I've arrived home tired and hungry, in need of something comforting, filling and quick. In this recipe, the spicy, buttery harissa coats the gnocchi and soaks into the broccoli florets, bringing a fiery kick to this easy midweek meal.

Harissa is easy to get in most decent-sized supermarkets: you should find it somewhere near the dried herbs and spices, with the other cooking pastes, spice mixes and sauces. And don't worry that you'll be buying a whole jar or tube only to use a couple of tablespoons: you can use more of the paste in the **harissa, spinach and ricotta cannelloni with toasted hazelnuts** recipe on page 180 and it's also great in tagines, with pasta, in soups or rubbed over the skin of a chicken before you roast it.

In this recipe, sautéing gives a crispier finish to the gnocchi and a buttery, caramelized layer underneath, but roasting is ideal if you just want a more hands-off approach. Roasting is also handy if you want to scale up the quantities, as even a two-person serving tends to fill a frying pan. With that in mind, I've written two versions of the recipe below: one using the roasting-pan method and one for the stovetop.

Serves: 2
Ready in: less than 30 minutes (stovetop method)
   or less than an hour (oven method)

Vegetarian   Vegan option

¼ cup (25g) walnuts, roughly chopped
Salt, to taste
1 small broccoli head
1 pound 2 ounces (500g) gnocchi
2 tablespoons (30g) salted or unsalted
   butter
2 tablespoons harissa, or to taste

The stovetop method:

1. First, toast the nuts in a large frying pan over a medium-low heat, stirring regularly. After a few minutes, they should begin to smell lightly toasted and nutty. Remove from the heat and transfer to a little bowl.

2. Bring a pot of salted water to a boil. While the water heats, prepare the broccoli: break the head into medium florets, then trim and peel the stalk before cutting it into ¼ inch (.5cm) rounds. Add the broccoli and gnocchi to the now-boiling water, reduce the heat slightly and simmer for 2 minutes. Drain well, letting the gnocchi and veg steam dry in whatever you've used to drain them for a couple of minutes (this will help them caramelize in the pan).

3. Melt the butter in your frying pan over a medium-high heat, then add the harissa and let it sizzle for a few seconds until your mouth begins to water. Add the gnocchi and broccoli to the pan, placing the florets bushy side down if you can—this will help them wick up all that butter and spice.

Cook for about 2 minutes, resisting the urge to stir—leaving everything in place will help it all to caramelize and brown. Give it a stir, then turn the heat down and cook for 4–5 minutes more, stirring occasionally. Season to taste, then scatter over the toasted walnuts when you dish it out.

The roasting-pan method:

1. Preheat the oven to 350°F (180°C) and get out an appropriate-sized roasting pan (a 6 x 8 inch/15 x 20cm pan will be big enough for a 2-person serving).

2. Toast the nuts in the roasting pan for 5–8 minutes, until fragrant. Use your eyes (and/or nose) to monitor how deeply they've toasted: if they burn, they'll be really bitter. Once they're ready, remove from the oven, tip into a little bowl and set to one side.

3. Boil a full kettle. Tip the gnocchi into a large heatproof bowl and pour over the boiling water. Leave the gnocchi to sit for 2 minutes, then drain. To prepare the broccoli, break the head into medium florets. Trim and peel the stalks, then slice into ¼ inch (.5cm) rounds.

4. Toss the butter in the roasting pan and melt in the oven for a couple of minutes. Stir in the harissa, then tip in the gnocchi and broccoli. Season with a little salt, mix everything well and roast for 25 minutes. Scatter over the toasted walnuts when you serve it.

Variations and substitutions:

If you don't have walnuts, almonds also work well for adding crunch, as do pine nuts or egusi. They can also be left out entirely.

You can use sweet potato or cauliflower gnocchi in place of the potato gnocchi if you fancy a change: you can get them in some larger supermarkets, usually in the refrigerated aisle. Gluten-free gnocchi can also be found in larger supermarkets.

In a pinch, you can swap the harissa for two tablespoons of red pesto and a pinch of chili flakes or powder. It'll be a very different dish, but still a quick and easy weeknight gnocchi idea.

You can use olive oil or a vegan butter in place of the butter here—it won't be quite as rich as the butter, but it'll still help the gnocchi crisp and caramelize.

EDEN RICE WITH BLACK BEANS
AND PLANTAIN

Some meals are just transparently brilliant—things like lasagna and golden-skinned roast chicken—while others, like this one, are perfect in a less flashy kind of way. What I love about this meal is that it's filling but varied, with verdant, garden-green rice (hence the name), hearty black beans and golden plantain. I come back to this recipe again and again and again when I want something that will satisfy body and soul.

You'll need to do some multitasking to get this meal to the table, but it's not difficult. Just make sure that you get all your ingredients out and prepped first: that means chopping the chilies, dicing the onion and so on before you get started with the cooking itself.

Serves: 4
Ready in: less than 55 minutes
Make-ahead and storage tips: page 323

Vegan

For the rice:
1½ cups (300g) white rice
10 ounces (300g) frozen chopped or
    whole leaf spinach, defrosted
1¾ cups (400ml) cold water
2 teaspoons olive or vegetable oil
4 garlic cloves, crushed or finely grated
1 bird's eye (Thai) chili, thinly sliced, or
    ½ teaspoon chili flakes
Generous pinch of salt

For the plantain:
2 ripe plantain, yellow-mottled
    with black spots
2 teaspoons olive or vegetable oil
2 teaspoons chipotle paste
Pinch of salt

For the black beans:
2 tablespoons olive or vegetable oil
1 large onion, finely diced
4 garlic cloves, crushed or finely grated
1 teaspoon dried oregano
1 bird's eye (Thai) chili or ½ teaspoon
    chili flakes, optional
2 x 14 ounce (400g) cans black beans,
    drained
4 tablespoons salted peanuts or
    cashews, roughly chopped
scant 1 cup (200ml) water, plus more if
    necessary
Salt, to taste

Special equipment: stick blender,
    food processor or blender, optional

1. Preheat the oven to 400°F (200°C).

2. Rinse the rice thoroughly in cold water, changing the water a few times until it's no longer cloudy. Drain the rice well and set to one side.

3. In a food processor or blender, or using a stick blender, blitz the defrosted spinach with the 1¾ cups (400ml) water. If you don't have a blender, just skip this step! The rice won't come out as vibrantly green, but it'll taste great all the same.

4. Heat the oil for the rice in a medium pot—one large enough to cook the rice, but not so large that the rice will cook in a really thin layer—and add the garlic and chili, sautéing it over a medium-low heat for a minute or so. It's ready when the raw garlic smell mellows a little, but make sure you don't let it brown and burn. Add the washed rice, spinach purée (or unblended spinach and water) and salt to the pot, stir well to combine, then bring to a simmer. As soon as it begins to boil, put a tight-fitting lid over the pot, turn the heat as low as possible (it helps to transfer the pan to the smallest burner if it isn't already on it) and cook for 15 minutes. Once the 15 minutes are up, turn off the heat but leave the lid on, letting the rice steam in the residual heat for 5 extra minutes. It'll stay warm like this until you're ready to serve it.

5. While the rice cooks, peel the plantain (cut off each end, score the skin along the plantain's length with a sharp knife, then pull the skin off like a coat) and cut on the diagonal into elegant slices around ⅜ inch (1cm) thick. Toss the slices with the oil, chipotle paste and salt, then lay out on a baking sheet. Bake for 10 minutes, then flip the slices and bake for a further 10 minutes.

6. Next up, make the beans—this is a really quick job. Heat the oil in a medium pan, then add the onion and cook over a medium heat for 6–8 minutes, until softened. Add the garlic, dried oregano and chili (if using) and sauté for a further minute or so. Add the drained beans, peanuts or cashews and scant 1 cup (200ml) water. Cook for 5 minutes, stirring often and mashing the beans against the side of the pan or under a spoon or spatula as you go. You want the beans to be broken and creamy, but there should still be plenty of whole beans to provide a craggy texture. If the beans start to dry out, add a splash more water. If they're too sloppy, just cook for a bit longer to evaporate away some of the liquid. Season to taste.

7. By the time that the beans are ready, the plantain should be just about ready to come out of the oven and the rice should have cooked and had its 5 minutes of resting time. Serve the beans heaped over the bright green rice and top with the golden, smoky plantain.

Variations and substitutions:

If you have fresh spinach, you can use it in place of the frozen spinach. Just blanch it (dunk it in boiling water, then quickly whisk it out and place in ice-cold water to stop the cooking process), drain, squeeze out any excess water and roughly chop it. You can then blend it with the water as above.

As an alternative to plantain, you could serve this with sweet potato or butternut squash. Peel and cut into ⅜ inch (1cm) slices, then coat with oil, spice and salt as above, then bake for 30 minutes, flipping the slices halfway through the cooking time. While I'll admit that it looks similar to plantain (and indeed they are related), banana is not an appropriate substitution.

If you prefer to fry the plantain—like you would for dodo or kelewele—forget about heating the oven and heat 1¼ cups (300ml) cooking oil in a large frying pan instead. Coat the plantain with the chipotle paste (or spices) and salt—no need to oil it. Heat the oil to 350°F (180°C) and fry the plantain slices for 2 minutes on each side.

If you don't have dried oregano, you can use dried marjoram, thyme or a dried herb mix. Instead of the chipotle paste, use 1 teaspoon smoked paprika and 1 teaspoon chili flakes.

More food, less work

SIMPLE RECIPES FOR WHEN YOU'RE LOW ON TIME OR ENERGY

Recipe list

Introduction

Everyone's idea of hard work is different—in the kitchen, especially so. For some people, a 6-hour cooking project is no big deal, but if they have to multitask during that time, things spiral out of control. For others, good cooking is about minimizing the physical exertion or strain, even if that means constant strategizing, negotiating and reworking a recipe inside their mind. Some can't commit to more than half an hour in the kitchen before the baby wakes up. The recipes in this chapter are about meeting you where you're at, whether the challenge for you is a disability or a baby in the next room. There are plenty of roasting-pan recipes here—like one for mozzarella-strewn orzo with broccoli—giving you the freedom to stick dinner in the oven and free up your mind and hands. There are also recipes that minimize strenuous chopping, stirring and mixing, if the physical side of cooking is something you struggle with: a soothing coconut, tomato and lima bean stew does just this. Towards the end of this chapter, you'll even find some low-effort cakes and desserts.

More food, less work

Further reading

Portugal Meets Mozambique by Jeny Sulemange
The Roasting Tin by Rukmini Iyer
The Quick Roasting Tin by Rukmini Iyer
Salt, Fat, Acid, Heat by Samin Nosrat
The Perfect Scoop by David Lebovitz
Jamie's 30-Minute Meals by Jamie Oliver
Real Fast Food by Nigel Slater
Nigellissima by Nigella Lawson
Simply Nigella by Nigella Lawson

IN-THE-OVEN TOMATOES AND LIMA BEANS IN A SPICED COCONUT BROTH

The effort-to-reward ratio for this dish is pretty spectacular: All you need to do is toss tomatoes in the oven to roast with garlic, fragrant nigella seeds (also known as black onion seeds or kalonji) and chili flakes. Halfway through the roasting time—during which the tomatoes become yielding and sweet—meaty lima beans and coconut milk are added, blending with the tomato juices to create a fragrant broth.

There are so many cuisines in which coconut milk becomes the basis for beautiful spiced broths: from south Indian vegetable ishtu to Malaysian laksa with its spice and noodles and Filipino ginataan dishes (ginataan means "cooked with coconut milk"). The inspiration for this particular dish is diverse, but what really brought it together was Jeny Sulemange's cookbook *Portugal Meets Mozambique*, all about the Mozambican food that Jeny cooks for Cantinho do Aziz, a restaurant with outposts in both Lisbon and, funnily enough, Leeds, in the UK. Jeny makes a side dish of lima beans cooked in tomatoey coconut milk, which inspired me to add pulses to this recipe (until that point it had just been a delicately spiced tomato and coconut dish). The beans really add heft and bite, making this a hearty meal when served with plenty of steamed rice.

In case you're not familiar with nigella seeds, they're the tiny jet-black seeds that you'll sometimes find studded into soft naan. You can find them in all large supermarkets, and I'd recommend having them in the cupboard for putting in flatbreads, soups and scattered over roasted vegetables.

Serves: 4
Ready in: less than 1 hour 15 minutes, of which
  1 hour is hands-off time while the dish roasts
Make-ahead and storage tips: page 323

Vegan

2¼ pounds (1kg) tomatoes
2 tablespoons vegetable, olive or
  coconut oil
Salt, to taste
4 garlic cloves, skin left on
1 teaspoon nigella seeds
½–1 teaspoon chili flakes, to taste

1 x 14 ounce (400ml) can coconut
  milk, preferably full-fat
2 x 14 ounce (400ml) cans lima
  beans, drained

Serve with: steamed white rice

1. Preheat the oven to 400°F (200°C). Get out a large, deep roasting pan—at least 9 x 13 inches (22 x 33cm).

2. While the oven heats, halve the tomatoes from top to tail.

3. Drizzle the oil into your roasting pan. Sprinkle the cut side of the tomatoes with plenty of salt (I start with about ½ teaspoon but often use more—the tomatoes really benefit from it) and arrange them in the oil with their cut edges facing down. Tuck the garlic cloves into the spaces between the tomatoes and scatter over the nigella seeds and chili flakes. Roast for 30 minutes in the preheated oven.

4. After 30 minutes, gently turn the tomatoes so that the cut sides are now facing up. Remove the roasted garlic cloves, take off their skins and crush the soft flesh into the coconut milk. Pour the garlicky coconut milk mixture all over the top of the tomatoes, then mix in the lima beans and return the pan to the oven for a further 30 minutes. Check the seasoning, then serve with rice.

Variations and substitutions:

To minimize chopping, you can use whole cherry tomatoes if that's what you have. Just toss them in the oil and salt, arrange in the roasting pan and proceed following the recipe above. They should pop and burst as they roast, but if they're still proving stubborn around the 30-minute mark, gently mash them to split their skins before pouring in the coconut milk.

Cannellini beans or gungo (pigeon) peas would also work nicely here.

If you can't get hold of nigella seeds, try black mustard seeds or cumin seeds instead, both of which will impart a very different flavor but will add crunch and interest nonetheless.

GNOCCHI WITH
CHILI CRISP SAUCE, CAPERS
AND PARMESAN

Who among us can honestly say they're not, at least on occasion, a petulant cook? I know I am because, despite twenty-something years on this planet so far, I'm still not completely fluent in the signals and distress calls of my own body. I ignore the brain fuzz and the distracted clicking between browser tabs and that feeling of whole-body heaviness, so that, by the time it registers that I'm hungry, I've gone way past the point of being a reasonable adult. Things can get ugly.

Because I know this about myself, I know I need simple, off-the-top-of-my-head meals for when the business of daily life gets in between me and my food. These meals need to be almost embarrassingly easy, both in terms of the processes involved in the recipe and the mental energy required to get started. (If my hunger is deep enough, even chopping an onion is enough to send me into a huff.) This gnocchi recipe is one that I fumble for again and again in these times of need: there's no chopping and barely any thinking required, and you can get it from pantry to table in less than 15 minutes.

You'll need chili crisp sauce for this: It's a Chinese condiment available in pretty much any Chinese grocery store and most supermarkets. Made with chili flakes, onion and fermented soybeans suspended in deep red oil, it's a crispy, crunchy condiment that's a little spicy, deeply savory and very, very moreish. For predictable and largely racist reasons, MSG has been unfairly maligned in the West, but in chili crisp sauce it brings the whole thing into perfect focus, like finding your glasses on top of your head and seeing life clearly for the first time all day. There's really no substitute for chili crisp sauce here—Lao Gan Ma is a widely available brand—so don't waste your time trying to make this dish without it. Along with the sharpness of the capers and the richness of butter and cheese, it's a dream.

Good news: this also works as a sauce for pasta! You may want to use a little bit more of everything though to make sure the pasta strands or pieces are all well coated with the buttery sauce.

Serves: 4
Ready in: less than 15 minutes

2¼ pounds (1kg) gnocchi

3 tablespoons unsalted butter

4 tablespoons capers in brine, well drained

2 tablespoons chili crisp sauce (I use Lao Gan Ma brand)

½ cup (60g) Parmesan *or* vegetarian alternative, grated

1. Bring a large pot of water to a steady simmer. Once it's ready, add the gnocchi and cook according to the instructions on the package. Drain the gnocchi, but set aside a few tablespoons of the cooking water.

2. In a large frying pan set over a medium-high heat, melt the butter. Once it's molten and sizzling, add the capers and chili crisp sauce (making sure you dig down in the jar to get spoonfuls of the crispy chili flakes—not just the oil floating on top) and sizzle for about 30 seconds, stirring all the time. Add the gnocchi to the pan along with a couple of tablespoons of the reserved cooking water, then stir or shake the pan until the gnocchi are well coated with a slick of red oil and everything's piping hot. This is best served straightaway with the grated Parmesan.

Variations and substitutions:

This recipe is my baby. I did try to veganize it, but there's really no match for butter and cheese as a foil for the punchy chili crisp sauce. This is a rare occasion when I'm gonna recommend you either take it as it is or leave it. However, if you can't eat gluten, gluten-free gnocchi can be found in larger supermarkets.

ROASTED OKRA, GREEN BEANS AND PANEER WITH GREEN CHUTNEY AND LIME

Okra—like farfalle pasta or tripe or rainbow bagels—is something that gets energetically slandered and just as vigorously defended about once a week on the internet. I hate going round in circles with all that crap, so I'll say only this: I really, really like okra any which way, but especially when it's cooked like this.

This is a stick-it-in-the-oven kind of meal, enlivened with the help of an Indian green chutney—made from cilantro leaves, chili and lime.

Serves: 4
Ready in: less than 45 minutes
Make-ahead and storage tips: page 323

Vegetarian   Vegan option

---

3 medium sweet potatoes
   (roughly 1¼ pounds/500g)
9 ounces (250g) paneer
7 ounces (200g) green beans
7 ounces (200g) okra
2 tablespoons coconut, vegetable
   or olive oil
1½ teaspoons chili powder
1½ teaspoons amchur,* optional
1 teaspoon cumin
½ teaspoon nigella seeds
Salt, to taste
½ lime, cut into wedges

For the green chutney:
4 cups (2 ounces/60g) fresh cilantro, stalks
   removed
1 thin green chili
1–1½ tablespoons lime juice
   (from roughly 1 lime)
¼ teaspoon cumin
2–3 tablespoons water
Salt, to taste

Serve with: rice or flatbreads
   (the **roti canai** on page 290 work well)
Special equipment: a stick blender
   or blender, optional

*This ground sour mango adds a lovely sourness to the dish but it's not vital. You can find amchur (or amchoor) in lots of South Asian grocery stores.

1. Preheat the oven to 400°F (200°C) and get out a large roasting pan. While the oven preheats, prep the veg and paneer. Start by peeling the sweet potatoes and cutting into 1¼ inch (3cm) cubes. Cut the paneer into 1–1¼ inch (2–3cm) cubes. Trim both the green beans and the okra,

cutting off the stem ends and then cutting the remaining veg into halves or thirds. Add the sweet potato, paneer, green beans and okra to your roasting pan, then toss with the oil, chili powder, amchur, cumin, nigella seeds and a generous pinch of salt. Roast in the preheated oven for roughly 25 minutes, or until the sweet potato is tender.

2. While the veg cooks, prepare the green chutney: Roughly chop the cilantro and chili and put into a food processor or blender. Add the lime juice, cumin, water and a generous pinch or two of salt and blend really well, until you have a loose paste or, in a pinch, a coarse pesto-like consistency. If you don't have a blender, a stick blender will just about do the trick, but you might need to add a splash more water to help the mixture blend together. If you don't have either of these gadgets, not to worry: just roughly chop the cilantro and chili and scatter them over the finished dish, sprinkling the cumin on top and adding an extra squeeze of lime.

3. Once the roasting is done, the veg should be tender and the paneer nicely browned. Drizzle the chutney on top and serve with lime wedges to add acidity. Serve with rice or flatbreads.

Variations and substitutions:

You can also spice the veg and paneer with chaat masala if you want. See page 23 for a chaat masala recipe and more info. Just add the chaat masala to taste.

The vegetables here can be adjusted according to what you have around: Butternut squash is a decent swap for the sweet potato. (Use a pre-prepared bag of cubed butternut squash if you want to minimize chopping. Paneer can also be bought pre-cubed.) Parboiled white potatoes (add them to a pan of cold, salted water, bring to a vigorous boil and cook for 3–4 minutes) would also work, and pre-cooked beets are nice here too. When I specified green beans, I meant anything labeled green beans, but you could use snow peas or sugar snap peas as an alternative. Chunky runner beans will be too robust unless you boil them before roasting.

To make this vegan, just swap the paneer for drained firm tofu—it works a treat.

WEEKNIGHT TOMATO AND SARDINE PASTA

Sometimes good cooking is about knowing which corners you can cut. In this ridiculously simple pasta recipe, the tomato sauce from canned sardines helps to make a near-instant pasta sauce—just pep it up with some garlic and chili and you're good to go.

Serves: 4
Ready in: less than 25 minutes
Make-ahead and storage tips: page 323

Salt, to taste
14 ounces (400g) pasta, any shape
2 tablespoons olive or vegetable oil
3 garlic cloves, crushed or finely grated
3 tablespoons tomato paste
½–1 teaspoon chili flakes, to taste
4 x 3.75 ounce (120g) cans sardines in tomato sauce
Scant ½ cup (100ml) water
3–4 ounces (100g) young leaf spinach or baby chard

Optional extras:
⅓ cup (60g) black olives, pitted and halved, or 2–3 tablespoons capers
Handful of fresh parsley leaves (roughly ½ ounce/10–15g), roughly chopped

1. Fill a large pot with water, add plenty of salt and bring to a boil. Once it's bubbling vigorously, add the pasta and cook according to the instructions on the package.

2. In a medium pan or frying pan, warm the oil over a medium-low heat. Add the garlic, tomato paste and ½ teaspoon chili flakes. Let sizzle for 2 minutes, stirring all the time—the tomato paste will turn a deeper red and the garlic will lose its raw smell.

3. Meanwhile, open the cans of sardines and lightly break apart the sardines with a fork—they'll break further into flakes as they cook. Add the sardines to the pan along with the water and bring to a simmer, then add the greens and cook for a further minute or two, stirring often, until the leaves collapse into the sauce. The sauce should be rich and deep red,

with sardine flaked through it and ribbons of deep green. It should be full-bodied, so let it simmer a few minutes longer if it's at all watery. Check the seasoning and add a pinch of salt and extra chili flakes if needed, then add olives or capers if you want to.

4. Drain the pasta well, then mix with the sauce. Serve straightaway, and sprinkle with parsley if you have it.

Variations and substitutions:

Defrosted frozen spinach can be used in place of the fresh spinach leaves. Alternatively, sauté a couple of handfuls of thickly sliced mushrooms in a little oil in a separate frying pan, then stir through the sauce once tender.

You can use a gluten-free pasta if required.

ROASTING-PAN ORZO WITH BROCCOLI AND MOZZARELLA

I have to credit my friend Rukmini with opening my eyes to the potential of the humble roasting pan. She's a magician in the kitchen—where other cooks (read: me) fuss, stir, season, fret and hover tethered to the stove, she just throws ingredients into a pan, puts the pan in the oven and lets heat and time do their thing. In all the time and headspace that these easy roasting-pan dinners free up, you could really carpe diem—seize the day— and make something of yourself. Or, if you're like me, you could just watch episodes of *Gilmore Girls* you've already seen a thousand times. You do you.

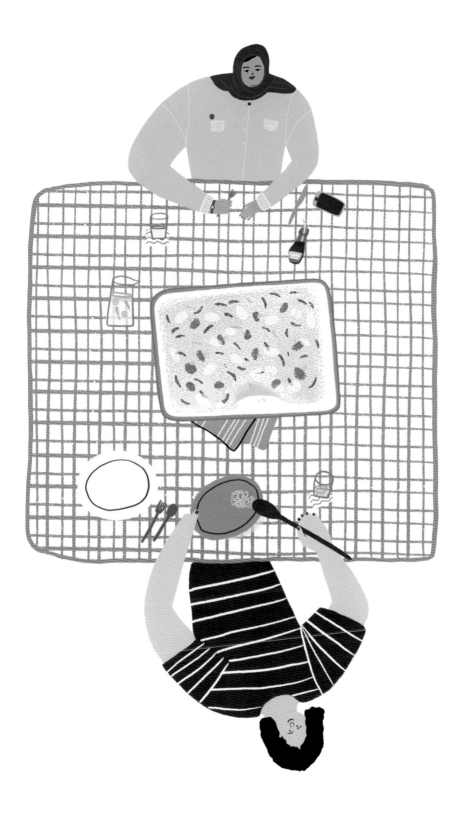

Serves: 4
Ready in: less than 45 minutes

Vegetarian   Vegan option

1 broccoli head, cut into small florets
2 tablespoons olive or vegetable oil
2 medium zucchini (roughly 14 ounces/400g), coarsely grated
2 cups (500ml) vegetable or chicken stock, very hot
1⅓ cups (300g) orzo pasta
2 teaspoons Dijon or wholegrain mustard
4-ounce (125g) mozzarella ball, torn into pieces, or 1 cup (4 ounces/125g) grated mozzarella

Handful of fresh basil leaves (about ½ ounce/10–15g), roughly torn
1 tablespoon lemon juice (from ½ lemon)
Lots of freshly ground black pepper
Salt, to taste

1. Preheat the oven to 400°F (200°C) and get out a large roasting pan, roughly 13 x 9 inches (22 x 33cm).

2. Toss the broccoli florets with 1 tablespoon of the oil in your roasting pan. Roast in the preheated oven for 10 minutes.

3. Add the grated zucchini, stock, orzo and mustard to the broccoli in the roasting pan, and stir well to combine. Pat down the orzo to make sure it's pretty much all submerged in the stock. Scatter the mozzarella on top, then bake for 20 minutes.

4. Once the pasta is cooked (it may be slightly al dente, but shouldn't be crunchy or chalky), remove from the oven, scatter over the basil, drizzle with lemon juice and the remaining tablespoon of oil and season to taste with plenty of pepper and salt. Mix everything really well, then serve straightaway—this dish tends to set firmer as it cools, so isn't good for making ahead of time.

Variations and substitutions:

To make this a vegan dinner, use a non-dairy mozzarella or leave the cheese out altogether, and make sure you use a vegan stock cube. You can swap the broccoli for pretty much any vegetables you have on hand: tomatoes work really nicely, as does butternut squash (you will need to cut it into small cubes). If you're going for that green, earthy vibe, kale is good, but should be thrown into the dish at the same time as the orzo, etc. You can also swap the basil for mint or parsley.

A reminder about grilled cheese

Cooking can be a real drag. When the day has been long and life's many other demands are circling, the last thing I want to do is lovingly coax spring greens to life, or add to the already looming washing-up pile. I don't want to cook, I don't want to be mindful, I don't want to be told about how vegetables are nature's *real* fast food. Sometimes in these moments I can recognize myself being petulant, and I pull myself out of my funk and into the kitchen, trying to soar above my own bad mood. But often this exhaustion is just a fact of life. Not every meal can be special; not every moment needs to be suffused with magic, self-improvement or romance.

So, although it's my role as a cookbook writer to help you find your way in the kitchen, I also want to make clear that this isn't something you necessarily need to do all the time. Unless cooking from-scratch meals three times a day is your true love, your career or a non-negotiable fact of your life, there is no need to rise to dizzying culinary heights every time you feel your stomach rumble. This is what instant noodles are for. This is when those feather-soft supermarket chocolate chip brioche buns will come to your rescue. This is the evergreen value of kebab shops, fried chicken places, curbside burger vans and sushi delivered to your door. I know that not all of these things will translate for non-Brits, but you have to find your own shortcuts, the quick-fix eats that feel right for you, wherever you are. That flexibility is exactly the point. It's important that you cook as you are. When you do get in the kitchen, I want you to have the luxury of being there with confidence and hopefully even with joy. But for ordinary days and ordinary moods, sometimes grilled cheese will do.

P.S. I have loved the months spent recipe testing, writing and editing this book, and all the culinary lessons I've learned en route. But I have to be honest with you: I'm desperate for the day when all the recipes are perfected and the last pan has been washed up, and I can just relax into a plate of chicken nuggets and fries. This is cooking—and eating—for real life.

EFFORTLESS COD IN RED LENTIL, TOMATO AND LEMONGRASS BROTH

Another roasting-pan recipe with absolute minimal prep work, chopping or messing around. In this recipe, the cod poaches in soupy, spicy, tangy red lentils, with lemongrass and a liberal amount of garlic, ginger and chili. The result is an intensely aromatic broth—somewhere between a Thai tom yum soup and an Indian lentil rasam—and perfectly tender, flaking fish. If you want to make this even easier—perhaps if you have trouble chopping things or performing fiddly tasks with your hands—there are some general tips in the introduction on pages 7–8, and some more specific pointers in the variations and substitutions below.

Serves: 4
Ready in: less than 1 hour 10 minutes, most of which is hands-off time while the dish roasts
Make-ahead and storage tips: page 323

Vegan option

---

2 tablespoons coconut or vegetable oil
4 scallions, thinly sliced
2 thin green chilies, thinly sliced (and deseeded if you want less heat)
4 garlic cloves, crushed or finely grated
1½-inch (4cm) piece of ginger, peeled and grated
4 cups (1 liter) water, freshly boiled
1 x 14 ounce (400g) can chopped tomatoes
1½ cups (200g) split red lentils
4 tablespoons lemon juice (from 2 lemons)
1 tablespoon fish sauce
1 lemongrass stick, slit along its length (stop just above the root, so the stalk holds together)
4 fresh or frozen cod fillets, skinless
Salt, to taste

Served with: steamed white rice

1. Preheat the oven to 400°F (200°C) and get out a large, deep roasting pan. I used a 13 x 9 inch (22 x 33cm) pan, which was perfect for making sure the fish was submerged in the soup, without the pan overflowing.

2. Combine the oil, scallions, chilies, garlic and ginger in the pan, then place in the preheated oven to roast for 5–10 minutes, keeping a close eye on

it all. This is just to blast the ginger and scallions, taking off that sharp pungency that can persist if you just cook them in water. You don't want the garlic to brown and burn though, so take care.

3. Add the freshly boiled water, the chopped tomatoes, lentils, lemon juice, fish sauce and lemongrass, and stir to mix. Return to the oven to cook for 20 minutes.

4. After 20 minutes, give everything a stir. Add the fish fillets to the mix, tucking them deep into the soupy lentils so that they poach, rather than roast. Cover the roasting pan tightly with aluminum foil and return it to the oven. How long this stage takes will depend on the kind of fish you're using and the size and thickness of the fillets: fresh fish will take roughly 12–18 minutes; frozen fish could take anywhere between 15 and 25 minutes. I'd recommend just checking the fish at the lower end of the recommended cooking time, seeing how cooked the center is and then proceeding carefully but confidently from there. It's ready when the flesh flakes but is still delicate: it shouldn't be jelly-like, frozen or, at the other end of the spectrum, dry and chalky.

5. Check the seasoning in the soupy lentils, adding salt to taste. Serve straightaway.

Variations and substitutions:

For ease of prep, particularly if you have limited mobility in your hands, you can swap the chopped fresh chilies for 1 teaspoon dried chili flakes. As ever, the garlic and ginger can be replaced with ready-prepared versions. Frozen diced onions work fine in place of the scallions, but add a few minutes to that initial blast in the oven.

In place of the cod, you could use hake, haddock or basa fillets.

If you have fresh tomatoes, these can be used in place of the canned chopped tomatoes. Roughly chop plum tomatoes, or halve cherry tomatoes. Cook as above, but add 4 tablespoons tomato paste as well at the same time.

You can make a vegan version of this, no problem. I very often make this as a lentil soup. Just leave out the fish sauce and, of course, the fish, and cook the lentils in their broth for 30 minutes, uncovered, in the oven. No need to return the mixture to the oven as in the fish version. You'll want to salt this generously in the absence of the fish sauce.

ROAST CHICKEN THIGHS WITH SPICED CAULIFLOWER, CRANBERRIES AND HERBS

This weeknight chicken dinner combines crisp-skinned roast chicken with cauliflower, sweet–sharp cranberries and the crunch of toasted nuts. What's more, it can all be cooked in a roasting pan, leaving you with more free time and less washing-up.

This recipe doesn't involve much chopping or other fiddly work, so may be useful if that stuff is ordinarily an issue for you. You can break the cauliflower roughly into florets if your knife skills aren't great. I wouldn't recommend using pre-cut frozen cauliflower florets though—they'll become mushy when roasted.

Serves: 4
Ready in: less than 45 minutes
Make-ahead and storage tips: page 323

Vegetarian option   Vegan option

8 chicken thighs, skin on and bone in
1½ tablespoons olive oil
1 teaspoon smoked paprika
1 teaspoon ground coriander
½–1 teaspoon chili powder, to taste
1 teaspoon dried thyme, oregano
   or mixed herbs
Generous pinch of salt
1 medium or large cauliflower
3 tablespoons (25g) pine nuts

For the dressing:
1 garlic clove, crushed or finely grated
1½ tablespoons olive oil
1 tablespoon apple cider vinegar, rice
   vinegar or white wine vinegar
2 teaspoons honey or maple syrup
Pinch of salt

To garnish:
Handful of fresh parsley leaves
   (roughly ½ ounce/10–15g)
¼ cup (40g) dried cranberries

Serve with: flatbreads and yogurt

1. Start by preheating the oven to 400°F (200°C). Get out a large, deep roasting pan, at least 13 x 9 inches (22 x 33cm).

2. Add the chicken to the pan along with the oil, spices, dried herbs and salt, then roast in the preheated oven for 15 minutes.

3. While the chicken roasts, cut or break the cauliflower into medium florets. (Save the leaves and stalk for use in other dishes—like the **no-waste whole cauliflower and macaroni cheese** on page 123 or for blending into soups.)

4. Once the chicken has roasted for 15 minutes, add the cauliflower and the pine nuts options and toss everything together really well to distribute the oil and seasonings. Return the dish to the oven for a further 25 minutes, until the chicken is cooked through (the juices should run clear) and the cauliflower florets are tender and mottled brown.

5. While the chicken and cauliflower finish roasting, prepare the dressing: whisk together all the ingredients until smooth and emulsified. Have the parsley leaves and cranberries ready.

6. When the dish is cooked, toss it with the dressing while still warm, then scatter with the chopped parsley and cranberries. Check the seasoning, then serve with yogurt and flatbreads.

Variations and substitutions:

I love the sharp-sweet pop of dried cranberries here, but you could alternatively use goji berries or—a much cheaper option—golden raisins or raisins. The sweetness is really welcome against the earthy cauliflower. For a fresher pop, use juicy pomegranate seeds instead.

Almonds, hazelnuts or walnuts can be used in place of the pine nuts. Roughly chop them first if you're using chunkier ones like walnuts or almonds.

Swap the chicken thighs for drumsticks if you want: they won't need quite as long in the oven though, so decrease the first part of the roasting (when the chicken is in the oven alone) to just 5–10 minutes.

If you're vegetarian or vegan, you can just make a chicken-free version of this, reconfiguring it as a kind of warm dressed cauliflower salad. Just double the amount of cauliflower, toss it in the oil, spices and so on and roast in the preheated oven for 25 minutes. Finish with the dressing and garnishes as above (be sure to use maple syrup rather than honey in the dressing if you're vegan).

SUMMER ZUCCHINI WITH HALLOUMI AND MINT

Sometimes I enter the kitchen in a daze, just drifting from cupboard to counter to fridge, opening doors and closing them again, not knowing where to even start. On days like this, it can help to have a recipe or two up your sleeve that require minimal thinking and effort: something that you can just prep, throw in the oven and then forget about until the oven timer goes off. In the empty time while it cooks and the smell of roasting garlic fills the kitchen, you can fall right back into your daydreams. Not all cooking needs to challenge or educate or enthrall you: sometimes cooking by numbers is enough.

Serves: 4 as a light meal
Ready in: less than an hour, most of which is free time
   while the zucchini soaks in brine and then roasts
Make-ahead and storage tips: page 323

Vegetarian   Vegan option

---

4 medium zucchini
Salt, to taste
1 tablespoon olive oil
½ teaspoon chili flakes
3 garlic cloves, skin left on
½ pound (225g) halloumi, cut into
   ⅜ inch (1cm) cubes
1 lemon

Handful of fresh mint leaves (roughly
   ½ ounce/10–15g), very thinly sliced

Serve with: bread (focaccia is
   particularly good for mopping up
   the juices), buttery polenta or
   steamed white rice

1. First, brine the zucchini. Trim the ends of the zucchini, then cut each zucchini into ⅜ inch (1cm)-thick slices along a slight diagonal. Put the slices in a large bowl with 2 tablespoons salt and cover with water. Leave for 20–30 minutes. It might seem counterintuitive, but soaking the zucchini like this actually draws a lot of water out of them (you can consult Samin Nosrat's brilliant *Salt, Fat, Acid, Heat* for a more in-depth explanation of this process). As a result, the zucchini will brown better in the oven and be less watery when cooked. Once they've brined for half an hour, drain the zucchini, rinse them and pat dry with paper towel. If you really can't be bothered with this step, that's fine: just chop the zucchini as instructed above and cut straight to roasting them.

2. While the zucchini soak, turn the oven on to 450°F (220°C) and drag the biggest roasting pan you have (or a couple of smaller roasting pans) out of the pantry. The zucchini will cook best if arranged in a single layer.

3. Toss the brined, drained and dried zucchini "coins" with the olive oil, chili flakes and some salt in your roasting pan and add the garlic cloves (they'll roast in their skins). Roast for 15 minutes, then scatter the halloumi cubes on top and put back in the oven for a further 15 minutes.

4. Once the roasting time is up, remove the pan from the oven and let it cool slightly—I find this dish is better served warm than piping hot. While the zucchini cools, zest and then juice the lemon, and combine the zest and juice in a small bowl. Squeeze in the soft, jammy garlic flesh from the roasted garlic cloves. Whisk together to create a garlicky, lemony dressing, and add a pinch of salt to taste.

5. Scatter the sliced mint leaves over the roasted zucchini and halloumi, drizzle over the dressing and stir well to combine everything. Check the seasoning, then serve with your chosen carb.

Variations and substitutions:

You can make a more autumnal version of this by swapping the zucchini for butternut squash and the mint for basil or parsley. Just roast the squash (peeled and cut into ¾ inch/2cm cubes), oil, chili and salt for 10 minutes, then add the garlic and roast for a further 15 minutes. Next, add the halloumi and continue as per the recipe.

If you don't have halloumi, paneer also works excellently. It's not as salty as halloumi though, so you might want to add extra salt to the dish. If you want to make a dairy-free version of this, you can leave out the halloumi altogether and toss in an extra zucchini to bulk it out. Or, if you live near a health food store or large supermarket, you might be able to get hold of vegan halloumi.

LIGHTNING-QUICK ASPARAGUS AND CHILI LINGUINE

Asparagus lovers tend to get on my nerves. I know this isn't fair. Maybe it's because asparagus has such a fleeting season (a few weeks around May and June), or because it can be a bit pricey, but its disciples tend to get puritanical about it. *You must, just must, have it with only hollandaise*, they might say. Sometimes they insist on *only a pinch of Maldon salt and the briefest of spells in a hot griddle pan! Let it speak for itself!* That's all well and good, but I need proper substance if I'm gonna come away from the table feeling like I've really eaten—not just tasted—some food. For that reason, I like asparagus with pasta: the starchy heft of the carbs provides a plain (and, crucially, filling) backdrop against which the flavorful, ever so gently sulfurous vegetable can shine.

Serves: 4
Ready in: less than 30 minutes

Vegan

Salt
1¼ pounds (500g) asparagus spears
14 ounces (400g) linguine, spaghetti or
  tagliatelle
3 tablespoons olive oil
4 garlic cloves, thinly sliced
½–1 teaspoon chili flakes, to taste
Freshly ground black pepper
4 tablespoons nutritional yeast *or*
  grated Parmesan, plus extra to serve

1. Put a large pot of well-salted water on the stovetop. Set it over a medium-high heat while you prepare the asparagus.

2. Gently bend each spear of asparagus until it snaps: the place where it breaks is the point where the woodier, more fibrous part of the stalk yields to the more tender flesh near the asparagus tip. Throw away or compost the tough bottoms. Cut off the asparagus tips—the bud-like arrowhead bit at the very end—and set to one side. Cut the rest of each spear into little slices, no bigger than ⅜ inch (1cm) across.

3. Next, the pasta: Break the bundle of pasta strands in half or into thirds so that they're more manageable when tangled up with the little bites of asparagus. When the salted water is at a steady boil, add the broken pasta, give it a quick stir and leave to cook according to the instructions on the package. Use a gluten-free pasta if required.

4. While the pasta cooks, place a large frying pan over medium heat and add the olive oil. Once the oil is hot, add the asparagus tips and slices and a generous pinch of salt. Sauté the asparagus for 5 minutes, stirring often, until the asparagus is tender but before it begins to brown too much.

5. Add the garlic, chili flakes and plenty of black pepper. Cook for another minute or two, until the garlic is fragrant and savory rather than raw and sharp. The garlic slivers should be light gold.

6. When the pasta is done—better that it's slightly al dente, or firm to bite, than overcooked, as you're going to be cooking it a little extra in the frying pan—drain it, reserving about half a mug of the starchy, salty cooking water.

7. Transfer the pasta back into its pan and set over a low heat. Add 4–6 tablespoons of the cooking water along with the asparagus and nutritional yeast or cheese. Beat everything vigorously using a spatula or wooden spoon, until the yeast or cheese is incorporated into a light, silky glaze that coats the pasta strands. If you need a little extra cooking water to bring it all together, add it. Check the seasoning, adding extra salt, pepper or chili flakes to taste. Serve straightaway, with extra cheese (or nutritional yeast) if you really rate yourself as a person.

MUSHROOM AND GOCHUJANG UDON NOODLES

This is my friend Leah's recipe. Gochujang, creamy peanut butter, soy sauce, a little sugar and tangy vinegar. It's the easiest dinner you can think of—just sauté the mushrooms, boil the noodles and mix together with the sauce—and so leaves you with more time to do the things that really matter, like scrolling the social media feeds of people you hate.

Gochujang is a sweet-salty Korean fermented chili paste, made with chilies and glutinous rice. It's a thick brick-red paste that works amazingly in stews (see the **spicy soft tofu and mushroom stew** on page 52) and with noodles. You'll find it in a squat red tub in lots of supermarkets and East Asian grocery stores, and any Korean food store.

Serves: 4
Ready in: less than 25 minutes
Make-ahead and storage tips: page 323

Vegan

---

1 tablespoon vegetable or sesame oil
14 ounces (400g) white, cremini or oyster mushrooms, thickly sliced
4 scallions, thinly sliced
4 tablespoons peanut butter
3–4 tablespoons gochujang, to taste
1–1½ tablespoons light soy sauce
2 tablespoons white wine vinegar, rice vinegar
  or cane vinegar (I used Filipino cane vinegar,
  the Datu Puti brand)
2 teaspoons white or brown sugar
11–14 ounces (300–400g) dried udon noodles or 1⅓–1¾ pounds
  (600–800g) fresh udon noodles

1. First up, get out a large, deep pot and fill with enough water to boil your noodles. Set the pot over a high heat to bring the water to a boil.

2. While the water heats, prepare the mushrooms. In a large frying pan or wok, heat the oil and add the mushrooms. If you're doing this in a frying pan, spread the mushrooms out as best you can, let brown on one side, then after 5–6 minutes of cooking over a medium heat, flip them over, add the scallions and cook for a further 4–5 minutes. If you're using a wok, you can cook the mushrooms over a high heat for 4–5 minutes, stirring pretty much continuously, until nicely browned and softened. Add the scallions and cook for just a minute or two more.

3. While the mushrooms are cooking, stir together the peanut butter, gochujang, soy sauce, vinegar and sugar for the sauce in a bowl. Add 3 tablespoons of the gochujang to start with, then increase if it could use more heat. I use 4 tablespoons, but use your discretion and taste as you go.

4. Add the noodles to the boiling water, and cook according to the instructions on the package. Dried noodles will of course take longer than the soft, fresh ones. Some straight-to-wok noodles will say on the package that they need no extra cooking, but I find they're best plunged into boiling water if only for 20–30 seconds. Once cooked, drain the noodles.

5. When the noodles and mushrooms are both cooked and the sauce is ready, it's time to bring everything together. Drain the noodles, then add to the frying pan or wok. Over a medium-low heat, add the sauce, and toss or stir everything until the noodles and mushrooms are slick with the sticky, salty sauce. Serve straightaway.

Variations and substitutions:

I love the meatiness of the mushrooms here, but if you really can't stomach them, leave them out. You can also replace them with onions and peppers, or those bags of prepared "stir-fry veg."

You can replace the peanut butter with almond butter or tahini (I'd use half the quantity of tahini, due to its slight bitterness) if you want.

Udon noodles are sold in lots of East Asian grocery stores and most big supermarkets. They cook to a really pleasing, chewy heft, so I'd recommend getting them if you can. If they're not an option, though, any medium or thick rice or egg noodle will do the trick. If you don't eat gluten, swap in a gluten-free noodle, use tamari instead of soy sauce and make sure that your gochujang is a gluten-free version, as some contain barley malt.

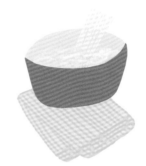

15-MINUTE
CREAM OF TOMATO SOUP

No chopping, no need to get the kitchen scales out, no gilding the lily. This is an easy soup for when you really can't face making an elaborate meal. This isn't meant to be a gentrified version of canned cream of tomato soup—there's no greater comfort than that lurid red-orange silkiness, and I'm not interested in replacing it. Neither am I suggesting that homemade is always best. But sometimes, just sometimes, a simple from-scratch recipe like this can nourish you in other ways, reminding you that you have the skills you need to care for yourself and can, when it comes to it, magic something from nothing.

Serves: 4
Ready in: 15 minutes
Make-ahead and storage tips: page 324

Vegan option

---

2 tablespoons olive oil *or* butter
2 garlic cloves, crushed or finely grated
3 x 14 ounce (400g) cans chopped
   tomatoes
2 teaspoons dried oregano, thyme or
   mixed herbs
1¾ cups (400ml) whole milk *or*
   1 x 400ml can full-fat coconut milk

1–2 tablespoons sugar, or more to taste
Salt, to taste

Serve with: thickly sliced bread
Special equipment: stick blender,
   food processor or blender

Heat the oil or butter in a large saucepan over a medium-low heat. Add the crushed garlic and let sizzle for a minute or two, stirring often, until it's sweetly fragrant and just beginning to turn golden. Make sure it doesn't brown or burn! Add the chopped tomatoes and herbs and bring to a gentle simmer. Let it bubble for 6–8 minutes, keeping a close eye on it and stirring regularly. It will thicken slightly during this time. Blend the soup with a stick blender if you have one, or in a blender or food processor if yours is suitable for blending hot liquids. Add the milk or coconut milk, then add sugar and salt to taste and don't be shy: tomatoes need it. If the soup has cooled a lot, return it to the pan and set over a low heat until it's warm. Don't let it bubble if you used cow's milk, or the milk may split. Serve straightaway with bread.

> ## Variations and substitutions:
>
> For a non-creamy soup, swap the milk or coconut milk for water. If you make it this way, you can also get away with leaving the soup chunky, which may be preferable if you don't have a blender or food processor.

POTATO, CARAWAY AND SAUERKRAUT SOUP

Store-bought sauerkraut adds instant depth of flavor and a gentle tang to this hearty potato soup, inspired by the flavors of Eastern and Northern European food. When coupled with the sweetness of onion and fragrant caraway seeds (read more about them in the **seeded rye cake with demerara crust** recipe on page 147), it makes for a delicious, easy and pleasingly filling lunch or dinner. See page 27 if you're wondering where to buy sauerkraut.

Serves: 4
Ready in: less than 50 minutes, of which half is
   carefree downtime while the soup simmers
Make-ahead and storage tips: page 324

Vegan

3–4 tablespoons salted or unsalted butter *or* 3 tablespoons olive oil
2 medium onions, thinly sliced
1 cup (200g) sauerkraut, drained
1 teaspoon caraway seeds
1⅓ pounds (600g) russet potatoes
6 cups (1.5 liters) water
Lots of freshly ground black pepper
Salt, to taste

Serve with: bread (preferably rye bread) and salted butter
Special equipment: stick blender, food processor or blender

1. Heat the butter or oil over a medium-high heat in a large, deep pot. Add the onion, sauerkraut and caraway seeds and sauté for 6–8 minutes, stirring often but letting the veg brown a little. While the onion and sauerkraut cook, peel the potatoes and cut into 1¼ inch (3cm) chunks. If the potato skins are thin and you want to minimize fiddly prep work, you can skip the peeling and just go straight to roughly chopping them.

2. Add the diced potato and the water to the pot, and bring the mixture to a simmer. Once it's bubbling, cook over a low heat for 20–25 minutes, or until the potato is perfectly tender.

3. Using a stick blender, blender or food processor (make sure yours is suitable for blending hot liquids), blitz the soup until smooth, then add plenty of black pepper and salt to taste. Serve straightaway with bread.

PEA GREEN SOUP

This very simple recipe uses Thai green curry paste alongside super-
sweet frozen peas. The result is a spiced, verdant pea soup, perfect
for when you need to inject life and color into a dreary day.

Serves: 4
Ready in: less than 30 minutes
Make-ahead and storage tips: page 324

Vegetarian option   Vegan option

2 tablespoons coconut, olive or
vegetable oil
1 medium onion, finely diced
3–5 tablespoons Thai green curry paste*
3 garlic cloves, crushed or finely grated
5½ cups (1¾ pounds/800g) frozen peas
3½ cups (800ml) water, freshly boiled
1 x 14 ounce (400g) can full-fat coconut
milk

2–4 tablespoons lemon or lime juice
(from 1–2 lemons or 2–4 limes)
Salt, to taste

Serve with: steamed white rice
or bread
Special equipment: stick blender,
food processor or blender

*Thai curry pastes vary wildly in heat, saltiness and depth of flavor depending on
which one you get. If it's a paste you use often, use your discretion and add it to
taste. If you're new to it, start by adding 3 tablespoons or so, then add more later
if necessary. A word of warning: if you need to add more to the soup, you'll have
to fry it for a couple of minutes in a small amount of oil in a little pan to cook off
the raw flavor.

1. Start by heating the oil in a large, deep pot over a medium heat. Add the diced onion and cook for 8–10 minutes, stirring every so often, until it begins to soften. There's no need to brown the onion here, so turn the heat down if necessary.

2. Add the Thai green curry paste (see note on previous page for more guidance) and garlic to the pan and sauté for a minute or two, until the raw garlic smell lifts and the paste is sizzling. Next, add the peas, water and coconut milk and bring the mixture to a simmer. Once it's bubbling, simmer gently for 10 minutes, adjusting the temperature as necessary.

3. Turn off the heat and then blend the soup with a stick blender or—in batches—in a food processor or blender (check if yours is safe for blending hot liquids). Add the lemon or lime juice to taste, then add salt if it needs it (as I mentioned, some green curry pastes are saltier than others). Serve on its own for a light meal, or with carbs for a more substantial dinner.

Variations and substitutions:

If you only have light coconut milk (the one with less fat) you can use this instead of full-fat, but the soup won't be as rich or velvety.

Scallions work well in place of the onion. Just use 4–5 of them, thinly sliced, greens and all. You could also swap in a sliced leek.

To make this dish vegetarian and vegan, make sure you use a curry paste that doesn't contain fish or shellfish.

ROASTED FIVE-SPICE CARROTS WITH BROWN BUTTER AND SESAME

Carrots become perfectly sweet when roasted. The aromatics of Chinese five-spice powder (ordinarily including cinnamon, Sichuan pepper, fennel seeds, cloves and star anise) work perfectly alongside this sweetness, especially with the mellowing influence of brown butter. This easy side dish is a toss-it-in-the-oven job, so it's easy to pull together while the roast dinner cooks.

This dish is based on a recipe for glazed carrots with five-spice powder by Rhonda Parkinson published on *The Spruce Eats*—if you want to make this but can't face turning on the oven, Rhonda's stovetop version is a good bet.

Serves: 4–6 as a side or part of a spread
Ready in: less than an hour, over half of which is
   hands-off roasting time
Make-ahead and storage tips: page 324

Vegetarian   Vegan option

1¾ pounds (800g) carrots
3 tablespoons unsalted butter
1 tablespoon Chinese five-spice powder
½ teaspoon chili flakes
Salt, to taste
2 tablespoons light soy sauce *or* tamari
3 tablespoons soft light or dark brown sugar
5 tablespoons (75ml) orange juice
1 tablespoon sesame seeds

1. Preheat the oven to 400°F (200°C) and get out a roasting pan roughly 13 x 9 inches (22 x 33cm) across its base.

2. While the oven heats, peel the carrots and cut into batons (for smaller carrots like Nantes carrots, you can just cut them in half along their length to give two long, thin pieces).

3. Add the butter to the roasting pan. Place in the preheated oven and cook until the butter is molten and sizzling, with light brown specks dotted through it (these spots are the toasted milk solids, which give browned

butter its nutty flavor). Exactly how long this takes will depend on the weight and thickness of your roasting pan, but it should take somewhere between 5 and 10 minutes.

4. Once the butter has browned, add the prepared carrots, five-spice powder, chili flakes and a pinch of salt, and toss to combine. Roast for 30 minutes, stirring halfway through, until the carrots are almost tender and beginning to brown at the edges.

5. Add the soy sauce or tamari, sugar, orange juice and sesame seeds to the roasting pan, and mix it all together, then return to the oven for a further 10 minutes or so, or until the glaze is reduced and syrupy. Exactly how long this takes will depend on the size of your pan, so keep an eye on it—if left too long, the glaze will burn. When the orange juice and soy sauce have turned from soupy mess to bubbling syrup, remove the pan from the oven and toss the carrots in this glaze.

Variations and substitutions:

If you want to make this vegan, swap the butter for olive oil and skip the step in which the butter is browned: just toss the carrots, five-spice powder, chili flakes and salt with the oil, then roast.

You can leave out the sesame seeds if you want to, or even replace them with roughly chopped hazelnuts, walnuts or pecans.

BOK CHOY WITH GINGER AND CLEMENTINE

This bok choy—browned in a pan with butter and garlic and brought to life with a squeeze of clementine juice—is exceptionally quick and works well as part of a vegetarian spread. I often serve this with the **roasted five-spice carrots with brown butter and sesame** opposite and the **charred Brussels sprouts with satay and crushed peanuts** on page 141.

Serves: 4 as a side or part of a spread
Ready in: less than 20 minutes
Make-ahead and storage tips: page 324

Vegetarian

Vegan option

---

3 tablespoons salted or unsalted butter
1 tablespoon vegetable or olive oil
4 heads bok choy
2¼-inch (6cm) piece of ginger, peeled and cut into matchsticks
4 garlic cloves, crushed or finely grated
½–1 teaspoon chili flakes, to taste
Juice of 4 clementines
Salt, to taste

1. In a large frying pan, melt the butter into the oil over a medium-high flame. Cut each head of bok choy in half, slicing from root to tip to give two long, thin halves. Lay the cut side of the bok choy halves face down in the hot butter and oil and let sizzle for 2–3 minutes, then turn over and sauté for a further 2 minutes.

2. Turn the heat down to medium, then add the ginger, garlic and chili flakes to the pan, nestling them into the spaces between the bok choy. Sauté for a minute or two, stirring gently every so often, until the garlic no longer smells raw. Add the clementine juice and toss everything together.

3. Let simmer for another minute or so until the clementine juice is slightly syrupy, then add a generous pinch of salt. Serve straightaway.

Variations and substitutions:

For a vegan version of this dish, just use a total of 3 tablespoons (40ml) oil instead of the oil-butter mix suggested above.

In place of the clementines, you can use the juice of 1–2 oranges.

CLOUD MASH

If you're cooking for a family, making mashed potatoes is easy. But when you're eating alone, going through the whole ordeal for just one portion can feel like a fuss. So here's a quicker way. It's nothing new—cooking a potato in a microwave—but it might just be new to you, as it was for me, and bring mashed potatoes back into the realm of the achievable, accessible and everyday. (The other option is instant mash, which I also love, but which doesn't always scratch the itch if you want to feel like you've really made a fuss of yourself.) Another perk of this method—in addition to its speed—is that it doesn't introduce any water to the potato as it cooks, which means you'll have perfectly fluffy, cloud-like mash.

Serves: 1
Ready in: less than 15 minutes
Make-ahead and storage tips: page 324

Vegan

1 large russet potato
2 tablespoons salted or unsalted butter *or* 1 tablespoon olive oil
2–3 tablespoons milk *or* non-dairy milk
Lots of freshly ground black pepper
Salt, to taste

1. The timings in this recipe are for a 700W microwave. If your microwave is more or less powerful than this, you might need to slightly adjust the cooking times.

2. Wash the potato and pierce its skin several times using a sharp knife. Place on a microwavable plate and microwave on full power for 4 minutes. Turn the potato the other way up, and microwave for a further 4 minutes. Leave to stand for 2 minutes to cool slightly.

3. When the potato has cooled very slightly, peel off the skin (it might help to wear plastic or rubber gloves to ensure you don't burn your fingers). Mash the steaming potato in a bowl until no lumps remain. Add the butter or olive oil, milk, pepper and salt, and tuck in.

Variations and substitutions:

There are as many ways to make mash as there are mash eaters. Roughly ¼ cup (1 ounce/30g) grated Cheddar wouldn't go amiss here. You could also add ½ teaspoon garlic powder, or 1 teaspoon Dijon or wholegrain mustard. Smoked paprika— around ½ teaspoon—lends a really nice smokiness, or a small handful of parsley leaves, finely chopped, will add pep and color.

10-MINUTE ZESTY
LEMON AND THYME PUDDING CAKE

There is no sight more perfect than a fat little pudding cake arriving at the dinner table. It should be said that this isn't custardy, soft American-style pudding, but pudding in the British sense of the word. Sometimes we Brits use pudding to refer to any dessert, and sometimes we mean something more specific: a rich, old-fashioned kind of pie or cake, usually steamed rather than baked. This one is a microwave pudding, doing away with the need to mess around with a steamer (although if you are a traditionalist, I've included steamed instructions in the variations and substitutions on page 101). It takes only 10 minutes from start to finish and yields a beautiful round little pudding that, when inverted onto a plate, is crowned with a halo of gold lemon curd. I use fresh thyme in this—it adds a sophisticated note to what is, in essence, a lemon mug cake. You don't have to follow my lead on this count, but in a world where people obsess about "real" cooking and the virtues of "slow food," it comforts me to know I can zap a zesty, sunny, thyme-scented pudding (something that feels fancy) in a cheap metal box.

If you want to serve more than four people, I'd recommend just making two of the puddings below rather than trying to cook an extra-large one: microwaves aren't the best at distributing heat, so I'm not convinced that this pudding works as well when scaled up.

Serves: 4
Ready in: 10–12 minutes (make sure your butter is softened before you start)
Make-ahead and storage tips: page 324

Vegetarian

---

6 tablespoons (80g) unsalted butter, softened, plus extra to grease the bowl

¼ cup (75g) lemon curd

½ cup (80g) superfine sugar

Leaves from 4–5 thyme sprigs (you'll need about 2 tablespoons leaves)

Zest of 1 lemon

1 medium or large egg, at room temperature

1 cup (100g) all-purpose flour

1 teaspoon baking powder

Pinch of salt

2 tablespoons milk

Serve with: yogurt or ice cream

Special equipment: deep microwavable bowl—any deep microwavable bowl will do (I used a deep soup bowl)—it just needs to be large enough to hold 2½ cups (570ml) water. Two and half cups of water will weigh about 570g, so test out the capacity of your bowl now if you're unsure.

1. Grease your bowl with a little butter. Cut out a small circle of parchment paper just large enough to cover the bottom of the bowl, and lay it down (don't worry if the paper crinkles). Measure the lemon curd into the bowl, letting it settle in a layer at the bottom on top of the parchment paper.

2. In a mixing bowl, combine the butter, sugar, thyme leaves and lemon zest. Beat really well for a couple of minutes, until lighter in color and fluffy. If you feel the mixture between your fingers, it should be silky and soft rather than heavy or waxy. Crack in the egg and mix until combined, then add the flour, baking powder and salt. Stir just until all the flour is mixed in and no floury patches remain, then stir in the milk to loosen the batter slightly.

3. Scrape the batter into your prepared bowl, gently heaping it on top of the lemon curd layer at the bottom and smoothing out the top.

4. Cook in the microwave for 4–6 minutes, until it's airy and the crumb has set. The top may be very slightly tacky still, but as long as a knife inserted into the middle of the pudding comes out clean, it is ready. In my 700W microwave, this takes exactly 5 minutes, but all microwaves differ, and yours may be more or less powerful than mine. Start off with 4 minutes, and add more time if necessary.

5. Once the cake is cooked, let it sit for a moment, then run a knife or spoon around the edge of the cake to loosen it. Place a serving plate upside down over the top of the bowl. In one smooth, swift movement—using a tea towel or oven mitts, please!—hold the bowl and plate together while flipping them over, so that the upturned bowl is now resting on top of the plate. Remove the bowl and gently peel off the parchment paper, if it hasn't been left in the bowl. Make sure all the lemon curd is pooled on top. Serve straightaway.

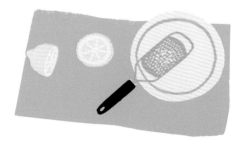

Variations and substitutions:

You can also use the **salted honeyscotch sauce** on page 259 to top this. Put a half batch of the honeyscotch sauce in the bottom of the bowl in place of the lemon curd, and leave out the lemon zest and the thyme. Another version that works nicely is with raspberry jam in place of the lemon curd—just straight swap one for the other.

If you have self-rising flour, you can use this instead of the all-purpose flour and baking powder. Or for a gluten-free version, swap the all-purpose flour for a gluten-free all-purpose flour blend.

To steam this pudding the traditional British way, prepare per the recipe but then cover the top of the bowl with a double layer of parchment paper, pleated down the middle to allow the cake to rise and expand as it cooks. Secure the parchment paper with string. Place the cake on a steamer rack in a large pot, with enough boiling water in the pot to create a steamy microclimate, but not so much that the boiling water is in direct contact with the bowl. Put a lid on, keep the water simmering over a medium-low heat and steam for 1 hour 15 minutes, topping up the water halfway through if the pot threatens to boil dry.

SALTED,
MALTED,
MAGIC
ICE CREAM

This ice cream is alarmingly moreish and very low hassle. Even if you think ice cream is too complicated or difficult for you, give it a go. It has just four ingredients, which you toss into a bowl, give a quick whisk and stick in the freezer until frozen. The only way you'll get ice cream more easily is if you slip on your shoes and pop to the store for a tub of Häagen-Dazs. No offense to Häagen-Dazs, which I enjoy very much, but this ice cream will be all the more special for being made by your own hand.

There's a lot of wild science behind smooth, rich ice cream. As food writer Charlotte Druckman put it in one essay: "To make ice cream, you're forced to complete an impossible task: freeze a solution that, despite being called ice cream, is more than half full of water, all while avoiding the formation of ice." It's the most frustrating, bewildering paradox, which makes it all the more magical when you master it. What's key in this recipe is sweetened condensed milk (high in milk proteins and sugars) and the malted milk powder (which contains flour and milk powder): these ingredients help "lock up" any errant water in the mix, preventing it from becoming icy as it freezes. As such, there's no need to churn this recipe: just put it in the freezer until it's set. If you're after a more technical ice cream recipe, try the **nkate brittle, cardamom and salted milk ice cream** on page 313.

Nigella Lawson, queen of no-churn ice creams, has recipes for coffee and brandied pumpkin versions on her website and in her books. Condensed milk also freezes well, so you could alternatively keep the remainder (decanted out of the can and into an airtight container) in the freezer for when your homemade ice cream cravings next strike.

Makes: roughly 2½ cups/600ml (serves 4)
Ready in: 6 hours 5 minutes (those 5 minutes are all the prep time—the remaining 6 hours are how long the ice cream needs to freeze!)
Make-ahead and storage tips: page 324

Vegetarian

¾ cup (200g) sweetened condensed milk
½ cup (60g) malted milk powder
1¼ cups (300ml) heavy cream
A couple of generous pinches of salt

Serve with: fresh berries, optional

1. After such a long preamble, this little recipe might seem a bit anticlimactic. All you need to do is whisk the sweetened condensed milk together with the malted milk powder until smooth, then add the heavy cream and salt and whisk vigorously until the mixture is pillowy and aerated. It's ready when softly whipped: if you lift the whisk from the bowl, the cream left behind should briefly hold its shape, rather than immediately flowing back to a flat surface. Add a little extra salt if you think it's needed—it will help to balance the malted sweetness.

2. Pour the mix into a suitably sized airtight container (at least 2½ cups/600ml capacity—by all means reuse a store-bought ice cream tub if you have one), clip on the lid and pop in the freezer for at least 6 hours, or preferably overnight. Depending on the temperature of your freezer, you might want to remove the ice cream ten minutes or so before serving to let it soften to a scoopable consistency. This ice cream is very rich, so I'd recommend pairing it with berries to balance the sweetness with fruity tang.

Variations and substitutions:

You can use a chocolate malted milk powder like
Milo or Ovaltine if that's all you can find at the
store. You can also swap the malted milk powder
for ½ cup (60g) hot chocolate mix or for ½ cup
(40g) cocoa powder (which is stronger as it's not
mixed with any milk powder or sugar). There's
no way to make this particular recipe vegan—
although you can find non-dairy condensed milk
and cream, they won't whip as well or give such
a smooth ice cream.

Hidden in plain sight

**MAKING
GREAT USE OF
KITCHEN STAPLES**

Recipe list

Introduction

You don't need to cook with "special" ingredients to make good food. The recipes here are about seeing familiar kitchen staples in a new light, from canned fish to peanut butter. There's a West African recipe for easy chili-stewed greens, and ugly leeks are given a new lease on life when cooked into a silky pasta sauce with butter and miso paste. There's also a recipe that revives stale bread in a sweet, spicy apple dessert. This is an exercise in trust: putting your faith in your battered old microwave, the cans at the back of your kitchen cupboard and, as ever, your ability to magic something delicious from everyday things.

Further reading

White Trash Cooking by Ernest Matthew Mickler

Rachel Ama's Vegan Eats by Rachel Ama

Hibiscus by Lopè Ariyo

Longthroat Memoirs by Yemisí Aríbisálà

Tin Can Cook by Jack Monroe

Japanese Cooking: A Simple Art by Shizuo Tsuji

Everyday Harumi by Harumi Kurihara

The Green Roasting Tin by Rukmini Iyer

Take One Tin by Lola Milne

The Cornershop Cookbook by Caroline Craig and Sophie Missing

Toast by Nigel Slater

Cook, Eat, Repeat by Nigella Lawson

Midnight Chicken by Ella Risbridger

Good Things in England by Florence White

Mrs. Beeton's Book of Household Management by Isabella Beeton

The Little Library Cookbook by Kate Young

The Hobbit by J. R. R. Tolkien

Cook Real Hawai'i by Sheldon Simeon with Garrett Snyder

In Pursuit of Flavor by Edna Lewis

Pride and Pudding by Regula Ysewijn

ONE-PAN SMASHED POTATOES WITH LEMONY SARDINES AND PESTO

This is a cooked lunch for days when I really can't be arsed making a cooked lunch. All you need to do is stick it all in a roasting pan and wait. It's particularly good if you find chopping difficult or need ideas for low-energy, low-stress cooking.

Serves: 4
Ready in: less than 1 hour 20 minutes, of which most is no-fuss time while the potatoes roast

Vegetarian option   Vegan option

1¾ pounds (800g) small potatoes, well washed
2 tablespoons olive oil
Pinch of salt
10 ounces (300g) frozen chopped or whole leaf spinach
2 x 6½ ounce (180g) cans sardines in oil or brine

½ cup (60g) black olives (Kalamata olives are particularly good)
6 tablespoons pesto
4 tablespoons lemon juice (from roughly 2 lemons)

1. Preheat the oven to 400°F (200°C). While the oven heats, prepare your potatoes, cutting any slightly larger ones in half, then toss them with the oil and salt in a large roasting pan (a 13 x 9 inch/22 × 33cm pan is a perfect size for this amount). Stick them in the preheated oven for 45–55 minutes.

2. In the meantime, take the spinach out of the freezer and defrost a little, either just in a bowl in a warmish room or in the microwave. You'll also need to drain the oil or brine from your canned fish, and pit and halve the olives.

3. Once the potatoes have had at least 45 minutes in the oven, test one for readiness by cutting it in half and having a poke at the middle with a fork. If it yields easily under the fork and is tender rather than crunchy (have a taste if need be), it's ready. If not, give them another 10 minutes.

4. Remove the potatoes from the oven and use a fork, spoon or even the bottom of a glass to "smash" them. You're not aiming to mash the

potatoes, just to squash them down hard enough that their skins burst and their steamy flesh fractures.

5. Dot the defrosted spinach over the potatoes, tucking it into any gaps between the potatoes. Break the drained fish into meaty chunks and scatter over the top. Sprinkle on the olives. Mix the pesto with the lemon juice, then pour this herby, lemony dressing over the lot.

6. Put the dish back in the oven for a further 10 minutes to heat everything through, then serve straightaway.

Variations and substitutions:

You can use fresh spinach in place of the frozen spinach here, but it's a bit more work. Pour a kettle of boiling water over the washed spinach leaves in a large bowl and let sit for a few seconds, then drain and immediately plunge the wilted leaves into very cold water. Frozen peas also work nicely in place of the spinach. Add 1–1½ cups (150–200g) peas to the dish exactly how you would the frozen spinach.

In place of the sardines, you could use canned mackerel or tuna. You can omit the fish if you're vegetarian or vegan, and use a vegetarian or vegan pesto (without Parmesan).

Small new potatoes work best here. Because you can leave the skins on, they steam nicely and don't dry out.
You can use bigger potatoes if you want,
cut into chunks no bigger than a golf ball.
Don't peel them unless the skins
are very thick and tough.

GOES-WITH-EVERYTHING GROUNDNUT SOUP

I didn't always appreciate peanut butter the way I should. I thought it was good for sandwiches, for dunking milk chocolate into and sometimes for milkshakes, but I hadn't tapped into the savory potential of this remarkable ingredient. More fool me. In Filipino kare-kare, peanut butter is cooked with bagoong (a deeply savory fermented shrimp paste) and, typically, beef. In Indonesian sate (or satay), skewers of meat are eaten with a peanut sauce. There are Indian peanut chutneys like the powdery shenga hindi, and sauces like Ecuadorian salsa de maní, which can be served with potatoes.

My introduction to this whole world of peanut butter dishes was through my own Ghanaian heritage. Nkatenkwan, or groundnut soup (groundnut being another name for peanut), is a West African peanut stew often cooked with goat or chicken. It's a robust, velvety soup with a lingering warmth from Scotch bonnet or habanero chili. There are variations of it across West Africa and beyond, with staunch advocates for every conceivable version. It even spread as far as North America, when enslaved West Africans brought with them the materials and the knowledge to cultivate and cook their prized groundnuts in a new, strange land. One result is Virginian peanut soup, which, despite its European influences, still carries within it the influence of those original West African cooks.

Considering the incredible spread of peanut-based soups, sauces and stews around the world, I don't think I'm overstating it when I say peanuts truly do have the range. So, when I tell you this nkatenkwan-influenced peanut soup goes with everything, I mean it! I've given a few suggestions in the variations and substitutions section on page 115, but the sky's the limit. This dish has been around the block—around the world, even—enough times; it can take whatever you throw at it.

Serves: 4
Ready in: less than 45 minutes, lots of which is easy simmering time
Make-ahead and storage tips: page 324

Vegan

---

1 tablespoon vegetable or red palm oil*
1 medium onion, finely diced
1 Scotch bonnet or habanero chili, pierced a couple of times
2¼-inch (6cm) piece of ginger, peeled and grated
4 garlic cloves, crushed or finely grated
1 teaspoon paprika
generous ½ cup (150g) smooth peanut butter

2½ cups (600ml) water
1 x 14 ounce (400g) can chopped tomatoes
1 vegetable or chicken stock cube

Serve with: omo tuo (page 116) fufu, or steamed rice
Special equipment: stick blender, food processor or blender, optional

*Red palm oil is a treasured West African ingredient—very different in taste and provenance from refined palm oil. Food writer Yewande Komolafe has written beautifully about this ingredient for the food website *Heated*. It's available in lots of large supermarkets in the international food aisles, in any African grocery store or online.

1. Heat the oil in a large deep pot. Toss in the onion, chili and ginger and cook over a medium heat for 10 minutes, stirring regularly, until soft and translucent. Add the garlic and paprika and sauté for a further minute or two. Once the garlic has cooked enough to take that sharp, raw edge off the smell, turn the heat right down and add the peanut butter, stirring to combine. Now add the water a little at a time, stirring well between each addition. First, the peanut butter will slacken to a loose paste, before collapsing into a creamy sauce as you keep on adding the water (doing things this way should stop the peanut butter from splitting in the sauce). Add the chopped tomatoes and crumble in the stock cube.

2. Turn the heat back up to medium, bring the mixture to a gentle simmer, then leave to cook for 20 minutes, stirring every so often. Turn the heat down if it's bubbling very vigorously.

3. Taste the soup now and see if it's hot enough and sufficiently salted for your tastes. To unlock some more of the fiery heat in the chili, squeeze it against the side of the pan under a wooden spoon a few times. Once you've reached the right spice level, remove the chili.

4. (At this point, you can blend the soup either using a stick blender or in a food processor or blender if you want it to be perfectly smooth, but check first that your blender is safe to use with hot liquids. This blending stage is by no means essential, though, and I don't usually bother.)

5. Serve the soup straightaway either by itself or with rice, omo tuo (page 116) or fufu. (If you're not familiar with fufu, it's made of starchy flours—often cassava and green plantain—cooked with water and mixed to a sticky, glutinous dough. It's perfect with soups and stews.) You can also serve the soup with one of the extras outlined on the next page.

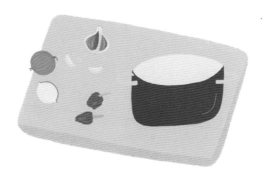

Variations and substitutions:

First up, about the chili. If you live anywhere near an African grocery store, or even a large supermarket, you should be able to get hold of these chilies. I always buy a bag of them and just toss them in the freezer—that way, they last for ages. (I also use them in the **chili-stewed greens with black-eyed peas** on page 117 and the **smoky chicken, okra and chorizo casserole** on page 175.) If you really can't get either Scotch bonnet or habanero chili, just add chili powder to taste instead, but know that, while you might get some heat this way, you'll be missing out on the beautiful, delicate flavor of the fresh chilies.

To make a chicken version of this soup: Brown four bone-in chicken thighs (skin on or off—whatever you prefer) in a couple of tablespoons of oil over a medium heat. After 4–5 minutes on each side, they should be beautifully bronzed. Remove the browned chicken and set aside, then make the soup in the pan as instructed in the recipe. Put the chicken back in when you add the chopped tomatoes. Bring to a simmer and cook for 30 minutes over a medium-low heat, adding more water as the stew cooks if necessary. It needs this extra time (compared to the plain groundnut soup) as the chicken needs time to cook through.

To serve this soup with roasted butternut squash: Before you start on the soup, peel a small butternut squash, halve it, remove the seeds and cut into slices about ½ inch/1.5 cm wide. Toss with some olive, vegetable or red palm oil and salt and roast in the oven at 400°F (200°C) for 30 minutes. While the squash roasts, prepare the soup. Serve with rice, pouring the peanut soup on top. Alternatively, you can follow vegan author Rachel Ama in adding peeled, diced sweet potatoes to the stew along with black-eyed peas. Add these to the pan along with the chopped tomatoes and then let simmer for 25 minutes, stirring occasionally. It's ready once the sweet potato is tender. I also like this soup a lot with plantain: just prepare and fry some plantain following the instructions in the **kelewele** recipe on page 238 (no need to marinate it when you're having it as an accompaniment to this full-bodied soup).

If you want to garnish the soup with something fresh: I'd recommend fresh tomatoes, diced and scattered on top. Cilantro leaves lighten this really nicely as well.

And finally, this soup is an epiphany when used as a kind of sauce with boiled potatoes—similar to how Ecuadorian salsa de maní might be served. Just peel, cut and boil your potatoes, and serve straightaway with the soupy peanut sauce poured over.

Hidden in plain sight

OMO TUO
Pounded rice dumplings

These Ghanaian rice balls are ideal with soup, especially the **goes-with-everything groundnut soup** on page 112. To make them, you cook basmati rice with lots of water, then beat it really well until it forms a chewy, sticky dough. You then squeeze the dough into fat dumplings a little smaller than a clenched fist. These balls can be added to a shallow bowl with soup: just use your fingers to pinch off small pieces of the rice dumpling and dip into the steaming soup.

Serves: 4
Ready in: less than 30 minutes

Vegan

1½ cups (300g) basmati rice
½ teaspoon salt, or to taste
3½ cups (850ml) cold water

1. Start by briefly rinsing the rice in a sieve under cold water. You don't need to rinse it as thoroughly as you might usually, as the sticky starch is structurally useful here—about 30 seconds should do it.

2. Drain the rinsed rice, then place in a medium saucepan. Add the salt and the cold water, then set over a medium heat and bring the water to a simmer. As soon as it's bubbling, put a tight-fitting lid on the pan and turn the heat down as low as it will go. Cook very gently for 15 minutes, then turn off the heat and let the pan sit—still covered—for 2–3 minutes.

3. Get out a sturdy wooden spoon. While the rice is still hot, beat it as energetically as you possibly can, mashing it against the sides of the pan as you go. The aim is to turn those separate grains of rice—which should

be mushy and sticky thanks to all that water—into a dense, chewy, pretty much homogeneous mass. It won't be completely smooth (unless you use a stand mixer, which is an option if you can't face all that stirring), but it'll come together as a kind of dough.

4. Fill a bowl with cold water and have it accessible to dip your hands in. As soon as the rice is just about cool enough to handle—it needs to be reasonably warm or it'll become dry and crumbly—wet your hands, then scoop roughly an eighth of the rice mixture out of the pan. Squeeze it between your dampened palms until you have a very compact ball, then set aside. Repeat with the remaining rice.

5. To make these look extra cute, and for a really dense, chewy texture, you can also squeeze these in plastic wrap: After you've shaped the balls by hand, set each one on a square of plastic wrap and then bring the excess plastic wrap up to cover the ball. Twist the plastic wrap shut as tightly as possible (like the twist end of a candy wrapper) to further compact the rice and give a smooth, taut ball. Set these aside until your soup or stew is ready, then remove the plastic wrap and place a couple of the rice balls in the middle of each bowl of hot soup.

CHILI-STEWED GREENS WITH BLACK-EYED PEAS

This recipe—greens simmered until silky in a chili-spiked tomato and red pepper sauce—is based on a Nigerian dish called efo riro. It's perfect with rice for a warming, fuss-free dinner and as good a way as any to bring new life to the old greens in your vegetable drawer. Ordinarily, efo riro might have iru (fermented locust beans), meat or fish in it, but this riff on the classic just uses black-eyed peas. If you want to try another version, Yewande Komolafe wrote an excellent one for her collection of essential Nigerian recipes in *The New York Times*.

I understand that in many places, it's become standard, even desirable, to keep oil in cooking to a minimum, but you're going to have to think beyond that for this dish. The oil in the sauce here carries so much of the flavor of the other ingredients, as well as adding a depth of its own. Especially if you choose to use red palm oil (available in lots of large supermarkets in the international food aisles, or in any African grocery store), this flavor will turn the dish from a pretty spartan greens-and-tomatoes affair to something luxuriously smooth. The oil also works some kind of magic on the Scotch bonnet chili, mellowing its heat. Speaking of the chili: feel free to use more if you like extra spice, or just add the chili pierced but whole to the simmering stew if you want a milder result.

Serves: 4
Ready in: less than an hour, most of which is
   hands-off time while the sauce simmers
Make-ahead and storage tips: page 324

Vegan

1 medium onion, roughly chopped
2 red peppers, roughly chopped
2-inch (5cm) piece of fresh ginger,
   peeled and roughly chopped
4 garlic cloves, roughly chopped
¼–½ Scotch bonnet chili, to taste,
   deseeded and roughly chopped
1 x 14 ounce (400g) can chopped
   tomatoes
5 tablespoons (75ml) olive or red
   palm oil
2 tablespoons tomato paste
1 x 14 ounce (400g) can black-eyed
   peas, drained
1 pound (450g) spring greens, Tuscan
   kale or chard, thickly sliced

about 1 cup (200–250ml) water
½ teaspoon turmeric
Salt, to taste

Serve with: steamed white rice
Special equipment: stick blender,
   food processor, blender or mortar
   and pestle

1. Use a stick blender, food processor or blender to blitz the onion, peppers, ginger, garlic, chili, chopped tomatoes, oil and tomato paste until smooth. (If you don't have a blender but do have plenty of time, you could also do this using a big pestle and mortar, pounding the onion, peppers, ginger, garlic and chili with a little oil, then adding the chopped tomatoes, the remaining oil and the tomato paste at the end.)

2. Bring this spicy scarlet mixture to a simmer in a large pan over a medium heat, then turn the heat down to low and cover with a lid. The lid is vital here: this mix tends to spit and spatter as it cooks. Cook very gently for 25 minutes, stirring regularly, until the paste is slightly thicker and the flavors have had a chance to come together.

3. Add the black-eyed peas, greens, water and turmeric to the pan, then simmer with the lid on for a further 20 minutes. Stir the stew every so often. If it's looking too thick, add a splash more water; if it's too thin, take off the lid to let it reduce.

4. Once the greens are silky and soft, turn off the heat and season to taste with salt. Serve with steamed white rice.

Variations and substitutions:

Scotch bonnet chilies are easy to get hold of in any Caribbean, African, or Latin American grocery store or larger supermarket, and their flavor is vital to this dish. Habanero chilies are comparable, if that's what you can get hold of. If you really can't get the fresh chilies, dried chili flakes—roughly 1 teaspoon—will provide some of the heat, but I'd warn that they won't give that same flavor.

I particularly love spring greens in this stew—they're ridiculously cheap, they're delicious and they keep their body once cooked—but fresh spinach or amaranth greens are also great options.

If you have a glut of fresh tomatoes, you can chop these and use them in place of the canned chopped tomatoes, but you may want to increase the simmering time slightly before adding the greens and beans in order to let the tomato flavor intensify.

YAJI-SPICED CELERY ROOT WITH GARLIC GREENS AND BULGUR WHEAT

Yaji, or suya spice, is a Hausa Nigerian spice blend used to make suya—grilled meat skewers almost blackened with a smoky, nutty, fiery dry rub. In an article for online food magazine *Vittles*, chef Joké Bakare, of London's Chishuru, outlines the anatomy of a good yaji:

Every yaji is different but the basic mix consists of ginger, garlic, Grains of Selim, false cubeb pepper, onion flakes, dried chili, paprika and salt, and in most cases bouillon powder . . . A really good yaji spice mix is a fine balance of bitter, musky and citrusy. Because some of the peppers are floral, you want to establish a fine balance so that no one overpowers the other and all work together in harmony.

Many versions use groundnut—or peanut—powder in the mix: these are, Joké explains, yajin-kuli. In another *Vittles* article, Emeka Frederick of Nigerian tapas joint Chuku's puts the groundnut powder center stage, listing dried ginger, cloves, red chilies, salt and Cameroon pepper as other ingredients in the blend. This mix creates what he calls "magic gold."

I've used yaji here to encrust chunks of celery root, whose earthiness is a great match for the spice if you're not a meat-eater. This recipe makes more yaji than you'll need right now: put the remainder in a small tub or jar and use it with meat or vegetable skewers. If you're lucky enough to live close to a Nigerian store, you can buy yaji premixed, but I'd recommend taste-testing it before you use it, because it can vary in heat from brand to brand. The version here can be made mild or fiery hot, depending on your tastes.

If you're after more ideas for yaji or suya spice or Nigerian cooking more generally, I'd recommend Lopè Ariyo's *Hibiscus* as well as *Longthroat Memoirs* by Yemisí Aríbisálà. For more plant-based Nigerian cooking, check out Tomi Makanjuola's website *The Vegan Nigerian*.

Serves: 4
Ready in: less than an hour
Make-ahead and storage tips: page 324

Vegan

For the yaji or suya spice mix:
⅔ cup (100g) roasted salted or unsalted
   peanuts
2 tablespoons smoked paprika
1–1½ tablespoons chili powder
2 teaspoons ground ginger
2 teaspoons garlic powder
2 teaspoons granulated onion
¼ teaspoon ground nutmeg
1–2 chicken or vegetable stock cubes,
   crumbled (use 1 if your peanuts are
   salted, or 2 if they're unsalted)

For the celery root:
1 large or 2 small celery root (you want
   2 pounds or so/800g–1kg), peeled and
   cut into 1¼-inch/3cm chunks
1½ tablespoons olive or vegetable oil

For the greens:
1 tablespoon olive or vegetable oil
3 garlic cloves, crushed or finely grated
7 ounces (200g) Tuscan kale, kale or
   spring greens, thickly sliced and
   stalks removed
½–⅔ cup (100–150ml) water
2 tablespoons lemon juice
   (from roughly 1 lemon)
Salt, to taste

For the bulgur wheat:
1½ cups (225g) coarse bulgur wheat*
3 medium tomatoes, diced
¼–½ medium red onion, finely diced
Salt, to taste

Special equipment: food processor
   or spice grinder, optional

*If you're not sure what grade of bulgur wheat you have—fine, medium or coarse—that's fine. It'll make a difference texturally, but for the purposes of this recipe the main difference will be in the cooking time. Fine bulgur wheat will cook faster, so if the wheat is tender (but still with some bounce) after a few minutes, take it off the heat and drain it.

1. Preheat the oven to 450°F (220°C). On the stovetop, bring a large pot of lightly salted water to a simmer.

2. In a food processor or spice grinder, blitz the peanuts until they're finely ground. Don't overdo this, or they'll release their oils and turn into peanut butter. You could also do this either with a rolling pin (put the peanuts in a sturdy freezer bag and give them a whack) or with a sharp knife (and a lot of patience) by chopping them over and over again. Mix the peanut meal with the rest of the yaji ingredients, then decant into a clean jar or tub—you'll need only some of the mix for this recipe.

3. Add the celery root chunks to the pan of simmering water on the stovetop. Boil for 6–8 minutes, or until almost tender but not quite cooked. Remove

the celery root with a slotted spoon, but leave the water in the pot—you can use this to cook the bulgur wheat in a moment.

4. On a large baking sheet, toss the cooked celery root with the 1½ tablespoons of oil and sprinkle over 4–6 tablespoons of the yaji mix. Roll the celery root chunks around until they're completely caked in the mix, then roast in the preheated oven for 25 minutes, or until the spice crust is slightly darker and nicely toasted.

5. While the celery root roasts, heat another tablespoon of oil in a large frying pan over a medium-low heat and add the garlic. Sauté for 1–2 minutes, then add the greens and ½–⅔ cup (100–150ml) water to the pan. Cover with a lid, then bring to a simmer and reduce the heat to low. Let the greens cook for 8–10 minutes, then remove the lid and cook, stirring occasionally, for a couple more minutes, until the water has evaporated and the greens are tender. Add the lemon juice and salt to taste.

6. To cook the bulgur wheat, bring the water that you used to cook the celery root back to a simmer. Add the bulgur wheat and simmer for 8–12 minutes, or until the bulgur is cooked but still slightly chewy. Drain the bulgur wheat and season to taste, then stir in the diced tomato and red onion. Serve straightaway, piling the nutty spiced celery root and garlicky greens atop the bulgur wheat.

Variations and substitutions:

You could also make this with rutabaga, cooking it exactly the same as you would the celery root. Another option is butternut squash, though I'd recommend skipping the boiling stage and instead adding 10 minutes to the roasting time.

Millet or quinoa would be good alternatives to the bulgur wheat if you can't eat gluten: they have different cooking times and methods, so just follow the instructions on the package. Fonio, a kind of West African millet, would work particularly well. For a really quick fix, try garri—a kind of cassava meal—or couscous.

You could also finish the celery root on the grill if you want. Instead of cutting it into chunks, cut into 1 inch (2–3cm)-thick slices, like burger patties. Boil the celery root as outlined above, then add the oil and the yaji spice mix. Grill over direct heat, turning occasionally, until the yaji is toasted and the celery root slices are smoky.

NO-WASTE WHOLE CAULIFLOWER AND MACARONI CHEESE

It was food writer and campaigner Jack Monroe who opened my eyes to the power of using the whole cauliflower. Until I saw a post on their Instagram about dicing the stalk and leaves of this magnificent vegetable, I'd just been using the florets and nothing else—a horrible waste by all accounts, but it was all I knew. It's a shame we're not more thoughtful about this kinda thing in general, because when you start using the whole cauliflower, you notice 1) just how small a percentage of the cauliflower the florets actually comprise and 2) how delicious the stalk and leaves really are—sweet and with a more gentle brassica flavor than the florets. This cauliflower and macaroni cheese is a smart, simple way of making use of all that goodness.

If the cauliflower you have doesn't have many (or any) leaves attached, you may want to consider using more cauliflower and/or pasta—those leaf "ribs" and greens add a lot of bulk to the finished dish.

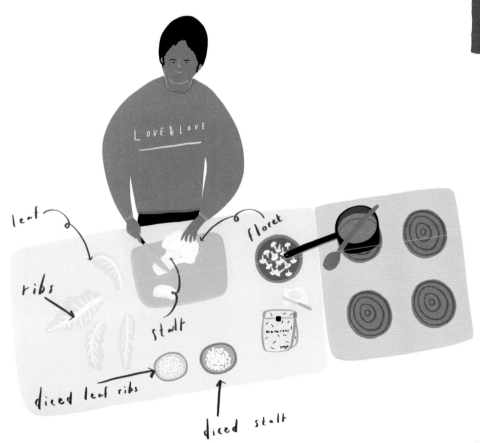

leaf

ribs

floret

stalt

diced leaf ribs

diced stalt

Serves: 6

Ready in: less than 1 hour 30 minutes,
  25 minutes of which are hands-off baking time

Make-ahead and storage tips: page 325

Vegetarian

Vegan option

---

1 large cauliflower (roughly 2¼ pounds/1kg), leaves and all

Salt

3 tablespoons salted or unsalted butter

4 tablespoons all-purpose flour

3¼ cups (750ml) whole or reduced-fat milk

3 cups (350g) grated Cheddar

1 tablespoon Dijon or wholegrain mustard

1 teaspoon paprika

¼–½ teaspoon chili powder, to taste

Lots of freshly ground black pepper

14 ounces (400g) macaroni

1. Preheat the oven to 400°F (200°C), and have a large roasting pan (roughly 13 x 9 inches/22 × 33cm) on hand.

2. Prepare the cauliflower. We want to make use of every part of the cauliflower here, so start off by breaking off all the leaves. Give them a good wash, then tear the green leafy part away from the thick "ribs" that run down the middle of each leaf. Finely dice the leaf ribs and put in one bowl. Cut the green leafy sections into very thin ribbons and put into a separate bowl. Next up, cut off the florets, cutting them into portions that are reasonably chunky, but small enough that you could feasibly eat it in one big mouthful. Put these prepared florets in a separate bowl. You'll be left with the knobbly stalk now. Trim off the skin from the very outside of the stalk and cut off the base. Finely dice what's left of the stalk, and add this to the bowl that you put the diced leaf ribs in.

3. Next, set a large pot of salted water over a high heat, and bring it to a boil. While the water heats, get out a second pot—a medium to large one—and set it over a medium heat. Add the butter to this second pot, then add the diced cauliflower stalk and leaf ribs. Stir well to combine, then put a lid on the pot and let the veg sweat for 13–15 minutes, stirring regularly.

4. Once the cauliflower has had a chance to soften, add the flour and stir well to mix it in. Let the flour and veg mixture sauté for a minute or two, to cook the flour. Add the milk a little at a time, stirring briskly as you go: at first it'll form a thick paste, before slowly loosening to a custard-like consistency and then a milky sauce. When the milk has all been mixed in, bring the mixture to a simmer while stirring constantly to make sure no lumps form. By the time the sauce starts to bubble, it should have

thickened slightly and will be similar to a white sauce that you might use in a lasagna. Turn off the heat and add the grated cheese, mustard, paprika, chili powder and black pepper.

5. By now, the pot of salted water should be boiling. Pour in the macaroni, give it a good stir to stop it clumping together and cook for 4 minutes. Add the cauliflower florets to the pot and cook for a further 4 minutes, then drain the pasta and florets together in a sieve or colander.

6. Tip the drained macaroni and cauliflower mixture into your roasting pan, then pour in the cheese sauce. Stir everything around so that the pasta is well coated. Scatter the ribbons of green cauliflower leaf over the top and gently press them down onto the sauce and pasta. Bake in the preheated oven for 20–25 minutes, until golden and sizzling—turn the oven down if the leaves on top are getting too dark. Let it sit for a few minutes before serving: it'll settle during this time and become easier to serve.

A vegan version:

1. First up, you need to soak 2 cups (9 ounces/250g) unsalted cashews in 2 cups (500ml) freshly boiled water, for 15 minutes or so. This is an alternative to the milk.

2. When it's time to cook, blend the cashew and water mixture until as smooth as possible—this will be easy in a blender, but can be done using a stick blender if that's all you have. Then add ½ cup (75g) nutritional yeast, 2 tablespoons olive oil, 2 teaspoons vinegar (white wine, cider, rice or cane vinegar are all fine) and ½ teaspoon salt, and blend until smooth. These additions are in place of the cheese.

3. Prepare the cauliflower as above. When you sauté the cauliflower, use oil instead of butter. Don't add any flour in this version (this sauce should be plenty thick enough already): just add the cashew sauce to the diced cauliflower stalk and leaf ribs and heat gently, stirring all the time, until steaming hot. Be sure to stir constantly as it may stick otherwise. You can then mix in the mustard, paprika, chili powder and black pepper listed in the main recipe, giving the sauce some color and bite.

4. Meanwhile, cook the macaroni and cauliflower florets as described in the main recipe. Assemble the pasta, cauliflower and sauce in your roasting pan, add the thin strips of cauliflower leaf and bake as instructed above.

BEETS WITH LENTILS, HALLOUMI AND CLEMENTINE

Beets take an age to cook if you buy them fresh, but that's why we can be grateful for vacuum-packed cooked beets: tender, sweet and with that truly lethal magenta juice (don't cook this in a white T-shirt). This is a reassuringly easy salad for when you know your body is craving nutrients, but you still need a dish with some physical heft. A salad is obviously never gonna fill you up in the way that a plate of pasta might (I'm a realist), but if you double the amount of halloumi here or add some bread on the side, you'll be set.

Serves: 4
Ready in: less than 20 minutes
Make-ahead and storage tips: page 325

Vegetarian

---

3 cups (500g) cooked brown, green or French lentils (from 2 x 14 ounce/400g cans, drained, or one large pouch)
2 tablespoons olive oil
½–1 tablespoon white wine vinegar or cider vinegar

5 clementines
½ pound (225g) halloumi, thickly sliced
Salt, to taste
14 ounces (400g) cooked beets, cut into fat wedges

1. In a medium saucepan, combine the lentils, olive oil and ½ tablespoon of the vinegar. Squeeze the juice from 3 of the clementines into the pan. Set the pan over a low heat—you're not aiming to cook this, just to warm the lentils through.

2. While the lentils warm, get out a frying pan and set it over a medium heat. Sauté the halloumi slices for a couple of minutes on each side, or until mottled with a cow print pattern of cream and copper brown. The cheese slices should be crisp outside and densely chewy inside. Break the remaining 2 clementines into segments.

3. Taste the lentils: if they need a touch more vinegar, add that now. Add salt to taste. Toss the lentils with the beets, halloumi and clementine segments and serve straightaway.

> **Variations and substitutions:**
>
> If you want to use dried lentils, use 1–1⅓ cups (6–7 ounces/ 175–200g) green, brown or French lentils and boil in lots of water for 20–30 minutes, or until tender. Drain, then use as specified above.
>
> To use raw beets, simmer them whole for 45–60 minutes, or until tender through to their middle, then peel off the skins while the beets are still warm.
>
> In place of the clementines, you can use orange. You'll need about 3 tablespoons orange juice (from roughly 1 orange) for the lentil dressing, and 1 orange to cut into segments.

FISH STICKS WITH
JAPANESE CURRY AND RICE

The anatomy of a katsukarē, or katsu curry, is simple. First there is katsu—the breadcrumbed cutlet element, usually pork or chicken. Then there is the curry or karē—thick, velvety and slightly sweet curry sauce, ordinarily cooked with chunks of carrot and potato. Finally, there's the steamed Japanese rice. Its origin story is less straightforward. Curries spiced with ground cumin and turmeric were transported from India to Japan by British colonial forces during the 1800s—one of the less disastrous instances of imperial meddling, but testament to the evergreen British compulsion to leave a heavy footprint wherever we go. Those curries were adapted, as foods so often are, to the tastes of the inhabitants of their adoptive country: Japanese cooks added a roux to thicken them (itself a French import, lending this thickener the name karērū) and, in another cross-cultural mishmash, even spiked them with Worcestershire sauce. The sauces became sweeter and more robust, and by the mid-twentieth century were beginning to gain popularity across Japan.

Not everyone was happy about this. In *Japanese Cooking: A Simple Art*, Shizuo Tsuji lamented the foreign influence on classic Japanese cooking. "Today the Japanese eat a mixture of Western, Japanese, and Chinese food . . . Japan must be the only country in the world where the everyday fare is such a hodgepodge." But when a food delights the palate, it captures hearts, and these kinds of protests couldn't do much to stop its progress. By the 1950s, these curries had found their way onto plates alongside tonkatsu—pork cutlets crusted with panko breadcrumbs and deep-fried—and katsukarē was born.

I approached this recipe with a degree of caution, keen not to continue the age-old tradition of culinary imperialism. But I humbly stand by this dish: fish sticks, breaded in golden crumbs, are a perfect easy swap for chicken or pork cutlets.

For this, I'd highly recommend using a store-bought Japanese curry roux block. This is the starch-thickened curry block, a bit like a massive stock cube, that will add thickness and flavor to your dish. You can get it in most big supermarkets, but if you go to an East Asian grocery store you should be able to find versions like S&B Golden Curry sauce mix. It's the most popular, easiest and arguably the most delicious way of making Japanese curry at home. If you can't get the ready-made roux, you can make your own though. Skip to the recipe for **homemade curry roux** on page 131.

If you want to learn more about Japanese cooking, I found Namiko Chen's website, *Just One Cookbook*, incredibly useful. You could also consult Harumi Kurihara's excellent cookbooks.

Serves: 4
Ready in: less than an hour
Make-ahead and storage tips: page 325

Vegetarian option   Vegan option

1½ cups (300g) short- or medium-grain rice*
1 tablespoon vegetable oil
1 medium onion, thickly sliced
1 medium apple, peeled and grated
1 large potato (5–7 ounces/150–200g), peeled and cut into 1 inch/2–3cm chunks
1¼ cups (100g) mushrooms, sliced
2 medium carrots, peeled and sliced

3–3½ cups (700–800ml) water
1½ tablespoons honey
12 fish sticks
3½ ounces (100g) store-bought curry roux or 1 batch homemade curry roux, see following recipe
Light soy sauce, to taste

Serve with: pickles or pickled daikon

*Sushi rice is a good option here, but a short- or medium-grain rice will do. I made this recently with a Thai medium-grain jasmine rice and it worked well. What you're looking for is a rice with plump grains that become chewy and slightly sticky when cooked—not the long, fragile, fluffy grains of basmati rice.

If you're making the curry roux from scratch, do that first, following the recipe on page 131.

1. Start by preparing the rice. The method will vary depending on the type of rice you use, so I'd recommend googling the cooking time if you're not confident. This is how I cook sushi rice: Wash the rice really well in cold water, continuing until the water runs pretty much clear. Cover the rice with water and soak for 30 minutes. Drain, then put the soaked rice in a small or medium saucepan along with 1⅔ cups (400ml) water (if you're making a bigger or smaller batch, just weigh your rice and then add 1⅓ of that amount of water). Set over a medium heat and bring to a simmer.

As soon as the mixture is simmering, turn the heat down as low as it'll go and put a tight-fitting lid on the pan. Cook for 12 minutes, then turn off the heat and let sit undisturbed—with its lid on—for 10 minutes. While you do all this, you can get started with the curry.

2. Preheat the oven to 400°F (200°C). Heat the oil in a medium saucepan over a medium heat. Add the onion and cook for 10 minutes, stirring, until the onion begins to soften. Add the apple, potato, mushrooms, carrots, water and honey and bring to a simmer. It won't look particularly exciting right now, but it'll come together when you add the curry roux. Simmer for 15 minutes over a low heat.

3. While the vegetables cook, lay out the fish sticks on a large baking sheet and cook in the preheated oven, baking them for a few minutes longer than specified in the instructions on the package—you want them to be really crisp.

4. While the fish sticks cook, return to the curry sauce. By now the vegetables should be tender. Briskly stir in the curry roux, mixing until it's smoothly dissolved into the stew. As the sauce starts to simmer again, you'll notice it begin to thicken, transforming from watery to rich and thick. When it thickens, add the soy sauce to taste if you think it needs more salt, or add extra water for a thinner curry.

5. When you're ready to serve, pour the curry sauce over the rice, then lay the crisp fish sticks on top. You can serve this with some thin slices of pickle or pickled daikon, if you want—the acidity is a good contrast with the smooth sauce.

Variations and substitutions:

Instead of the fish sticks, you can of course use chicken schnitzel—baked or fried and sliced—or panko breadcrumbed pork if you prefer. For a vegetarian version, breadcrumbed and fried pumpkin or eggplant are good options.

Homemade curry roux

As I mentioned in the previous recipe, I'd recommend buying a ready-made block of curry roux if you can. If that's not an option, here's how to make your own.

Makes: just over 3½ ounces (100g), enough for 4 servings of curry
Ready in: less than 20 minutes
Make-ahead and storage tips: page 325

Vegetarian   Vegan option

⅓ cup (75g) salted or unsalted butter *or* ¼ cup (60ml) vegetable oil
⅓ cup plus 2 tablespoons (50g) all-purpose flour

2 tablespoons mild curry powder
1½ teaspoons cumin
½ teaspoon chili powder
¼–½ teaspoon salt

Melt the butter or warm the oil over a medium-low heat. Once it's hot, add the flour and cook very gently for 5–10 minutes, stirring the mixture every minute or so. This stage requires patience, but it's worth it: the butter and flour mixture will darken slightly to a light golden brown as it cooks, and if you try it you'll notice the raw flour taste has given way to a nutty, toasted flavor. If you've used vegetable oil, the roux won't darken in the same way, but it's still worth cooking it for a few minutes to thoroughly cook off the raw flour flavor. Once the roux has cooked, add the curry powder, cumin, chili powder and salt (use the full ½ teaspoon if your butter was unsalted; use less with salted butter). Cook for a further 30 seconds, then remove from the heat. The roux is now ready to use.

ROASTED CARROTS WITH CHICKPEAS, GARLIC YOGURT AND HERBS

Everyone has their own Old-Man-Yells-at-Cloud gripe that they just can't let go. Some people can't get over the fact that some people do (or do not) keep their ketchup in the fridge; other people can't stop themselves ragging on pineapple-topped pizza. My favorite bugbear is the fact that people don't tend to pay enough attention to cheap vegetables. Every time we start sounding off about our chosen gripe, we feel ourselves calcifying into exactly the kind of embittered moaner we swore we'd never be. This is one of life's small pleasures.

This recipe is one of a handful coming up in this chapter that puts cheap veg center stage. By combining plenty of different textures and flavors (sweet roasted carrots, spiced chickpeas, garlicky yogurt, the tang of pickled onions and fresh herbs), you can bring new life to vegetables that might usually be confined to a supporting role.

Serves: 4 as a main with bread or rice, or 6–8 as a side dish
Ready in: 1 hour
Make-ahead and storage tips: page 325

Vegan

1¾ pounds (800g) carrots
2 tablespoons olive oil
½–1½ teaspoons chili flakes, to taste
Salt, to taste
4 garlic cloves, skin left on
1 small red onion, thinly sliced
Scant ⅔ cup (150ml) white or red wine vinegar
2 x 14 ounce (400g) cans chickpeas, drained
¾ cup (75g) walnuts, crumbled into chunks
1 tablespoon paprika
2 teaspoons cumin seeds or 1½ teaspoons cumin
1 heaping cup (250g) plain yogurt, dairy or non-dairy
Handful of fresh herb leaves (roughly ½ ounce/
    10–15g)—cilantro, parsley, basil or mint all work

Serve with: flatbread, pita or rice

1. Preheat the oven to 350°F (180°C) and haul a big roasting pan (you'll want one at least 13 x 9 inches/22 × 33cm across its base) from the depths of the kitchen cupboards.

2. While the oven heats, peel the carrots and trim off their tops and bottoms. Cut each carrot in half lengthways to give two long strips, then chop each of these into 1 inch (2–3cm) chunks (I like to cut on a diagonal to create tapered pieces). Toss the prepared carrots with 1 tablespoon of the oil, the chili flakes (how much you use will depend on how spicy you like your food) and a good pinch of salt, and tip into your roasting pan. Toss the garlic cloves on top and put in the preheated oven for 30 minutes.

3. Put the onion slices in a small bowl with the vinegar, pressing the onion down so that it's all covered by the liquid. Leave to soak until everything else is cooked—during this time, the onion will lose some of that pungency, so you don't have to worry about knocking anyone out with your breath later on.

4. Toss the drained chickpeas and walnut pieces with the remaining tablespoon of oil, the paprika, the cumin seeds or ground cumin and a pinch of salt. Once the carrots have roasted for half an hour, take the pan out of the oven and carefully pluck out the garlic cloves, setting them to one side. Tip the spiced chickpeas and walnuts into the roasting pan, roughly stir until everything is well mixed, then return to the oven for a final 20 minutes.

5. To prepare the garlic yogurt, pop the fragrant roasted garlic cloves from their skins—you'll notice they're a lot more mellow than acrid raw garlic—and crush into the yogurt, stirring to combine.

6. When the carrots and chickpeas are nearly done, roughly chop or tear your chosen herbs. Drain the vinegar from the onions. Take the roasting pan out of the oven, scatter over the beautiful pink onion slices and dot over the garlic yogurt. Scatter over the herbs and serve.

Variations and substitutions:

You could swap the carrots for butternut squash, celery root or sweet potato if that's what you have. To ensure that everything cooks in the right time, cut the veg into pieces the same size as the carrot chunks described in step 2. Buy pre-cut veg if that makes your life much easier.

In place of the yogurt, you could crumble some feta over the dish once everything's cooked. Torn mozzarella would also work well if you swap the cumin or cumin seeds for a couple of teaspoons of dried oregano or thyme.

The spices in the chickpeas can be switched up however you see fit: smoked paprika is delicious, as are nigella seeds (half a teaspoon or so should do) or a generous sprinkling of citrusy sumac.

The walnuts can be swapped for sunflower or pumpkin seeds or be omitted altogether.

BUTTERED MISO LINGUINE WITH LEEKS

I love how weird leeks are: scrubby, mud-caked roots at the bottom, rising through a bright white belly to broad green leaves. They're stately but cumbersome (why do they never fit in the vegetable drawer?), and even though their livery is impeccable, they can make your eyes water. Yet with a little heat, plenty of butter and some patience, they collapse into the most perfect, deeply savory tangle. Someone on Twitter described the joy of pressing rounds of leek under a wooden spoon while they cook, and the pieces "birthing" the inner rings of leek from their middles. This is the kind of joy you can expect from leeks: strange, kind of slimy and deliciously real. They deserve more love than they ordinarily get, so here's a pasta dish that lets them take the limelight.

Serves: 4
Ready in: less than 40 minutes
Make-ahead and storage tips: page 325

Vegetarian

Salt, to taste
4 small to medium leeks
6 tablespoons (85g) salted or unsalted butter
14 ounces (400g) linguine
4 tablespoons crème fraîche or sour cream

1½ tablespoons white miso
½–1 teaspoon chili flakes
  or ½ teaspoon chili powder,
  to taste
Lots of freshly ground black pepper

1. Put a large pot of salted water on the stovetop over a high heat, bringing the water to a boil.

2. While the water heats, trim your leeks: remove the wiry root end and the very top, where the leaves fade to a deep green and are coarser and tougher than the white and lighter green parts. Halve the remaining leek stalk and cut into finger-width slices.

3. In a separate medium or large pot, heat the butter over a medium heat, then add the chopped leeks and a pinch of salt. It will look like a lot of butter, but it's vital to this dish so have faith. Stir everything to combine, then put a lid on the pan and let the leeks sweat for 15 minutes, stirring regularly and turning down the heat if they're beginning to brown or stick. When the leek is ready, it should be tender, yielding and slippery. Turn off the heat.

4. By this point, your water should be boiling. Add the pasta to it and cook according to the instructions on the package. I'd err towards the lowest end of the recommended cooking time—especially in a creamy sauce like this, it's important that pasta isn't too soft. As Marcella Hazan puts it, when overcooked, "pasta becomes leaden, and it loses buoyancy and its ability to deliver briskly the flavors of its sauce." Once cooked, drain the pasta but reserve a couple of tablespoons of the cooking water.

5. Add the drained pasta to the pot with the leeks, then add the reserved cooking water, the crème fraîche or sour cream, white miso, chili flakes and black pepper. Stir everything together over a very low heat, stopping as soon as it's mixed. Turn off the heat and check the seasoning, adding salt if necessary, then serve straightaway.

Variations and substitutions:

If you can't eat gluten, gluten-free pasta can be found in most supermarkets. The linguine can of course be swapped for any other long pasta, such as spaghetti, tagliatelle or pappardelle.

I use white miso, or shiro miso, for this dish, which is delicate but deeply savory. I also use it in the **hearty lentil ragù** on page 283, so you don't need to worry about having nothing to do with the rest of the jar. It's also a great addition to the **pantry brownies** on page 151. If you don't have any miso, you can just leave this out! Alternatives to the miso and chili seasoning include 1 tablespoon Dijon or wholegrain mustard, or a generous pinch of nutmeg and 1½ teaspoons paprika.

BAKED SEMOLINA WITH MUSHROOM AND MOZZARELLA

This is truly a stir-together job, with only about 10 minutes of hands-on prep time. The result is a roasting pan of creamy, garlic semolina studded with roasted mushrooms and herbs—an all-in-one dinner that doesn't need side dishes or bring any other kind of complication into your busy life.

Serves: 4
Ready in: 1 hour, nearly all of which is
hands-off time while the dish roasts

Vegetarian

Vegan option

2 tablespoons olive oil
1 pound (400–500g) mushrooms,
   halved or quartered
3 garlic cloves, skin left on
2 tablespoons fresh thyme leaves
   or 2 teaspoons dried thyme

½–1 teaspoon chili flakes, to taste
1½ cups (250g) semolina flour
4 cups (900ml) hot chicken *or*
   vegetable stock
1 generous cup (125g) mozzarella, torn
   or grated

1. Preheat the oven to 400°F (200°C). In a large roasting pan, roughly 13 x 9 inches (22 x 33cm), toss the olive oil with the mushrooms, garlic, most of the thyme and all of the chili flakes. Roast for 25 minutes, until the mushrooms are starting to brown and the garlic is fragrant.

2. When the mushrooms are nearly roasted, whisk together the semolina flour and stock in a large mixing bowl. The semolina will start thickening as soon as the stock is added.

3. Once the mushrooms are ready, remove the pan from the oven and pluck out the garlic cloves. Pop the garlic cloves out of their skins—they should by now be soft and fudgy—and crush into the semolina mix, stirring everything together. Add the semolina to the roasting pan and mix so that everything is evenly distributed: the semolina may sink to the bottom at first, but it'll sort itself out as it cooks. Sprinkle the mozzarella and the remaining thyme over the top, then return the pan to the oven for a further 30 minutes, or until the semolina is set. It should be very thick, almost custardy, but not too stodgy or firm.

4. Serve straightaway as the semolina will become much firmer as it cools, losing that luxurious smoothness. That said, you could probably slice and serve it like a quiche once it's cold, so it could make for good lunchbox fodder.

Variations and substitutions:

As long as you stick roughly to the amount of liquid and semolina in this recipe, you can switch it up pretty much however you want. Rosemary can take the place of the thyme, or you could follow the lead of Rukmini Iyer, who adds a dressing of chopped parsley and lemon to her sweet potato and mushroom polenta in *The Green Roasting Tin*. Alternatives to the mushrooms include small chunks of butternut squash or sweet potato, large pieces of red pepper, okra or broccoli florets (broccoli and okra will only need 10–15 minutes or so in the oven before the addition of the semolina, or they may burn).

If you're looking to replace the semolina with polenta, I'd recommend consulting a recipe like Rukmini's rather than trying to directly adapt from my one—if you mess up the liquid amounts or cooking times, you could end up with either a grainy slop or a house brick.

If you'd rather make a vegan version of this, just leave out the cheese and check that your stock cube is vegan. You could also add a couple of tablespoons of nutritional yeast to the semolina mix.

WHATEVER-YOU'VE-GOT FRIED RICE

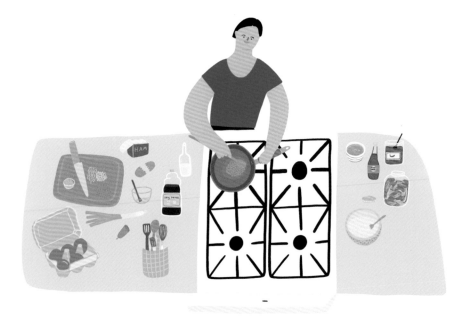

I want you to have a look through the ingredient list, pick whatever combination of veg, fun stuff and flavoring you fancy, and build your perfect fried rice around that. The essentials—rice, oil, soy sauce and pepper—are the only non-negotiables in this particular recipe: make this as maximalist or pared back as you want, guided both by your appetite and by the state of your pantry.

There are so many ways to make fried rice. There's garlicky Filipino sinangág, Chinese-Peruvian chicken fried rice and Thai khao pad sapparod with pineapple and shrimp. In Korea there is kimchi bokkeumbap, or kimchi fried rice, while Indonesia and Malaysia have nasi goreng, made with syrupy kecap manis. Nigerian fried rice is pepped up with Maggi seasoning and often bulked with iron-rich liver. There are countless permutations and combinations of the below ingredients that you can experiment with, but here are a few good options to get you started:

- scallions, sweet corn, carrots, peas, egg, sesame oil
- garlic, peas, egg, bacon, chili flakes
- scallions, sweet corn, red pepper, egg, Spam, pineapple
- garlic, peas, carrots, red pepper, ackee, chili flakes (a good vegan option)
- garlic, scallions, egg, kimchi, sesame oil

Serves: 4
Ready in: 20 minutes

Vegetarian option   Vegan option

The essentials:

4 cups (650g) cooked and cooled rice (from roughly 1¼ cups/250g uncooked rice)*

1–2 tablespoons vegetable oil

2 tablespoons light soy sauce *or* tamari

Lots of freshly ground black pepper

The veg (I'd recommend choosing three or four of these):

3 garlic cloves, crushed or finely grated

4 scallions, thinly sliced

1 x 11½ ounce (325g) can sweet corn, drained

2–3 medium carrots (roughly 7 ounces/200g) carrots, diced, or 1 x 11 ounce (300g) can carrots, drained and diced

1 cup (150g) peas, defrosted

1 red pepper, diced

The fun stuff (I'd recommend choosing at least one of these):

4 eggs, any size

1 x 7 ounce (200g) can Spam, diced

4 thick slices smoked or unsmoked bacon, diced

1 x 19 ounce (550g) can ackee, drained and roughly chopped (a great alternative to the eggs, if you're vegan)

1¼ cups (7 ounces/200g) kimchi, roughly chopped

1 x 8 ounce (225g) can pineapple, roughly chopped

The flavorings (you don't have to use any of these, but using one will add extra interest!):

½ tablespoon fish sauce

½–1½ teaspoons chili flakes or gochugaru (see page 53), to taste

Chili sauce, such as sriracha, to taste

1 teaspoon sesame oil

*I usually have basmati rice left over, but you can make this with short- or medium-grain rice as well. Whatever you use, just cook it according to the instructions on the package, cool it as quickly as possible, then chill in the fridge to firm it up—preferably overnight. If you try to make this with freshly boiled or steamed rice, it will end up gummy, wet and sticky.

1. The method for making this is going to depend on what combination of ingredients you use, so you're going to have to trust your intuition slightly here. I'll do my best to run through a few basics of method and the order to add ingredients, though, so you won't be going it completely alone.

2. You're going to need a wok or a really generously sized frying pan for this. If you're making the full four portions following the quantities given above, you may need to use two frying pans if you don't have a big wok, otherwise you risk scooting the rice straight out of the pan as you stir.

3. This is a fast-paced recipe, so make sure you've chosen the combination of ingredients you want to include and have them measured out, chopped (if necessary) and set out in separate bowls so they're easy to grab and add to the pan when it's their turn.

4. If you want to add egg to your fried rice, that's the first step: lightly beat the eggs and add, if you have it, a little sesame oil. Over a medium-high heat, add the lightly beaten eggs to a teaspoon or two of vegetable oil in the pan. Cook quickly, stirring often, until the eggs are scrambled—this might take only a minute in a wok, or very slightly longer in a frying pan. Remove the scrambled egg pieces from the pan and set to one side.

5. If you're using Spam or bacon, cook this next. Heat a little of the oil in your frying pan or wok over a medium-high heat. Add the diced Spam or bacon and cook for 1–3 minutes (it'll be much faster in a wok than a frying pan), stirring often, until lightly browned.

6. Next up, add your garlic, if you're using it. If you already browned your meat in the wok or pan, just add your garlic now. If you haven't used any meat, just heat a splash of oil in your wok over a medium-high heat and add the garlic. Cook for 30 seconds to 1 minute, or until the raw acrid garlic smell changes.

7. If you're using any raw veg, like diced fresh carrots, red pepper or kimchi, you should add these to the wok or frying pan next, to join the Spam, bacon and/or garlic, depending on what you're using. They'll need a minute or two over a medium-high heat to start softening—make sure you stir pretty much constantly.

8. Now, it's time to bring everything together. To the hot wok or frying pan, add whichever of the following ingredients you've chosen to use: scallions, sweet corn, canned carrot, peas, ackee, kimchi or pineapple. Add the rice, breaking it apart with a fork or wooden spoon as best you can to separate the grains. Return the pre-scrambled eggs to the pan, if you're using them. Add the light soy sauce or tamari and, if you're using it, any fish sauce, chili flakes or chili sauce. Mix everything really well and sauté over a medium-high heat, stirring often, until the rice is piping hot. This should take only 4–5 minutes in a wok, but just keep an eye on it and keep going until it's hot through.

9. To finish the rice, drizzle over a little sesame oil, if you're using it. Serve straightaway.

CHARRED BRUSSELS SPROUTS WITH SATAY AND CRUSHED PEANUTS

The sweet–salty richness of satay sauce (this one is *very* loosely based on Indonesian satay sauces) works well with the slight bitterness of Brussels sprouts, I think. It's also a way to make this ubiquitous midwinter vegetable feel a little bit less like itself: the culinary equivalent of giving it a stick-on mustache and a trench coat.

This works well as a side dish or as part of a vegetable spread—try it with the **roasted five-spice carrots with brown butter and sesame** on page 94 and the **bok choy with ginger and clementine** on page 95. Double the quantities below if you want to serve this as a main with rice or noodles.

Serves: 4 as a side
Ready in: 35 minutes
Make-ahead and storage tips: page 325

Vegan

To garnish:
1 banana shallot or ¼ medium red onion, thinly sliced
½ cup/120ml white wine vinegar or cider vinegar
2–3 tablespoons salted peanuts, roughly chopped

For the Brussels sprouts:
14 ounces (400g) Brussels sprouts
2 tablespoons vegetable or olive oil
4 garlic cloves, crushed or finely grated
½ teaspoon cumin seeds
½ teaspoon chili flakes
Generous pinch of salt
1–2 tablespoons lemon juice (from roughly ½–1 lemon), to taste

For the satay sauce:
4 tablespoons smooth or crunchy peanut butter
1 tablespoon light brown or superfine sugar
2 teaspoons light soy sauce *or* tamari
1–2 tablespoons lemon or lime juice (from ½–1 lemon or 1–2 limes), to taste
½ teaspoon chili flakes
¼ cup (50–60ml) water, freshly boiled

1. Preheat the oven to 400°F (200°C) and get out a large roasting pan, roughly 13 x 9 inches (22 x 33cm). Meanwhile, soak the shallot or onion slices in the vinegar in a small bowl—this vinegar will mellow the allium harshness.

2. Next, trim the Brussels sprouts, if yours didn't come pre-trimmed: Just cut off the very bottom (where the sprout attaches to the stalk) and remove any discolored leaves from the very outside. Slice all the Brussels sprouts in half from root to top.

3. In the roasting pan, toss together the Brussels sprouts, oil, garlic, cumin seeds, chili and salt. Roast in the preheated oven for 15–20 minutes, until the Brussels sprouts are nicely browned, with the outer leaves beginning to darken and crisp. They should be just about tender.

4. While the Brussels sprouts roast, make the satay sauce: Stir together the peanut butter, sugar, soy sauce (or tamari), lemon or lime juice and chili flakes, then add the hot water a little at a time, stirring until the sauce is smooth and thick. Add a little extra water if it needs it, or add extra soy sauce or citrus to taste.

5. Add the lemon juice (start with 1 tablespoon, then add more to taste) to the roasted Brussels sprouts and mix together. To serve, heap the Brussels sprouts onto a serving dish, drizzle over the satay sauce and sprinkle on the peanuts. Drain the vinegar from the shallot or red onion, and sprinkle the lightly pickled slices over the dish.

Frozen peas and other miracles

With frozen peas, the universe claps back at food purists. They are perfect, preserved in the moment of perfect sweetness (and it really is a moment—the sugars in peas begin converting to starches as soon as the pods are picked) so that we can enjoy them at their best, at our convenience and with only a couple of minutes of cooking. If you've ever tried to pick and shell your own peas, you'll know what a blessing this is. I feel lost if I don't have a bag in the freezer.

It's easy to take foods like this for granted. Simple fresh foods—vine-ripened tomatoes, unwaxed Amalfi lemons, fish straight from the net or off the line—are ideal fodder for folklore. We can talk about the farmer who dug it up or the village where the boat docked, building up a story about what "real" food is really made of. When it comes to foods that have passed through the sterile apparatus of the large farm or factory, things get more complicated. How do you spin a myth about mechanical arms, blast freezers and conveyor belts? In classical Greek tradition, you needed the logos, the words, facts and reason, but you could only really hit to the heart of an issue if you captured the mythos—story, emotion and meaning. It's hard for us to get excited about something if we can't tell a story about it, and it's hard for us to tell stories about things that haven't had a human touch.

We can try, though. If we create a mythology of processed foods, we might talk about the Italian summer captured in a can of tomatoes. We could get excited about orange juice, concentrated to the purest sap so that it can be transported and resurrected, with water, in some less sun-drenched place, whether that's a school cafeteria or a suburban supermarket. We would be grateful that saltwater fish could reach the deepest mainland in cans, in frozen fillets and, if we're lucky, as fish sticks. There are canned soups, bringing warming goodness to the kitchens of those who aren't able to cook. Watch a *How It's Made* video and you'll see how the manufacture of even the simplest frozen veg is an epic undertaking, as filled with heroic endeavor as any odyssey. (The Viennetta making-of videos are a personal favorite, but that's an aside.)

Like any food, these cans and packages have their moral complexities. There are brands of canned tomatoes from Italy that have been linked to modern-day slavery and horrific working conditions, just like commercial fishing—bringing you your tuna salad sandwich—has the potential to deplete fish stocks. But working conditions can be appalling for migrant fruit pickers, too, harvesting fresh berries that are sold for $10 a half-pint at organic grocery stores. Vegetable preppers work for poverty wages peeling and chopping onions at wholesale markets, ready to be sold to high-end restaurants, cooked and then fed to wealthy diners. While these issues tend to worsen when economies of scale come into play, they're not exclusive to processed foods. The enemy isn't so much the machinery as the money that drives it.

I guess all of this is a roundabout way of saying that I'm grateful for these modern food miracles. If you live alone and on a tight budget, you can buy powdered or evaporated milk for convenience and to minimize waste. In the UK, Ghanaians living in London can buy packages of dried crayfish, a taste of home, on Rye Lane. In Earl's Court, Filipinos find bottled calamansi juice, even when the fresh fruit is nowhere to be found. We have instant mashed potatoes, for homes, schools and cafeterias where time is short and budgets are low. We can bottle tomatoes so we have ketchup for french fries and preserve deep-sea-salty anchovies in little cans. Best of all, there are frozen peas (thank god) and all the perfect meals you can make with them. Coming up next is a recipe for **pea, mint and chili toast with crispy paneer**, or you could flick back to page 92 for a **pea green soup** that makes use of Thai green curry paste.

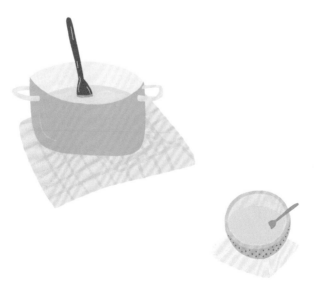

PEA, MINT AND CHILI TOAST WITH CRISPY PANEER

This easy recipe is golden: just mash peas with fresh herbs and chili flakes, pile on top of toasted bread, then top with crispy pieces of paneer. Think avocado toast, but peas.

Having a few toast dinners like this up your sleeve can be a lifesaver, especially if you struggle to find the time or energy to cook from scratch every night. The fact that you're having "just toast" means that, no matter how elaborate your choice of topping, you'll still come out feeling like you gamed the system. Nigel Slater, a vocal supporter of toast in all its forms, has described the dual pleasures of toast: it is a food to be eaten with your hands, which makes it feel right, natural and convenient, but it's also a comfort food, sending us back to some of our earliest memories of being nourished. Nigella Lawson, in *Cook, Eat, Repeat*, treats us to the secret of double-buttered toast and hot buttered toast with anchovies. In *Midnight Chicken*, Ella Risbridger touches on the ability of this most simple food to nourish us even through grief. It's sick food and treat food and everything in between but, most importantly, it's easy.

Serves: 1
Ready in: less than 15 minutes
Make-ahead and storage tips: page 325

Vegetarian

For the herby peas:
¾ cup frozen peas
½–1 tablespoon lemon or lime juice (from roughly ½ lemon or 1 lime)
2 teaspoons olive or vegetable oil
¼ teaspoon chili flakes, to taste
A few fresh mint leaves, roughly torn or chopped
A few fresh cilantro leaves, roughly torn or chopped
Good pinch of salt

For the crispy paneer:
1 teaspoon olive oil
2 ounces (60g) paneer, coarsely grated

To serve:
2 slices of bread
Olive oil
1 garlic clove, halved

Special equipment: food processor or blender, optional

1. Start by preparing the peas. In a bowl or jug, soak the peas in about 2 cups (500ml) of freshly boiled water for 5 minutes.

2. While the peas soak, prepare the paneer. In a small frying pan over a medium heat, warm the oil. Add the grated paneer and sauté, stirring very often, for 3–4 minutes. It's ready when it turns a mottled terra-cotta color against the milky white. If you carefully pluck a sliver from the pan, cool it and bite it, you'll notice it's now got a light crunch and toasted flavor. Transfer to a sheet of paper towel to drain—it'll become crispier as it cools.

3. Drain the peas now and either mash really well with a fork or pulse briefly in a food processor or blender. You want a coarsely textured pea mixture—not a perfectly smooth purée. Stir in the lemon or lime juice, oil, chili flakes and torn mint and cilantro leaves. Season with salt to taste.

4. Toast your bread, then drizzle with some olive oil and rub a cut side of the garlic over the bread. The garlic hit won't be overpowering, I promise. Top the bread with the herby pea mixture and then finish with the crispy paneer.

Variations and substitutions:

The peas can be swapped for mashed avocado if you want a guacamole kind of vibe.

Use chopped fresh red or green chilies in place of the chili flakes for a fresher heat. Play around with the herbs however suits you: fresh parsley or basil would also work, or you can leave out the herbs altogether for a more back-to-basics lunch.

If you're not planning on kissing anyone immediately afterwards, add some thinly sliced or finely chopped red onion on top of the peas and paneer.

Halloumi would work in place of the paneer if that's easier for you to get ahold of, but it's likely to become chewy, rather than crisp, when fried. It'll be saltier, too, so mind how vigorously you season the pea mixture.

SEEDED RYE CAKE WITH DEMERARA CRUST

Caraway seeds are tiny, dusty brown seeds that taper to a wispy point at one end. It's hard to describe their flavor, but they have a sharpness to them, very slightly aniseedy, perfumed and earthy. It's the flavor you'll most likely recognize from rye bread, but it also comes to life in some sauerkrauts, Nordic spirit aquavit and (the inspiration for this recipe) traditional British seed cakes. I'll tell you now: if you don't like caraway, you're not going to like this cake. I don't want to undersell this recipe—I like it a lot—but I also have to be realistic. If you do like caraway though, you'll love this.

A seed cake is just a simple butter cake flavored with caraway, like the plain seed cake from Florence White's 1932 book *Good Things in England*, or any one of Victorian cookery guru Isabella Beeton's four (!) seed cake recipes in the 1861 classic *Mrs. Beeton's Book of Household Management*. Food writer Kate Young—author of *The Little Library Cookbook*—has written about them, too, drawing inspiration from Bilbo Baggins's seed cake in *The Hobbit*. It's an old-timey kind of cake: something that will make you feel like a scullery maid or a medieval prince—or, indeed, a hobbit—when you eat it.

Hidden in plain sight

Serves: 6–8 in fat slices
Ready in: 55 minutes, most of which is hands-off baking time, but you'll need to let it cool before eating!
Make-ahead and storage tips: page 325

Vegetarian

½ cup (110g) unsalted butter, softened
3 tablespoons vegetable or olive oil
⅔ cup (150g) superfine sugar
3 medium or large eggs, at room temperature
¾ cup (100g) all-purpose flour
¾ cup (75g) dark rye flour
1 tablespoon poppy seeds
2 teaspoons caraway seeds
2 teaspoons baking powder
1 teaspoon ground coriander
¼ teaspoon salt
1 tablespoon demerara sugar

Special equipment:
2 pound (900g) loaf pan, roughly 8½ x 4½ inches (11 x 22cm) across its top

1. Preheat the oven to 350°F (180°C) and line a 2-pound (900g) loaf pan with parchment paper.

2. In a large mixing bowl, combine the butter, oil and superfine sugar and beat for a few minutes with a wooden spoon (or with an electric mixer if you're lucky enough to have one), until the butter is completely smooth and the mixture is homogeneous. If you rub it between your fingers, the grittiness of the sugar should have almost disappeared, and the fat should feel light and silky.

3. Add the eggs and beat everything together—it might be slightly curdled at this point, with tiny pockets of the butter mixture suspended in the slippery egg, but don't worry about this. Add the flours, poppy seeds, caraway seeds, baking powder, ground coriander and salt, and gently stir together until everything comes together into a smooth, silky, spoonable batter.

4. Spoon the batter into the lined pan and sprinkle over the demerara sugar. Bake for 40–45 minutes, or until well risen and crackly on top. A small knife plunged into the deepest part of the loaf should come out clean, with no wet batter stuck to it. Let cool before slicing and serving.

Variations and substitutions:

I use a mix of butter and oil in this cake to balance richness with moisture, but you can also make this with all butter or margarine (use ⅔ cup/150g in total) or all oil (in this case, use 1 cup plus 1 tablespoon/135ml in total) instead.

If you have self-rising flour, you can use this in place of the all-purpose flour, just decrease the amount of baking powder to 1 teaspoon. Dark rye flour adds a nutty richness to this cake, but you can swap it for the same amount of either all-purpose flour or whole wheat flour if that's what you've got. If you can't eat gluten, omit the all-purpose and rye flours and instead use 1 cup plus 2 tablespoons gluten-free all-purpose flour blend.

In place of the demerara, you can use granulated sugar on top of the cake. You can also use superfine sugar in a pinch, but it won't add the same crunch.

ORANGE, OLIVE OIL AND BLACK PEPPER CAKE

When I asked my friend what this book was missing, she told me "fancy bitch cakes." I knew immediately what she meant. This fragrant cake sounds more complex than it really is, and will help you bust a few pantry staples—olive oil, pepper—out of their savory rut. Because this uses oil rather than butter, there's no need to laboriously cream the fat and sugar together: all it takes is a quick stir and then you can sit back while it bakes, feeling like your true fancy bitch self.

A quick note: it'll seem like you're adding a lot of pepper to the batter, but the heat mellows dramatically in the oven. Whatever you do, don't use ready-ground black pepper or very fine, powdery stuff: it'll make the cake taste musty and give it a grayish color.

Serves: 6–8 in chunky slices
Ready in: 1 hour, but you'll need to let it cool before eating!
Make-ahead and storage tips: page 325

Vegetarian

For the cake:
7 tablespoons extra-virgin olive oil
½ cup plus 1 tablespoon superfine sugar
Zest and juice of 2 large oranges
2 medium or large eggs, at room temperature
⅓ cup (175g) all-purpose flour
2 teaspoons baking powder
¾ teaspoon freshly ground black pepper (coarse, not fine and powdery)
¼ teaspoon salt

For the syrup:
¼ cup (60ml) orange juice (from the juiced oranges)
¼ cup (60g) superfine sugar

Serve with: Greek yogurt or crème fraîche, optional
Special equipment: 2 pound (900g) loaf pan, roughly 8½ x 4½ inches (11 x 22cm) across its top

1. Preheat the oven to 350°F (180°C) and line a 2-pound (900g) loaf pan with parchment paper.

2. Get out a large mixing bowl for making the cake batter in. Combine the olive oil, superfine sugar and orange zest in the bowl, and stir briskly to combine. Add the eggs and beat until smoothly mixed in, then add the flour, baking powder, pepper and salt. Mix until the batter is thick but smooth, then add ¼ cup (60ml) of the orange juice to loosen the batter.

3. Spoon the cake batter into the lined loaf pan and bake for 45–50 minutes, or until a small knife inserted into the middle of the cake comes out clean. By this point, it should be well risen and a rich copper color on top. Don't worry if it's cracked: This tends to happen with loaf cakes, as their depth means the top sets before the middle is done cooking. As the batter continues to bake, it forces the just-set top open and the cake cracks. If your loaf is looking particularly craggy, take that as a sign that you've got a particularly good rise.

4. As soon as the cake is out of the oven, make the syrup. Combine ¼ cup (60ml) of the remaining orange juice and superfine sugar in a small saucepan. Set over a medium heat and stir for a few minutes, until it just starts to bubble. Pierce the loaf all over with a skewer or toothpick, then, while both syrup and cake are still hot, slowly pour the syrup over the top, giving it a chance to seep into the sponge. Leave to cool completely, then remove the cake from the pan and serve in fat slices. This cake is particularly good with Greek yogurt or crème fraîche.

Variations and substitutions:

If you have only self-rising flour at home, you can use this in place of the all-purpose flour (but omit the baking powder). To make a gluten-free version of the cake, swap the all-purpose flour for a gluten-free all-purpose flour blend, following the rest of the recipe as written.

A lemon version of this cake works really well. Swap the orange zest for the zest of 3 lemons, and replace the orange juice with the same quantity of lemon juice—¼ cup (60ml) in the cake and ¼ cup (60ml) in the syrup.

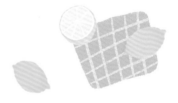

If you need to leave out the black pepper here, that's fine! Alternative additions might be: chopped fresh rosemary, fresh thyme leaves or even white or dark chocolate chunks.

PANTRY BROWNIES

The very best, fudgiest, most chocolaty brownies are those made with a lot of dark chocolate. But let's be realistic: by the time your sweet-toothed cravings are baying for brownie blood, you've probably already eaten all the chocolate in the house. With that in mind, this is a brownie recipe for when you weren't planning to make brownies at all: a cocoa-based emergency recipe for when the craving strikes but your cupboards are pretty much bare.

A quick note: Cocoa powder is *not* the same as hot chocolate mix! The latter is bulked out with sugar and often with milk powder, too—ideal for sweet, milky hot chocolate, but it doesn't have the chocolaty kick you'll need for these brownies.

Makes: 8–10 brownies
Ready in: less than 40 minutes, but you'll need
   to let the brownies cool before tucking in
Make-ahead and storage tips: page 326

Vegetarian   Vegan option

⅔ cup (160ml) vegetable, olive or coconut oil
⅔ cup plus 2 tablespoons (175g) soft light
   brown sugar
2 medium or large eggs
3 tablespoons milk, dairy or non-dairy
¾ cup (100g) all-purpose flour
½ cup (50g) cocoa powder
1½ teaspoons instant coffee granules
1 teaspoon vanilla extract, optional
½ teaspoon salt

Special equipment: 9 x 6 inch (15 x 22cm) baking pan or 8 inch (20cm) round
   springform pan

1. Preheat the oven to 350°F (180°C) and line your pan with parchment paper. If you don't have this exact pan size and shape, an 8 inch (20cm) round pan is very close in volume and is a fine alternative. It's also worth noting that if you make half of the above quantity, it'll fit perfectly in a 2 pound (900g) loaf pan—ideal for an emergency stash.

2. Whisk together the oil and light brown sugar in a large bowl (melt the coconut oil first, if that's what you're using and if it's solid). Add the eggs and the milk.

3. Into this wet mix, whisk the flour, cocoa powder, instant coffee granules, vanilla extract (if you have it) and salt. Stir until the batter is more or less smooth, with no big clumps. Pour into the prepared baking pan and bake for 15–20 minutes. When ready, it shouldn't be liquid or wobbly if you shake it, but a knife inserted into the center should still come out with a small amount of gooey batter on it. Give them a few minutes more if necessary, but err on the side of fudgy and underdone rather than cakey and overbaked. Once they're completely cool, cut into pieces and serve.

Variations and substitutions:

To make vegan brownies, forget the eggs, and use ⅔ cup (160ml) non-dairy milk instead of the 3 tablespoons specified above. For a gluten-free version, make the brownies as written but use a gluten-free all-purpose flour blend in place of the all-purpose white flour.

These are also delicious made with butter! Just swap the oil for ¾ cup (180g) melted butter, and decrease the amount of milk from 3 tablespoons to 1 tablespoon.

Swap the soft light brown sugar for superfine sugar if that's what you have.

Occasionally I make these with miso, which adds a gentle salty, umami edge. Leave out the salt in this case, and whisk 1–2 tablespoons white miso into the batter, to taste.

If you or your family don't consume caffeine, you can of course use a decaffeinated coffee or leave the coffee granules out altogether. At the other end of the spectrum, if you're a coffee aficionado and don't keep granules in the house, just use strong espresso in place of the 3 tablespoons milk (or a long black or white coffee in place of the ⅔ cup [160ml] non-dairy milk, if you're making the vegan version).

As far as additions go, the world's your oyster here. I kept the ingredient list as short as I could get away with, but if you happen to have walnuts or pecans, chunks of dark or white chocolate, freeze-dried berries or fudge pieces in the pantry, by all means, toss them in.

LEMON MOCHI SQUARES

I first read about butter mochi on Kathy YL Chan's blog, *Onolicious Hawai'i*. Mochi is a kind of Japanese rice sweet, made with glutinous rice flour for a springy, elastic texture, but in the popular Hawai'ian butter mochi things are switched up a little: the rice flour is baked into a large "cake" with lots of butter, combining that pleasing mochi density with the richness of a cake. Butter mochi also typically contains coconut milk, marrying that Japanese influence with the flavors of Filipino bibingka. The resulting texture is bouncy rather than crumbly, cakey or aerated.

Just like the butter mochi they're based on, these lemon mochi squares draw on a couple of influences. They inherit their squidgy texture from butter mochi, of course, but I've swapped the usual coconut milk for extra egg and lots of lemon zest and juice. The result is something like a mochi lemon tart, a sweet-sour, sunny slice of heaven.

If you're after a true butter mochi recipe, Kathy YL Chan's is a great start, or you can find some wonderful riffs on traditional Hawai'ian foods in *Cook Real Hawai'i* by Sheldon Simeon with Garrett Snyder.

Makes: 12–16 squares
Ready in: less than 45 minutes (you'll want to let them cool before eating though)
Make-ahead and storage tips: page 326

Vegetarian

⅓ cup (75g) unsalted butter, melted
1 cup (200g) superfine sugar or granulated sugar
Zest and juice of 4–5 lemons
    (you'll need ⅔ cup [160ml] lemon juice)
4 medium or large eggs
1¼ cups (150g) glutinous rice flour (mochiko)*
1 teaspoon baking powder
½ teaspoon table salt

Special equipment: 8 x 8 inch (20 x 20cm) or 9 x 6 inch (15 x 22cm) baking pan

*It's vital that you get glutinous rice flour—not plain rice flour—for this. If you go to any East Asian grocery store, you should be able to find it. If that fails, it's easy to buy online.

1. Preheat the oven to 350°F (180°C) and line a medium baking pan with parchment paper: I've made this in both a 9 x 6 inch (15 x 22cm) rectangular pan and an 8 x 8 inch (20 x 20cm) square dish to great success, so make sure yours is roughly this size.

2. In a large mixing bowl, combine the melted butter, sugar, lemon zest and juice and eggs, and whisk briskly until smooth. Add the glutinous rice flour, baking powder and salt, and whisk until no lumps of the rice flour remain. If you want a pinch more salt, add this now.

3. Pour the batter into the lined pan and bake in the preheated oven for 35–40 minutes. The batter will puff up during the baking time and sink slightly once it's out of the oven. When freshly baked, the mochi "cake" will be soft with a thin, mottled bronze crust, but as it cools and sets it'll become chewy and fudgier. When it's cool, cut into smallish squares and place in the fridge until you're ready to eat it.

SPICED APPLE PUDDING WITH BROWN SUGAR CRISP

This is a very useful dessert if you have leftover bread sitting around: it's a lot like an apple crumble but uses fresh breadcrumbs in place of the usual flour. When tossed with sugar and melted butter, the breadcrumbs bake to a perfectly crisp, crunchy topping over the jammy apples. I first read about apple brown betty (made with apples and cubes of stale bread) in Edna Lewis's *In Pursuit of Flavor*, and played around with the recipe from there. She suggests serving this with a custard sauce. Don't mind if I do.

These quantities make a large roasting dish (roughly 13 x 9 inches/22 × 33cm) of pudding, but you can make a half quantity in an 8 inch (20cm) or 9 inch (23cm) round springform cake pan or oven dish.

Serves: 6–8

Ready in: roughly an hour, most of which is the baking time

Make-ahead and storage tips: page 326

Vegetarian   Vegan option

For the brown sugar crisp:

1½ cups (150g) fresh white or whole wheat breadcrumbs (from roughly 5 medium slices of bread)

⅓–½ cup (75–90g) demerara sugar

1 cup (75g) rolled oats

¼ teaspoon cinnamon

⅓ cup (75g) salted or unsalted butter

For the filling:

1¾ pounds (800g) apples*

2–3 tablespoons superfine or granulated sugar

1 teaspoon cinnamon

1 teaspoon ground coriander

½ teaspoon ground ginger

¼ teaspoon ground nutmeg

4 tablespoons apple juice or water

Serve with: custard, ice cream or heavy cream

Special equipment: food processor, optional

*You want apples with enough sharpness to stand up to the sweet breadcrumb topping.

1. Preheat the oven to 350°F (180°C). Get out a large roasting pan, roughly 13 x 9 inches (22 x 33cm).

2. Start by preparing the topping: If you haven't already done so, blitz your bread into crumbs in a food processor. If you don't have a food processor, you'll want to let the bread stale slightly (just leave it out overnight) before crumbling it as finely as possible into a bowl. Mix the breadcrumbs with the sugar (adding this to taste, depending on whether you have a sweet tooth), oats and cinnamon. Melt the butter—either on the stovetop or in the microwave—then stir into the breadcrumbs to form a damp, rubbly mixture.

3. Peel the apples and cut into ⅜ inch (1cm) slices—the size doesn't matter too much, so cut into thicker wedges if that makes your life easier. Add the apples to the roasting pan and toss with the sugar (to taste—sharp apples will need a little more sugar than sweeter ones) and spices, then drizzle over the apple juice or water.

4. Scatter the breadcrumb mixture in a thick layer over the top, then place in the preheated oven to cook for 40–45 minutes, or until the apples are tender and the topping is crisp.

Variations and substitutions:

To make a vegan crumble, swap the ⅓ cup (75g) butter for ¼ cup (60g) melted coconut oil and 1 tablespoon non-dairy milk.

In place of the demerara sugar in the topping, you can use superfine or granulated sugar if that's easier—you'll lose the toffee brown sugar flavor, but it'll still be great.

Play around with the spices however you please. You could keep things simple by just limiting it to cinnamon, or leave out any spices you don't happen to have in the pantry.

If you've had the good fortune to go blackberrying recently, you can add 1–1¾ cups (150–250g) blackberries to the apple mixture.

I wouldn't recommend using dried breadcrumbs— they tend to brown too much in the oven. Just make a traditional flour-based crumble topping instead: Mix 1⅓ cups (160g) all-purpose or whole wheat flour with ¼ teaspoon cinnamon in a large mixing bowl. Rub in ½ cup (110g) cold butter (or ⅓ cup/80g coconut oil) using your fingertips, until the mixture resembles fine breadcrumbs. Stir in ½ cup (100g) sugar (soft light brown, demerara, superfine or granulated are all fine) and 1 cup (75g) rolled oats. Drizzle over a tablespoon or so of water or apple juice to make the mixture clump. Scatter over the apples and cook as instructed in the recipe.

CREAMY MANGO AND GINGER PUDDING POTS

Some foods taste and feel exactly the way their name sounds. The best of these are soft, wobbly, sweet things, food like *pudding* or *blancmange*, which fill your mouth with mellow, rounded sounds. *Syllabub* is the same, starting light and sweet before collapsing into childish comfort. Recently, I found out about *flummery*—a sweet set pudding first documented in England in 1623. In Wales, it was known as llymru. Early recipes soak oats in water before straining, the starch from the oats acting as a thickening agent, like adding flour to a sauce. In my shamelessly adulterated version, cornstarch takes the place of the oats and coconut milk replaces dairy. Mango and fiery ginger lift this jelly-like, puddingy, perfectly *flummery* treat out of the seventeenth-century English kitchen and into the here and now.

If you're the kind of person who gets stressed out by dessert and all the technical know-how you think it requires, this one's for you. This pudding is easy to make, needing only to be mixed, brought to a boil on the stovetop and then chilled. It's a great use for pantry staples as well: coconut milk, canned mango and cornstarch. No baking, no fuss, no messing around. I like to make this for an easy weeknight dessert, but because it's not overwhelmingly sweet, you can also have it with yogurt and/or granola for breakfast. It even spreads well on toast (think of it as a mango curd).

Vegan

Makes: 6
Ready in: 5 hours, most of which is setting time in the fridge
Make-ahead and storage tips: page 326

¼ cup (45g) cornstarch
3 tablespoons (45g) superfine or
  granulated sugar
Pinch of salt
1 x 400ml can full-fat coconut milk
  (low-fat coconut milk won't be
  creamy enough)
2 cups (400g) mango pulp
2 tablespoons lemon juice (from
  roughly 1 lemon)

2-inch (5cm) piece of ginger, peeled
  and finely grated

Serve with: coconut yogurt *or* softly
  whipped heavy cream; Sesame Snaps
  or peanut brittle, all optional
Special equipment: 6 small ramekins

1. In a medium saucepan, stir together the cornstarch, sugar and salt until well combined. (This will help prevent the cornstarch clumping when you add the liquid.) Pour in the coconut milk, mango pulp and lemon juice and add the grated ginger. Whisk everything together until smooth.

2. Set the saucepan over a medium heat and cook, stirring constantly with a whisk or a rubber spatula. Make sure that you stir nonstop, covering the entire base of the pan—otherwise the mixture will become lumpy! (If you do get any lumps, just whisk them out as well as you can and pass the mixture through a sieve afterwards if necessary.) By the time the mixture begins to bubble, it should be thick and creamy. Turn off the heat and taste for sweetness and acidity, adding a little extra sugar or lemon juice to taste.

3. Pour the mixture into your serving dishes. Leave to cool to room temperature, then transfer the puddings to the fridge to chill for at least 4 hours. (Ordinarily, I cover custard with plastic wrap or parchment paper to prevent any skin from forming. But I find that these puddings don't develop much of a skin, perhaps because they're not made with cow's milk. They will darken very slightly and set a little firmer where they come into contact with the air, but this actually makes it easier to garnish them without breaking the surface. If you're 100% skin-averse, just lay little pieces of plastic wrap or parchment paper directly onto the surface of the puddings while they're still warm, let them cool and chill, then remove the plastic wrap before garnishing and serving.)

4. Garnish (if you want to) with coconut yogurt or softly whipped heavy cream on top. The Sesame Snaps or peanut brittle can either be bashed into rubble using a rolling pin then scattered on top, or broken into larger shards to jut architecturally out of the puddings. Serve straightaway.

Variations and substitutions:

You can find mango pulp in large cans in most supermarkets and in many South Asian or Southeast Asian grocery stores. I get it from a corner store just a few minutes away from my apartment. If you absolutely can't find it, you can also use very ripe fresh mango for this at a push: just blitz the flesh of two large mangoes in a food processor until smooth, then pass through a sieve to remove any stringy fibers. You might want to add a touch more sugar if using fresh fruit, as canned mango pulp tends to be sweetened.

You could also make this as one larger pudding if you can't face messing around with individual portions. Just use a medium shallow oval dish instead of the ramekins.

Swap the lemon juice for white rum if you're after a slightly more grown-up riff on this.

Wild appetites

FOOD FOR EVERY MOOD, CRAVING AND OCCASION

Recipe list

Introduction

When cooking for a special occasion, it's all too easy to feel a bit Mrs. Pepperpot about it all. In Alf Prøysen's children's stories, Mrs. Pepperpot bustles about her errands all business-like and brisk and smartly coiffed until, without fail, she shrinks to the size of a pepperpot. In the face of this shrinking, you'd think she might put her daily chores on hold, but the books are something like a field guide to martyrdom: standing at a few inches tall, she insists on finishing making a stack of thirty pancakes for when her husband returns from work, or picking bilberries or spring cleaning. I don't think cooking needs to be a trauma like this. With that in mind, these special occasion recipes—for everything from hangover breakfasts to Hanukkah, midsummer feasts and birthdays—are ones that will excite your guests without exhausting you.

Further reading

Mrs. Pepperpot Stories by Alf Prøysen

The Essential Book of Jewish Festival Cooking by Phyllis and Miriyam Glazer

The Book of Jewish Food by Claudia Roden

Modern Jewish Cooking by Leah Koenig

The Cooking Gene by Michael W. Twitty

Vegan Soul Kitchen by Bryant Terry

Five Quarters by Rachel Roddy

The Violet Bakery Cookbook by Claire Ptak

The New Way to Cake by Benjamina Ebuehi

The Taste of Country Cooking by Edna Lewis

The Pastry Chef's Guide by Ravneet Gill

How to Be a Domestic Goddess by Nigella Lawson

Feast by Nigella Lawson

The Christmas Chronicles by Nigel Slater

Wild appetites

KIMCHI AND POTATO HASH

It took me a very long time to come around to the idea of savory breakfasts. Things like maple syrup-drenched waffles and fluffy pancakes just seemed so special and rare—I always felt like I was cheating myself if I passed up any opportunity to have them. So, that meant savory breakfasts were off the cards, and my sweet tooth raged unchecked.

Maybe this is my tastes changing as I get older, or maybe it just took a while to shake off the pancake scarcity mindset, but I now relish the chance to indulge in starchy, spicy, pickled, umami flavors in the morning. This savory potato hash ticks every one of those boxes, with all that savory clout of kimchi and butter and tangy cheese.

If you're new to kimchi, it's a fermented vegetable dish, very popular in Korea and in some parts of China, too, typically made of napa cabbage, and often with radish, carrots, scallions or chives as well. It is beautiful and complex and, when made the traditional way, bears the imprint of the hand that made it, with each leaf tenderly massaged with salt before being rubbed with a paste of gochugaru (Korean red pepper flakes), fish sauce and plentiful garlic. This mix of expertise and biology (each person's hands will have a slightly different ecosystem of microbes) means that a batch of kimchi will be different each time, and marked with the sonmat—or hand taste, in English—of the person who made it. Artist Jiwon Woo created an art project called *Mother's Hand Taste (Son-mat)*, which explores these intersections. I would definitely recommend checking it out if you're interested. But, if you're just here for breakfast (or lunch, or dinner, let's be honest), let's crack on.

Serves: 4
Ready in: less than 1 hour 10 minutes, much of which is quiet time while everything roasts, so you can chill
Make-ahead and storage tips: page 326

Vegetarian

¼ cup (60g) salted or unsalted butter or 3 tablespoons olive oil
1¾ pounds (800g) potatoes (preferably russets), peeled and cut into 1¼ inch (3cm) cubes
2 tablespoons gochujang (see page 87)
Generous pinch of salt

1¼ cups (200g) cabbage kimchi (vegetarian if required), roughly chopped
7 tablespoons kimchi juice*
⅔ cup (160ml) water
4 eggs, any size
2 scallions, thinly sliced
⅔ cup (75g) grated Cheddar, optional

*By this I mean the beautiful red liquid that kimchi comes with in its jar or package. Pour out as much as you can, and gently squeeze the kimchi itself to extract a little more. If you're short of the full amount, no worries—just make up to ½ cup/100ml with some water.

1. Preheat the oven to 400°F (200°C) and get out a large roasting pan—at least 13 x 9 inches (22 x 33cm).

2. Once the oven is hot, put the butter into the roasting pan and place in the oven for 3–4 minutes, until it has slumped into a pool of molten, sizzling gold. Add the peeled and chopped potatoes, gochujang and a good pinch of salt. Mix everything until the potatoes are slicked with deep red oil, and roast in the oven for 20 minutes.

3. Add the kimchi, kimchi juice and water to the pan. Mix everything together, then return the dish to the oven for a further 20 minutes.

4. Last up: the eggs. Create four hollows in the potato mixture. These are the cozy nooks in which the eggs will cook. Crack one egg into each hollow—don't worry too much if any of the egg white leaks out into the surrounding mix. Scatter over the sliced scallions, then sprinkle the grated Cheddar evenly over the top, if using. Now, place the roasting pan back in the oven until the egg whites are set and the yolks are cooked to your liking (I like them runny). I've found that the time this takes varies quite a lot—anywhere between 5 and 12 minutes—but keep an eye on it and you'll be just fine.

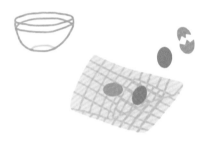

Variations and substitutions:

Kimchi is pretty essential here, although there are plenty of good potato hash recipes online if you like the idea but not this version of it. I can get kimchi in both of the big supermarkets near my house. You'll also find it in any Korean store, if you're lucky enough to live near one, and in lots of decent-sized Chinese groceries too—it's often in a plastic package in the fridges here, whereas in the supermarket you're more likely to find it in an unchilled jar.

Gochujang is a fermented Korean chili paste—read more about it on page 87, where I use it in the **mushroom and gochujang udon noodles,** so you don't need to worry about being left with a whole tub of it. If you really can't get hold of it, that's fine—swap it for 1 tablespoon tomato paste, 1 teaspoon superfine or granulated sugar and either ½ teaspoon chili powder or a couple of teaspoons sriracha or other chili sauce, to taste. Gochujang typically contains barley malt, so take care to find a gluten-free version if you can't eat gluten.

POTATO LATKES

A latke is a simple thing, typically made from potato, onion, egg and sometimes flour or matzo meal. But it is more than that. According to Phyllis and Miriyam Glazer in *The Essential Book of Jewish Festival Cooking*, the latke is "a poor man's food that graces rich men's tables . . . It preserves within it an ancient holiday tradition and a centuries-long Jewish culinary tale. It has a soul." Latkes are traditional Hanukkah fare, fried in oil to commemorate the ancient miracle of a temple's menorah kept alight for eight long days with oil that should have lasted only for one.

The traditional latke is a potato one, but there are countless ways to riff on the classic. Claudia Roden has a recipe in her excellent *The Book of Jewish Food* for apple latkes. For *The New York Times*, Martha Rose Shulman has written recipes for butternut squash and sage latkes, and a leek, kale and potato version. Leah Koenig includes a recipe for beet latkes in her cookbook *Modern Jewish Cooking*, while food writer and historian Michael W. Twitty has a Louisiana-style version with celery, scallions, cayenne and garlic. It's not my place to mess with tradition here, so I've gone down a more conventional route with these potato latkes. If you're after something with a similar vibe but very different execution, there's a recipe for **green plantain, coconut and chili rösti** just after this one.

You can enjoy these with breakfast or as a starter or a side dish.

Makes: 16–18 (serves 4–6 people, depending on what you serve them with)
Ready in: 45 minutes
Make-ahead and storage tips: page 326

Vegetarian   Vegan option

---

2 pounds 2 ounces (1kg) russet potatoes
2 medium onions
2 eggs, lightly beaten
1 teaspoon salt
⅔ cup or more (150–200ml) vegetable or olive oil

Serve with: sour cream, optional
Special equipment: food processor with grater attachment, optional

1. Preheat the oven to 325°F (160°C) and get out a baking sheet—this is just to keep the latkes warm while you fry them in batches.

2. Start by peeling the potatoes. Grate the potatoes and onions using the coarser grating side of a box grater. Alternatively, if you have a food processor with a grater attachment, you can save yourself some tears and use that.

3. Using your hands, squeeze as much liquid from the grated potato and onion as possible, collecting the liquid in a small bowl. Pour most of the liquid away, but keep just the starchiest dregs at the bottom of the bowl.

4. Place the grated veg in a mixing bowl and stir together with the egg, salt and the little bit of starchy liquid you reserved.

5. Heat the oil in a heavy frying pan over a medium heat. Once the oil is shimmering hot, scoop out heaped tablespoons of the latke mixture and dollop into the hot oil. Press down lightly on the top of each mound to flatten the mixture into a thick pancake. Cook the latkes for 5 minutes on one side, then flip and cook for a further 5 minutes. If they're browning too quickly, turn the heat down. If they're still pallid after 5 minutes on each side, turn up the temperature to get a perfect golden crisp. When they're ready, they should be lacy and shatteringly crisp around the edges, and feel firm to the touch.

6. Drain the cooked latkes on paper towel, then transfer to the preheated oven to keep warm while you cook the rest of the mixture in batches. These are at their best when served hot with sour cream.

Variations and substitutions:

To make a vegan version of these, omit the egg but add 4 tablespoons of all-purpose flour to help bind the potato together.

GREEN PLANTAIN, COCONUT AND CHILI RÖSTI

These rösti cakes are unbelievably crunchy, frying to a deep golden brown in the pan. You can serve them in pretty much any context in which you might eat a hash brown or a latke, whether as a side or starter with sour cream or as an accompaniment to a Full English breakfast (they also come into their own when eaten with fried egg, callaloo and bacon). You'll need green plantain—the unripe, firm-fleshed ones—for this recipe as their high starch and low sugar will help the rösti to crisp and hold together as they cook. Don't even think of using yellow or black plantain or, worse still, banana. You can switch the flavorings if you want, though: skip to the variations and substitutions section for pointers.

Makes: 12 small rösti (serves 4–6)
Ready in: 40 minutes—you'll spend most of that time standing
  by the stove frying and flipping the rösti, so put the radio on
Make-ahead and storage tips: page 326

Vegan

2 large green plantain (roughly
  1¼ pounds/500g)
3 ounces (100g) fresh coconut, optional
2–2½-inch (5–6cm) piece of ginger,
  peeled
6 scallions, thinly sliced
1–2 thin green or red chilies,
  thinly sliced
1 egg or 2 tablespoons milk, dairy
  or non-dairy

4 tablespoons all-purpose flour
½ teaspoon salt
⅔ cup or more (150–200ml) sunflower
  or vegetable oil
1 lime, cut into wedges

Special equipment: food processor,
  optional

1. Preheat the oven to 325°F (160°C) and get out a baking sheet—this is just to keep the rösti warm while you fry them in batches.

2. Peel the plantain by slicing off each end, scoring a knife down the length of the skin and peeling it off like a coat. Using a box grater (or the grater attachment of a food processor, if you have one), coarsely grate the plantain. Finely grate the fresh coconut flesh, if using, and the ginger. Combine the grated plantain, coconut, ginger, scallions and chili in a mixing bowl.

3. To the mixing bowl, add the egg or milk, flour and salt, then beat vigorously (or massage with your hands) to bring everything together.

You should be left with a mixture that's neither dry nor runny—if it's very liquid, add a touch more flour; if it's too dry to hold together, massage it between your hands for a minute to help everything bind, then add a splash of milk if necessary.

4. Heat the oil in a large frying pan over medium heat. Test the heat of the oil: if it sizzles as soon as a little of the plantain is dropped in, it's ready. Using your hands or a couple of tablespoons, scoop generous mounds of the mix into the hot oil until you have roughly 6 rösti in the pan. Bear in mind that this recipe makes enough for roughly 12 rösti in total, which means you'll have to cook in two batches. Press each mound of rösti mix down under a spatula, flattening and compressing them until they're roughly ⅜ inch (1cm) thick: the better compacted they are, the better they'll hold together. Fry for 5 minutes on one side, then flip and fry for a further 5 minutes on the other side. Once fried, the rösti should be croissant-brown on each side and feel crisp and firm.

5. Transfer the cooked rösti to a large plate lined with paper towel to mop up any excess oil. If you need to keep these warm while you sauté the second batch, transfer to the baking sheet in the preheated oven. Serve hot with lime wedges to squeeze over the salty, savory, carby fritters.

Variations and substitutions:

If you can't get hold of fresh coconut flesh (usually you can get boxes of it in large supermarkets, doing away with the need to crack your own coconut), just leave it out. I wouldn't recommend replacing it with desiccated coconut, as this may brown too quickly when frying.

In place of the scallions, you could use ½ an onion, coarsely grated along with the plantain.

If you only have self-rising or bread flour in the cupboard, you can swap this instead of the all-purpose flour. To make these gluten-free, you can use a gluten-free all-purpose flour and make sure you use a gluten-free non-dairy milk if you also want these to be vegan.

If you want to try making these with sweet potato, you can, though the texture will be softer and the taste sweeter. If you really can't get hold of green plantain, I'd recommend looking at the previous recipe—**potato latkes**—for an alternative.

Food for
the thirty-second
of neverember

I have an email in my drafts folder that might be the saddest thing I've ever written. The subject line is *halloween*. The recipient is me. The body of the email is divided into subheadings, which speaks to my enthusiasm. It goes something like this: *to make: pumpkin cheesecake, sweet potato and gochujang soup, peanut butter and salted dark chocolate cookies. to buy: halloween creme eggs. crafts: halloween tic-tac-toe. films: black christmas, texas chainsaw massacre, the love witch.* With every line, it gets sadder. The last line is the worst of all: *to invite*, I have gone to the trouble of writing, *???*

I do a lot of this kind of "planning," for occasions that I know in my heart will never really happen. I think a lot of us do this. It feels good somehow, when the concerns of the real world weigh so heavy, to just escape into daydreams about meals we'll never cook, for friends we're yet to make, in a kitchen we'll never be able to afford. When you've just got home from a shift at a brand-new job, your body aching and your head pounding, somehow this is as good a time as any to start imagining what it'd be like to, who knows . . . lacquer a pheasant. Or, while you're standing at the stove with your eyes glazed over, waiting for potatoes to boil, this might be when you fantasize about cooking a massive, drumlike timpano—a pasta and egg and meat construction almost big enough to see from space, and showcased in the 1996 film *Big Night*. (I recommend *Big Night* with all my heart, by the way. It is one of those gems that is both emotionally rich and replete with people to crush on.)

That is a lot of the appeal of cookbooks: They give us a chance to dream about being richer, less stressy and better fed than we really are. We read them and imagine ourselves cooking perfect but unfussy feasts for people who will then have no choice but to love us. All of this happens in a kitchen like something from a Nancy Meyers film. Again and again, I come back to this aspirational element in food writing, trying to understand it so that I can move away from it, but I know deep down that it's a vital part of the recipe, this spark of futile hope. We dream big not because we really expect those food fantasies to come true, but because there's so much pleasure in the dream itself. And when we flex our imaginative muscles this way—whether we're dreaming of Willy Wonka–style concoctions, or racks of lamb, or a Halloween cheesecake for a cast of imaginary friends—we get a sense of what food ideas hold our attention and even delight us, and which ones we can do without. This wishful thinking is as much a part of the cooking process as any other. It's how we get acquainted with our appetites and, by extension, with ourselves.

I'd encourage you to do as much of this kind of dreaming as you can be bothered to do. Imagine unimaginable foods, because why not? Plan for dinners that will never, ever happen. Notice the foods that come up again and again. (I have another email draft, a more cheering one, with 150 different ice cream flavor ideas. Ice cream is a repeat fixture in my dreamscapes.) If you can do all this while you're on the clock, all the better: escape into a world of hot ice cream and chocolate fountains and singing blackbirds baked into pies while you're at work, on somebody else's dime. Whether you send emails or push a mop, nobody else knows what's a-cooking in the space between your ears.

WATERMELON WITH PEANUTS, SUMAC AND LIME

I am not by any stretch of the imagination a salad evangelist. I like them, sometimes even love them, but I usually struggle to drag myself away from the hot, starchy, heavy foods that bring me comfort and fill me up. It takes exceptional circumstances—in this recipe's case, a heat wave—for me to break tradition and have a light lunch. When I first made this salad, on what felt like the thousandth consecutive 90°F+ day one August, I was stunned by the cooling sweetness of watermelon alongside salty peanut crunch. It's the best salad I know.

If you've not used sumac before, it's a spice made from ground berries—blood-red with a tart, citrusy flavor—and often used as a seasoning on rice or meat. It works really well alongside the sweet watermelon. You should be able to find it in large supermarkets or Turkish or Middle Eastern grocery stores. It's not vital, though, so leave it out if you can't get it.

Cut to the **pickled watermelon rind** recipe on page 287 if you want to use up the rinds this recipe leaves behind. Bryant Terry has some great no-waste watermelon recipes in his cookbook, *Vegan Soul Kitchen*.

Serves: 2 (for lunch) or 4 (as a side)
Ready in: less than 15 minutes

Vegan

---

1 small watermelon or a sizable wedge of a larger watermelon (you want around a generous pound/500g)
¼ medium red onion or 1 banana shallot, thinly sliced
Handful of fresh mint leaves (roughly ½ ounce/10–15g), sliced into fine ribbons
3 tablespoons salted peanuts, roughly chopped

1 tablespoon lime juice (from roughly 1 lime)
1 tablespoon extra-virgin olive oil
1 teaspoon sumac, optional
½ teaspoon chili flakes
Pinch of salt (preferably flaky sea salt)

1. Start off by preparing the watermelon: Cut in half and then into fat wedges, then remove the dark green skin and the watery white rind. Cut the remaining pink flesh into "tiles" roughly ¼ inch (.5cm) thick. The exact measurements really don't matter—I cut mine to pieces a little larger than a Scrabble tile, but what really matters is that you have flattish pieces rather than fat chunks or wedges. The seeds are edible, so don't worry about removing them unless you really dislike them.

2. Arrange the watermelon "tiles" on a large plate or serving dish. Scatter over the onion or shallot slices, the mint leaf ribbons and the roughly chopped peanuts. Drizzle over the lime juice and oil, then sprinkle the sumac (if using), chili flakes and salt on top. Serve straightaway.

> ### Variations and substitutions:
> If you can't eat peanuts, salted cashews or almonds (roughly chopped) would be a fine substitute.

SMOKY CHICKEN, OKRA AND CHORIZO CASSEROLE

This warming stew channels a few disparate culinary influences. Here, there is the Creole holy trinity of pepper, celery and onion, but also Spanish chorizo and, as ever, a West African flavor—from the okra as well as from Scotch bonnet chili. It's the kind of meal that's understated and unfussy but somehow coolly rises to whatever occasion you cook it for, whether that's a Sunday lunch or a family gathering.

Serves: 4
Ready in: 1 hour 15 minutes if you cook it slowly in the oven,
  or 1 hour if cooked on the stovetop
Make-ahead and storage tips: page 326

---

2 tablespoons olive or vegetable oil
4 chicken thighs or 6 drumsticks,
  bone in*
2 peppers, any color, cut into
  ¾ inch (2cm) chunks
1 large onion, finely diced
1 celery stick, diced
¾ cup (150g) chorizo, diced
2 tablespoons all-purpose flour
2 tablespoons tomato paste
2 teaspoons dried thyme
1½ teaspoons smoked paprika

3 garlic cloves, crushed or finely grated
1 Scotch bonnet chili
1 x 14 ounce (400g) can pigeon peas,
  navy beans or black-eyed peas,
  drained
1 x 14 ounce (400g) can chopped
  tomatoes
About 2 cups (400–500ml) chicken
  stock
2 cups (6–7 ounces/175–200g) okra
Salt, to taste

Serve with: couscous, polenta, millet, pearl barley,
  mashed potatoes or rice (this is particularly good
  alongside the jollof rice on page 178)
Special equipment: large oven-safe casserole dish,
  optional

*It's your call whether you leave the skin on or take it off. I don't mind chicken skin in a stew, but some people feel strongly about it. In 2018, *MasterChef* judge Gregg Wallace got in trouble for his big opinions on this matter when he berated contestant Zaleha Kadir Olpin's chicken rendang, (wrongly) insisting that the skin should be crispy. If you want to serve separate crispy chicken skin on top, see the tips in the **tinolang manok** recipe on page 30.

1. Get out a large pan: an oven-safe casserole dish is best if you want to finish this dish in the oven, but if you have only a plastic-handled saucepan, you can use that—just follow the stovetop instructions later on. If you do have a suitable casserole dish, preheat the oven to 400°F (200°C) now.

2. Add a couple of teaspoons of the oil to your pan and set it over a medium-high heat, then brown the chicken pieces for 4–5 minutes on each side, until the skin begins to lightly crisp. The chicken won't be cooked through at this point, and that's fine. Remove from the pan and set aside.

3. Pour the remaining oil into the pan and warm over a medium heat, then add the peppers, onion, celery and chorizo. Sweat everything together for 10 minutes, stirring often and scraping up any chicken scraps from the bottom as you go. It's ready when the vegetables have begun to soften and the chorizo has released its paprika-stained oil.

4. Stir in the flour, tomato paste, thyme, smoked paprika and garlic. Cook for 2 minutes or so, stirring as you go.

5. Pierce the Scotch bonnet chili once or twice with a small sharp knife and add to the pan, along with the beans, chopped tomatoes, stock and browned chicken pieces. Bring the stew to a simmer. You can now choose whether to finish this stew in the oven or on the stovetop.

6. To finish this in the oven: Put a lid on, transfer the dish to the preheated oven and cook for 30 minutes. While it cooks, prepare the okra, removing the ends then cutting the lengths into thick slices. After 30 minutes, add the okra, stir well and then return to the oven—uncovered this time—for 15 minutes.

7. To finish this on the stovetop: Bring to a simmer, then cover with a lid and cook for 20 minutes over a very low heat, stirring every 5 minutes so that the flour-thickened sauce doesn't stick at the bottom. While it simmers, prepare the okra, removing the ends then cutting the lengths into thick slices. After 20 minutes, add the okra, cover the pan again and cook gently for a further 10 minutes.

8. Once the stew is cooked, season with salt if necessary, then check the heat levels. If it needs more spice, squeeze the Scotch bonnet gently under a spoon to extract more of that fire. Remove the Scotch bonnet before serving so that nobody gets a nasty surprise. You can also strip the chicken from the bone at this point if you want to, cutting or tearing the

meat into manageable chunks and then returning it to the stew before serving. This is good served with pretty much any carb but comes into its own when eaten with rice, like the **jollof rice** on the following pages.

Variations and substitutions:

If you want to forgo the chorizo, that's fine. Increase the amount of smoked paprika to 1 tablespoon. Alternatively, swap the chorizo for smoky bacon pieces.

I love the flavor of Scotch bonnet, but you could use other fresh chilies if that's more convenient. Finely chop mild red or green chilies, or thinly slice birds's eye chilies. If chili powder or flakes work better for you, use one of those instead—1–2 teaspoons should be about right, depending on how spicy you like things.

For a pearl barley stew, swap the beans for ½ cup (100g) pearl barley, and increase the amount of stock to 2¾ cups (675ml). You may want to cook the stew for an extra 10 minutes or so to make sure the barley is tender.

You can swap the canned beans for frozen or canned garden peas if you want. The okra is beautiful here but could be replaced with 5 ounces (150g) or so fresh or frozen spinach leaves.

To make this gluten-free, swap the all-purpose flour for a gluten-free all-purpose flour blend or for 1 tablespoon cornstarch.

JOLLOF RICE

No party is a party without jollof rice, although nothing can sour the mood of a party quite like people's arguments about which country's jollof is best. This fiercely fought-over West African rice dish is bright red and deeply spiced, and has a delicate smokiness—in this case from smoked paprika—running through it, though there are countless variations and riffs on this popular recipe. It's easy too: just cook basmati rice in a chili-spiked tomato sauce until the grains are fluffy and tender. This is good served with spiced and roasted chicken thighs or alongside the **smoky chicken, okra and chorizo casserole** on page 175.

Serves: 4
Ready in: 45 minutes
Make-ahead and storage tips: page 326

Vegan

For the rice:
1½ cups (300g) basmati rice
2 tablespoons vegetable or olive oil
1 red pepper, diced
½ medium onion, finely diced
4 garlic cloves, crushed or finely grated
2 tablespoons tomato paste
1 teaspoon mild or medium curry powder
1 teaspoon smoked paprika
1 teaspoon dried thyme
Salt, to taste

For the sauce:
½ medium onion, roughly chopped
½–1 Scotch bonnet chili, seeded, to taste
3 tablespoons water
1 x 14 ounce (400g) can chopped tomatoes
1 chicken or vegetable stock cube

Special equipment: stick blender, food processor or blender

1. Start by soaking the rice: rinse it really well in a few changes of water, then cover with fresh cold water and leave to sit for 15 minutes or so.

2. Heat the oil in a medium saucepan over a medium heat, then add the diced pepper and onion. Sauté for 8–10 minutes, stirring occasionally, until the onion starts to soften.

3. While the onion and pepper are cooking, make the sauce. Combine the onion and Scotch bonnet (make sure it's seeded, and add less if you don't like heat) with the water, chopped tomatoes and stock cube. Blitz with a stick blender or in a food processor or blender to get a smooth sauce.

4. Return your attention to the sautéing onion and pepper now. Add the garlic, tomato paste, curry powder, smoked paprika and thyme. Sauté for a further minute or two until the garlic smells cooked, the tomato paste is deep red and the spices are fragrant. Add the sauce to the pan, then mix well and let simmer for 3–4 minutes.

5. Drain the rice really well, then add to the pan. Mix to combine everything, patting down the rice so that it's all at least partially submerged in the sauce.

6. Cook over a medium heat until the mixture begins to bubble and sputter, then turn the heat down as low as it'll go, cover the pan with aluminum foil and then put on a lid. (The foil is just to keep as much steam in as possible. If your pan lid is tight-fitting, and if you can cover any steam holes, you can skip the foil.) Cook for roughly 16–20 minutes, or until the rice is cooked and no longer chalky. Turn off the heat and leave to sit for 5 minutes with the lid still on. Uncover the pan, fluff up the rice, add salt if necessary and then serve.

Variations and substitutions:

In place of the Scotch bonnet, you can use ½–1 teaspoon chili powder.

Use a pound or so (400g) fresh tomatoes, roughly chopped, in place of the canned tomatoes if you want.

To add interest, you could add any of the following, stirring them in when you add the rice to the sauce in the pan: a couple of handfuls of shredded roasted or grilled chicken, thinly sliced okra, frozen mixed chopped veg or peas.

HARISSA, SPINACH AND RICOTTA CANNELLONI WITH TOASTED HAZELNUTS

There are some party pieces you covet but know you'll never be able to fully integrate into your world. Into this category, I put the silver glitter thigh-high boots I once bought from the Topshop on Southend High Street, and returned two days later. See also: leather skirts, ice cream cakes and scallops. I am drawn to these things with an almost frantic hunger, but truly they're just too wild to ever jell with the scruffy reality of my life.

So, when I find a big, showy recipe that also feels *right* somehow—comfortable, delicious, not a weekend-long affair—I cling to it. This is one such recipe. Harissa and spice add depth to the tomato sauce, while the toasted hazelnuts, molten mozzarella and marbling of yet more harissa atop turn this into a perfect spectacle. It's classy as hell. If you have leftover harissa, it can also be used in the **gnocchi with harissa butter and broccoli** on page 55.

Serves: 6
Ready in: less than 2 hours
Make-ahead and storage tips: page 326

Vegetarian

For the sauce:
¼ cup (60g) salted or unsalted butter
1 medium onion, finely diced
4 garlic cloves, crushed or
    finely grated
2 teaspoons paprika
1 teaspoon cumin seeds
1 teaspoon ground coriander
¼ teaspoon cinnamon
2 x 14 ounce (400g) cans chopped
    tomatoes or 24 ounce (680g) jar of
    passata
1½ tablespoons white wine vinegar,
    red wine vinegar or balsamic
    vinegar
1 tablespoon sugar (any kind will do)
2–4 tablespoons harissa, to taste
scant ½–1 cup (100–200ml) water,
    optional
Salt, to taste

For the cannelloni:
1⅓ pounds (600g) fresh spinach
2 cups (500g) ricotta
⅓ cup (50g) toasted or blanched
    hazelnuts, halved
Pinch of ground nutmeg
Salt, to taste
about ½ pound (240g) cannelloni
    tubes (18–20 tubes)

To top:
½ pound (250g) mozzarella, torn into
    small pieces
⅓ cup (50g) toasted or blanched
    hazelnuts, halved
2 teaspoons harissa

Serve with: crisp green salad
Special equipment: piping bag,
    optional

1. First, let's make the sauce: Melt the butter in a medium pan over a medium heat and add the diced onion. Sauté for 8–10 minutes, stirring often, until the onion is beginning to soften and turn translucent. Add the garlic, paprika, cumin seeds, ground coriander and cinnamon, and sauté for a minute or two, or until the raw smell of garlic lifts away and the spices begin to toast. Add the chopped tomatoes (or passata), vinegar, sugar and harissa (different harissa brands have wildly different spice levels, so add this to taste).

2. Once the sauce is bubbling, turn the heat down to low and leave to very gently simmer for 15 minutes, stirring every so often. When it's ready, add a little water if necessary, starting with scant ½ cup (100ml) and adding extra if needed. The sauce should be rich and velvety, but still needs to be loose enough to balance the heartiness of the pasta filling. Add salt to taste.

3. For the cannelloni filling, start by rinsing the spinach leaves under cold water (the water left on the leaves will help to steam the spinach, so do this even if your spinach comes pre-washed). Place the washed and still-wet leaves in a large saucepan. It'll look like a lot of spinach—it may come all the way to the top of the pan—but we've all seen the memes: this forest of green will collapse down to a thimbleful in no time.

4. Place a lid on the spinach pot and set over a medium heat. Let cook for 4–6 minutes, stirring a couple of times, then remove the lid. By this point, the leaves should have collapsed into a silky tangle. Turn the heat down slightly and cook with the lid off now, for roughly 10 minutes—or slightly longer if necessary—until the spinach has dried out a little and is lubricated without being sopping wet. Keep stirring while you wait. Obviously the mixture is never going to be dry (and we wouldn't want that anyway), but dripping leaves will do you no favors.

5. Once the spinach is ready, add the ricotta, hazelnuts, nutmeg and plenty of salt to taste, and beat really well to mix everything and partially break up the leaves.

6. Turn on the oven now while you assemble the dish: it needs to be at 350°F (180°C). Get out a 13 x 9 inch (22 x 33cm) deep roasting pan. Spread half of the tomato sauce evenly into the bottom of the roasting pan. Now fill the cannelloni with the spinach and ricotta filling: This is easy if you have a piping bag (just cut a wide hole at the end and pipe the mixture in) but you can also do this just fine, as I did, by using your fingers. It's messy, and there's really no other way of saying it than: poke the spinach mixture into the tube from each end. OK, that's quite enough of that.

7. As you fill the cannelloni, lay the tubes down on top of the sauce in the roasting dish, arranging them so that they fit snugly. Pour the remaining half of the tomato sauce over the top. Scatter over the mozzarella and hazelnuts, then dot on little dollops of harissa.

8. Bake the dish in the preheated oven for 30 minutes, or until the sauce is bubbling and the mozzarella is molten and golden. Let sit for 5 minutes to give it a chance to settle, then serve with a crisp green salad.

Variations and substitutions:

If you can't get hold of cannelloni, you can make this with lasagna sheets. It's a bit more effort, but works well if needs be. You'll need approximately 12 dried lasagna sheets, each broken neatly down the middle to give you two squarish halves. Lightly grease a large baking tray, and have extra oil at hand. Working in batches to avoid overcrowding the pan, parboil the lasagna for 3 minutes in lots of boiling, salted water. Stir often so the sheets don't stick together. Use tongs to fish the lasagna pieces out of the water and lay them on the oiled tray. Layer up the lasagna pieces, rubbing oil on them as you go so they don't stick to each other. When they're cooked, start filling them: spoon some of the spinach and ricotta mixture along one edge of the pasta, then roll it up. If the pasta wraps right around itself, use a bit more filling next time to fill it out; if the pasta roll won't "close," use less filling next time. Proceed as in the recipe.

In place of the hazelnuts, you can use pine nuts. They're pricey but they work well. Alternatively, you can leave out the nuts altogether if you want to.

If you have a big batch of twaróg (from the recipe on page 273) you can use this in place of the ricotta.

You can also make a non-spiced version of the tomato sauce. It will be miles away from the version here, but if it's good enough for Italians, it's good enough for me. Just leave out the paprika, cumin seeds, ground coriander, cinnamon and harissa.

A half batch of this recipe will fit well in a 9 x 6 inch (15 x 22cm) or 8 x 8 inch (20 x 20cm) pan. A quarter batch fits in a 2 pound (900g) loaf pan.

CHICKEN, BROWN BUTTER AND MUSHROOM PIE

This chicken pie feels special but doesn't involve too much stress or sweat. Skip to the end and you can find tips for preparing it in advance, making an easier single-crust version or replacing the homemade pastry with store-bought, although I have to say that even if you make the most elaborate version of this recipe, it's still not an ordeal. I made this for Christmas dinner last year and honestly had the most chill Christmas Day of my life so far.

Brown butter in this pie takes the place of the usual cream. It enriches the filling and adds a nutty, toasted flavor that I really love alongside the mushrooms and chicken.

Serves: 6
Ready in: less than 2 hours 30 minutes, most of which is
    idle time while the pastry chills and the pie bakes
Make-ahead and storage tips: page 327

For the filling:
½ cup (110g) salted or unsalted butter
1½ pounds (750g) chicken thigh fillets,
    cut into 1¼ inch (3cm) chunks
2 leeks, thickly sliced
9 ounces (250g) mushrooms, thickly
    sliced
3 tablespoons fresh thyme leaves
    or 2 teaspoons dried thyme
2 tablespoons all-purpose flour
½ cup (120ml) white wine, optional
1¼–2 cups (300–450ml) chicken stock
1 tablespoon Dijon or wholegrain
    mustard
2 tablespoons sour cream
    or crème fraîche
Salt, to taste

For the pastry:
2 cups (250g) all-purpose flour, plus
    extra for dusting
¼ teaspoon salt
⅔ cup (150g) unsalted butter, chilled
¼ cup (60ml) cold water

To glaze:
1 egg, lightly beaten

Serve with: aligot (page 188),
    cloud mash (page 97) or just
    boiled potatoes
Special equipment: ideally a 9 inch
    (23cm) pie plate, but an 8 x 8 inch
    (20 x 20cm) roasting pan would also
    work; food processor, optional

1. First, make the filling. In a large saucepan, melt just a couple of teaspoons of the butter. Add the chicken pieces to the pan in batches and fry over a medium-high heat for a few minutes, until lightly browned. The meat doesn't need to be cooked through: this stage is more about getting a fond—the brown, sticky residue at the bottom of the pan—that will add color and depth to your sauce. Once you've got a light fond, remove the chicken and set to one side.

2. Now you're going to make the brown butter. Add the remaining butter to the pan and set over a medium heat. Watch as it melts, then starts to sputter and fizz. After a couple of minutes, you'll notice the milky white pools in the molten butter start to color, speckling the gold with brown flecks. It should smell nutty and toasted at this point. Take care when doing this: if the butter cooks for too long or at too high a temperature, those milk solids will blacken and burn, making the mixture bitter.

3. Once the butter is browned, add the leeks, mushrooms and thyme. Turn down the heat slightly, then let the vegetable mixture sweat and soften for 10 minutes or so, stirring regularly.

4. Add the flour to the vegetables and mix well, then sauté for a minute or two. Pour in the wine, if using, then turn up the heat and stir constantly while the wine bubbles and the alcohol cooks off. After a couple of minutes, turn the heat down again and add the chicken stock (1¼–1¾ cups/300–400ml if you used white wine, or slightly more if you didn't), mustard and the browned chicken pieces. Bring the mixture to a simmer, then cook gently for 6–8 minutes, until the chicken pieces are cooked.

5. Add the sour cream or crème fraîche, then check the seasoning, adding a pinch of salt if necessary. Set the mixture aside to cool slightly while you prepare the pastry.

6. To make the pastry, combine the flour and salt in a large mixing bowl (or the bowl of a food processor if you have one). Get out your chilled butter—it really does need to be cold—and cut into small cubes. Add the butter cubes to the bowl and combine with the flour mixture, until the fat is almost completely worked into the flour and the mixture resembles a fine crumble. If you're doing this by hand, you just need to rub the flour and butter briskly between your fingertips. In a food processor, pulse until you have a very delicate, floury rubble. Add the water and mix briefly but assertively, until the floury crumble comes together into a smooth dough—you can knead or process it a little here, just to bring the mixture together, but it's important not to overdo it or the pastry will toughen.

7. Divide your dough into two portions, one twice the size of the other, and flatten each into a disc shape. Wrap each portion in plastic wrap or parchment paper and put in the fridge to chill for about 30 minutes.

8. By the time the pastry has chilled, your chicken filling mixture should also be cool enough to work with: time to assemble the pie. Turn on your oven to 350°F (180°C) and get out your pie dish.

9. Unwrap the larger piece of pastry and dust your work surface and the pastry with a little flour. Roll the pastry out until it's big enough to line the base and sides of your pie dish—it should be roughly ⅛ inch (2mm) thick. If it cracks while you do this, don't panic: just press it back together firmly. Transfer the pastry to the pie dish and cut off any overhang, reserving these offcuts. Spoon the filling mixture into the pastry shell.

10. Unwrap the smaller portion of pastry and add any offcuts from the pie base, squeezing the dough together. On a floured surface, roll out the pastry until it's large enough to cover the pie, then drape it over the filling. Trim off any excess pastry and use a fork or your fingers to crimp the pastry together so that the base fuses with the lid. Glaze the pastry lid by brushing it with the lightly beaten egg, then cut a cross or small hole into the center of the lid, to let steam escape as the pie cooks.

11. Bake the pie in the preheated oven for roughly 40–50 minutes, or until the filling is bubbling and the pastry is tender and a deep gold.

For a weeknight, single-crust pie:

A from-scratch double-crusted pie might be asking too much for a weeknight. If you switch the recipe to a single crust pie, it takes out some of the worry work and drives down the cooking time. Make half or a third of the pastry quantity specified in the recipe (or use 7–9 ounces/200–250g of store-bought shortcrust pastry), and use it to top the pie. Because you're not piling the filling on top of the pastry in this case, you don't need to wait for the filling to cool before assembling the pie: just fill, roll, top, glaze and go. Bake for around 25–30 minutes.

Variations and substitutions:

If you can't face making your own pastry, don't sweat it! You can use roughly 1 pound or so (500g) store-bought shortcrust pastry.

I find chicken thighs are most tender when cooked in this pie, but it's really a matter of preference. You can use pretty much any cut, as long as it's off the bone, skinless and suitable for cutting into decent sized chunks. Chicken breast will be firmer and slightly drier.

If you don't like mushrooms, just leave them out and add an extra leek and a little more chicken to make up for it.

Tarragon is a great alternative to the fresh thyme in this, if you like its aniseedy, grassy notes. Use the leaves from 3–4 sprigs, but instead of adding at the beginning, add as the filling finishes simmering to preserve their delicate flavor.

ALIGOT
The cheesiest mashed potatoes

Aligot is a French recipe for mashed potatoes that are pretty much equal parts potato and dairy, ideal for those days when plain carbs just won't cut it. The special thing about the heinous spud-to-cheese ratio in this dish is that the potato begins to take on the qualities of the cheese it's cooked with: rather than mashing to fluffy clouds, it becomes stretchy, molten and golden, like the pools of mozzarella on top of a good pizza. There's some debate over the correct cheese to use here: in her *Guardian* column, Felicity Cloake opts for a mixture of Lancashire and mozzarella, while Tejal Rao suggests Comté or Gruyère for *The New York Times*. Tomme fraîche is traditional, but in the spirit of cross-Channel irreverence I've gone for Cheddar and Comté here, for a balance of tang and bounce.

Aligot is perfect with dark, leafy greens cooked really simply: I like kale or spring greens simply boiled, salted and buttered. It's also great with sausages or with the **chicken, brown butter and mushroom pie** on page 184. If you want a simpler, more everyday kind of mash, check out the super quick **cloud mash** on page 97.

Serves: 4–6 as a side
Ready in: 35 minutes, about half of which is
   hands-off while you boil the potatoes
Make-ahead and storage tips: page 327

Vegetarian

1⅓ pounds (600g) russet potatoes
Salt, to taste
⅔ cup (160ml) light cream or whole milk
⅓ cup (75g) salted or unsalted butter
1 cup (100g) grated mature Cheddar
1 cup (100g) grated Comté

Special equipment: potato ricer, optional

1. Peel the potatoes, then halve smaller ones and quarter large ones. Place the potatoes in a large saucepan of cold, well-salted water. Place over a high heat and bring to a boil, then simmer the potatoes for 14–18 minutes, or until they feel very tender—but not waterlogged or falling apart—when pierced with a fork. Drain the potatoes through a sieve, then leave them in the sieve to steam dry for a couple of minutes.

2. While the potatoes rest, gently heat the cream (or milk) and butter in the saucepan you cooked the potatoes in. If you used a very heavy pan, the residual heat of the pan may be enough to warm the cream and melt the butter; otherwise, set the pan over a low heat until the mixture is warm. Once it's warm, turn off the heat.

3. If you have a potato ricer, you can use this to purée the still-hot potatoes into the pan with the cream and butter now. Otherwise, just use a spoon to push the potatoes through a sieve: it'll slowly worm its way through the sieve holes in a way that you'll find delightful if you like pimple-popping videos on YouTube, or unnerving if not. If your sieve has very fine holes, you may not be able to do this. In that case use a potato masher to mash the potatoes very, very thoroughly. Whatever method you use, make sure you get out every last lump: aligot stands or falls on the smoothness of the potatoes. Mix the potatoes, cream and butter really well.

4. Add the grated cheese to the pan and turn on the heat as low as it'll go. Vigorously stir in the cheese until the potatoes are smooth and almost elastic, with the potato dragging in cheesy strands as you spoon it. Check the seasoning and add salt if needed. Serve straightaway.

Variations and substitutions:

Feel free to play around with the cheeses however you please. If you make this with all Comté (or all Gruyère), it will be mellower but more stringy and elastic. If you make this with all Cheddar, it'll have a looser, softer consistency but a stronger cheesy tang. Another option is to swap the Comté for a 4 ounce (125g) ball of mozzarella, for a milder flavor but unbeatable stretch.

SAUSAGE AND POTATO STEW WITH ROSEMARY DUMPLINGS

There aren't many things lovelier than dumplings. The word, the concept and the food itself—as broadly as you wanna define it, from custard-filled steamed buns to pan-fried gyoza—are all perfect. Here's a dumpling-topped stew that I turn to when I need something that feels special but not fussy, pleasantly hearty but without leaving you breathless.

Serves: 4

Ready in: less than 1 hour 30 minutes, much of which is downtime while the stew simmers unattended

Make-ahead and storage tips: page 327

Vegetarian option   Vegan option

For the stew:

1 ounce (30g) dried porcini mushrooms, optional

4 cups (1 liter) hot chicken *or* vegetable stock

2 tablespoons olive or vegetable oil *or* butter

8 pork *or* vegetarian sausages

2 medium onions, thinly sliced

Leaves from 2 fresh rosemary sprigs or 1 teaspoon dried rosemary

2 large or 4–5 medium russet potatoes (roughly 4 ounces/400g), peeled and cut into 1¼ inch (3cm) chunks

9 ounces (250g) fresh mushrooms,* thickly sliced

1 tablespoon Dijon or wholegrain mustard

3 tablespoons all-purpose flour

*White, cremini or oyster mushrooms are all good options.

Lots of freshly ground black pepper

Salt, to taste

For the dumplings:

1¼ cups (150g) all-purpose flour

2 teaspoons baking powder

Leaves from 1 fresh rosemary sprig, finely chopped

Pinch of salt

6 tablespoons water

2 tablespoons olive or vegetable oil

1. First, if you're using them, soak your porcini mushrooms: Place them in the hot chicken or vegetable stock in a large jug or mixing bowl, and leave to rehydrate while you brown the sausages and cook the onion. If you want to leave these out, just prepare the stock.

2. Get a large, deep pot out of the cupboard—a heavy cast-iron one will be particularly good here, but use whatever you have. Heat a couple of teaspoons of the oil or butter over a medium-high heat and add the sausages. Fry for 4–5 minutes, turning them regularly, until they're browned on the outside (they don't need to be cooked all the way through just yet). Remove the sausages from the pan, cut each one into four or five fat chunks and set aside.

3. Put the remaining olive oil or butter into the pan and add the onion and rosemary leaves. Cook for 10–12 minutes over a medium heat, stirring often, until the onion begins to brown and collapse. Add the sausage pieces back to the pan, along with the potatoes, mushrooms, mustard, porcini mushrooms (if using) and stock. Stir, scraping the brown fond from the bottom of the pan as you go—this adds so much flavor to the sauce. Bring to a simmer, then cook the stew over a low heat for 15–20 minutes, or until the potatoes are tender.

4. While the stew cooks, prepare the dumpling dough: Mix the flour, baking powder, chopped rosemary and salt in a mixing bowl. Add the water and oil and mix until just combined to a sticky, shaggy dough. If you overmix the dough, the dumplings will be chewy: you need to mix it only until no streaks of dry flour remain. Set aside while you finish the stew.

5. In a small bowl, stir the flour together with a couple of tablespoons of the stew sauce to form a loose paste. Scrape this into the pan and stir well to combine, then let the stew simmer just a minute or two more to let the sauce thicken. Check the liquid levels: if there's not enough stewing liquid to cover the vegetables and sausages, add a splash of water. Check the seasoning, adding black pepper and pinch of salt if you think they're needed.

6. Scoop the dumpling dough into eight rough, sticky mounds on top of the stew. Put a lid on the pan and turn the heat down until the mixture is at a very gentle simmer (any higher than this, and the flour might make some of the stew stick to the bottom of the pan). Cook for 30 minutes, leaving the lid on the whole time so that the dumplings puff up, steam and cook to perfect feathery fluffiness. Serve straightaway, while the dumplings are still fresh.

Variations and substitutions:

To any mushroom haters: You can swap out the fresh mushrooms for carrots if you must, but if you do this I'd still recommend leaving in the dried porcini mushrooms as they add a deep, umami flavor to the broth, particularly if you're using vegetarian sausages. If you really hate the texture, you can even blend the soaked porcini with their soaking liquid so that you have all the flavor but without the delicious slippery, sluggy mushroom mouthfeel. Alternatively, you can find porcini mushroom stock cubes online.

The potato can be replaced with carrots, rutabaga, celery root or pumpkin. The onions can be swapped for leeks if that's what you've got, but if you do this you should sweat the leeks with the mushrooms for 10 minutes over a low heat rather than trying to brown them as with the onions.

If you have any red or dry white wine, you can add a glass to the sweated vegetables and let the alcohol cook off for a few minutes before you add the remaining stew ingredients. If you do this, use a little less stock.

If you have self-rising flour in the house, you can use that in place of the all-purpose flour for the dumplings—just leave out the added baking powder. If you can't eat gluten, use a gluten-free all-purpose flour mix in place of the all-purpose flour specified for the sauce and dumplings (and make sure you're using a gluten-free meat or vegetarian sausage).

Finally, if you like the freedom of just sticking things in the oven, you can finish the stew there rather than on the stove. Preheat the oven to 350°F (180°C) while you prepare the stew base, and make sure you use an oven-safe pan. Once you've scooped the dumpling dough on top of the stew, put the whole pan in the preheated oven with the lid off and roast for 30 minutes.

CACIO E PEPE LASAGNA

Cacio e pepe is ordinarily pasta with grated pecorino cheese and lots of black pepper. In a little of the pasta cooking water, the cheese emulsifies to create a slippery, salty sauce flecked with fiery pepper pieces. In this wildly unconventional take on that classic, I've incorporated the pecorino and black pepper into an intensely creamy lasagna—no meat, no ragù, no veg, just cheese.

I know I'm playing with fire here. There's an infamous clip from *This Morning* in which Holly Willoughby suggests that a macaroni and cheese, if it had ham in it, would be a bit like a "British carbonara." Gino D'Acampo freezes, fork midair, in shock. "If my grandmother had wheels," he fires, "she would've been a bike!" There are times when a dish is a dish is a dish: it is itself, and it's not there to be played around with. Especially if a food culture is seldom taken seriously, the greatest respect you can give it is to make recipes as they were intended, as tradition dictates, without trying to reinvent the wheel for a Western, and often white, palate. But I really don't think there's any risk of Italian food being underappreciated or under-respected in our foodscape. Cacio e pepe will live to tell the tale, under the Italian sun and in fancy small-plates pasta restaurants. Besides, you don't need to take my word for it: Italian chef Rita Sodi has made a name for herself with a 21-layer cacio e pepe lasagna in her Manhattan restaurant, I Sodi. If it's good enough for her . . .

Serves: 6
Ready in: roughly 1 hour 20 minutes, 35 minutes of which is baking and resting time
Make-ahead and storage tips: page 327

Vegetarian

Wild appetites

For the béchamel sauce:
6 tablespoons (90g) salted or unsalted butter
¾ cup (90g) all-purpose flour
5 cups (1.2 liters) whole or reduced-fat milk (low-fat milk isn't rich enough for this outrageous dinner)
Pinch of ground nutmeg
Lots of freshly and coarsely ground black pepper
Salt, to taste

To assemble:
Vegetable oil, to grease
15 dried lasagna sheets
1¾ cups (175g) pecorino, Parmesan or Grana Padano *or* vegetarian alternative(s), finely grated
2 cups (200g) coarsely grated mozzarella
Lots of freshly and coarsely ground black pepper

Serve with: crisp green salad or steamed greens with lemon

1. Start by making the béchamel sauce. This white sauce will be the foundation of the lasagna. In a medium to large saucepan, melt the butter over a medium-low heat. Once it's sizzling, add the flour and whisk to combine. Let cook for 2–3 minutes, whisking all the time, until the flour is slightly toasted and the paste is bubbling. Add the milk very gradually, whisking all the time and keeping the pan on the heat. At first it'll create a thick, gummy paste, then slacken to a custard-like soup before relaxing back into milkiness. Add the nutmeg, then increase the heat slightly and bring to a simmer, stirring all the time so the sauce doesn't become lumpy. By the time it's bubbling, it should have thickened slightly. Turn off the heat and season with lots of coarsely ground black pepper and a little salt—you'll need more or less salt depending on whether your butter was salted, but best to err on the side of under-seasoning this sauce, as you'll be adding lots of salty cheese when you assemble everything.

2. Once the béchamel is ready, preheat the oven to 400°F (200°C) and get out a large roasting pan. Bring a large pot of salted water to a boil, and lightly grease a couple of baking sheets with vegetable oil. Have your cheeses ready and grated and your black pepper at hand.

3. Working in a couple of batches, parboil the lasagna sheets for 4 minutes in the boiling water. If you stir the pasta as soon as it goes in the water, it shouldn't stick. Once cooked, pluck the sheets from the pan with tongs or a couple of forks, and lay them out on your greased baking sheets (if you tip the lasagna sheets into a colander together, they'll congeal into a thick pasta brick).

4. Now, assemble the lasagna: You'll need a large 13 x 9 inch (22 x 33cm) roasting pan. Start with an introductory ladleful of béchamel, spreading it across the bottom of the roasting pan—you'll need about a sixth of the sauce. Next, lay down three lasagna sheets, followed by a generous ladle of béchamel, a sprinkle of hard cheese, a sprinkle of mozzarella and a good couple of pinches of black pepper. You'll repeat these layers— lasagna, sauce, cheese, pepper—another four times, so you'll be using roughly a fifth of the ingredients for each layer.

5. Bake the lasagna in the preheated oven for 30 minutes. It's ready when it's bubbling, with mottled patches of bronze and gold across the top. Let sit for 5–10 minutes to settle and firm before serving with something fresh and green.

CRÊPES WITH MUSHROOM, RICOTTA AND THYME

I have food writer Rachel Roddy to thank for this dish: Her recipe in the *Guardian* for cheesy Italian crespelle taught me that the tomato element here needs to be only a drizzle, not a full-on immersive sauce. Rachel's books about Italian cooking—specifically Roman and Sicilian cooking—are great if you want to broaden your repertoire.

Serves: 4
Ready in: roughly 1 hour 15 minutes, or less if you're speedy with your crêpe cooking
Make-ahead and storage tips: page 327

Vegetarian

Vegan option

For the crêpes:

1 cup (125g) all-purpose flour

Pinch of salt

1⅔ cups (400ml) milk

4 medium or large eggs

2 teaspoons olive oil or butter, for frying

For the filling:

2 tablespoons olive oil or butter, plus extra for greasing the tin

1 pound 2 ounces (500g) mushrooms, thinly sliced

3 tablespoons fresh thyme leaves or 2 teaspoons dried thyme

4 garlic cloves, crushed or finely grated

Lots of freshly ground black pepper

Salt, to taste

1 cup (250g) ricotta

¾ cup (75g) mozzarella, coarsely grated

To top:

2 tablespoons tomato paste

Scant ½ cup (100ml) water

1 tablespoon fresh thyme leaves or ¾ teaspoon dried thyme

½ cup (50g) mozzarella, coarsely grated, optional

1. First, make the crêpe batter: Combine the flour and salt in a large mixing bowl, then whisk in the milk until the batter is lump-free. Add the eggs one at a time, stirring well to mix everything together smoothly. Let the batter rest while you prepare the filling.

2. In a large frying pan (or a large saucepan, if that's a better size), heat the olive oil or butter over a medium-high heat, then add the mushrooms and thyme. Sauté for 7–9 minutes, stirring often, until the mushrooms are lightly browned and collapsing. Turn the heat down slightly, then add the garlic and cook for 1–2 minutes, until no raw white garlic remains. Season to taste with black pepper and salt, then set aside the filling while you make the crêpes.

3. Preheat the oven to 350°F (180°C).

4. Set a large nonstick frying pan (or crêpe pan if you have one) over a medium heat and grease with a little of your olive oil or butter. Once very hot (if you hold your hand about 6 inches [15cm] above the pan, you should be able to feel its heat), add a ladle of the crêpe batter, swirling the pan well to evenly coat the bottom. Cook for 1½ minutes or so, then flip the crêpe and cook for a further 30–60 seconds. Exactly how you do this is up to you, so play around until you find a technique that works for you, whether with a theatrical in-air somersault or a more pedestrian fish spatula flip. Adjust the heat as necessary to give light brown spots and crisp edges, but without burning the crêpes. Layer the crêpes on a plate once cooked.

5. In a medium bowl, stir the ricotta until smooth, then mix in the mozzarella and plenty of freshly ground black pepper. In a separate bowl, prepare the tomato topping by whisking the tomato paste with the water until you have a loose sauce.

6. It's time to start assembling everything. Grease a large roasting pan, roughly 13 x 9 inches (22 x 33cm), with a little olive oil or butter. One at a time, smear the crêpes with a generous spoonful of the ricotta mixture, spreading it across in a line, about a third of the way up the crêpe. Heap some of the mushrooms on top, then roll up the crêpe with its ricotta and mushroom filling to create a fat cigar. Lay the rolled crêpe in the greased dish and repeat with the remaining crêpes.

7. Drizzle the tomato paste and water mixture in zigzags over the top of the crêpes, then sprinkle with thyme and—if you're using it—the extra grated mozzarella. Bake in the preheated oven for 20–25 minutes, until sizzling.

A vegan version:

For the crêpes, you'll need to adapt the batter—without eggs, it needs a lot more flour in order to hold together. The crêpes will need to be slightly thicker too. Whisk together 2½ cups (300g) all-purpose flour with 1½ tablespoons of superfine or granulated sugar and a pinch of salt in a large bowl. Gradually whisk in 3¾ cups (900ml) oat or soy milk (these work better than other plant milks for giving body to the batter) and stir in 2 tablespoons olive oil. Set the batter aside to rest while you fry the mushrooms as outlined in the recipe (in oil rather than in butter, obviously). When you're ready to cook the crêpes, fry them in an oiled pan as described in the main recipe, but be gentle with them: they're fragile without the binding power of eggs, so you'll want to loosen the edges with a spatula and then flip assertively. If they're very soft, cook them for an extra 30 seconds or so on each side.

Instead of the ricotta and mozzarella mixture, make a cream as follows: In a blender or food processor (or using a stick blender), blitz 10 ounces (300g) silken tofu (not firm tofu!), 1 tablespoon olive oil, 1 tablespoon nutritional yeast, 1 tablespoon lemon juice, 1 teaspoon Dijon mustard (or ½ teaspoon English mustard), lots of freshly ground black pepper and a generous pinch of salt. Once smooth and well seasoned, it's ready to use exactly like the ricotta and mozzarella mixture above. Fill, roll, arrange, garnish and bake the crêpes as specified in the main recipe.

All about birthday cakes

I know there are those who would say that any cake made to celebrate a birthday is a birthday cake, but those people are more sensible than me. I like to make a fuss: that means that birthday cakes need to be silly, sweet and wildly over the top, never too restrained or classy. If you insist on being grown-up about it all, the **seeded rye cake with demerara crust** on page 147 or the **orange, olive oil and black pepper cake** on page 149 may be of interest to you. But if you're really in the market for fun, I'd recommend using the recipes for the **sour cream vanilla cake** or the **marbled chocolate and almond cake** on the pages that follow as templates for your birthday fun.

What you do next with your cake is really up to you, but I have a few suggestions in case you're in need of guidance. First of all, make your cake of choice in a round pan (I've included instructions and baking times for this in the relevant recipes)—this allows you to fill and frost the cake more ostentatiously than a sensible loaf pan shape would allow. If you made a thick round cake, you'll probably want to use a large knife to slice it into two thinner layers; if you used a couple of shallower pans, your cakes will already be the right thickness. Now, to fill the cake. Jam is an excellent choice—I like raspberry or blackcurrant, both of which add a welcome sharpness to balance the sweet. In the **sour cream vanilla cake**, you can swap the vanilla extract in the batter for lemon zest: this will set the scene perfectly for a lemon curd filling or, if you fancy it, the **salted passion fruit, pineapple and coconut curd** on page 320. For the **marbled chocolate and almond cake**, you could go all out with a dulce de leche filling or even the **salted honeyscotch sauce** on page 259. If you plan on eating your cake the same day, jam and softly whipped cream are heaven in either a chocolate or a vanilla cake. Whipped cream and fruit (strawberries or raspberries work well) are also a winning combination—just make sure the fruit isn't too wet, and don't leave the cake sitting around on a picnic bench in the midday sun or it'll begin to disintegrate.

If you want to frost your cake, you have a few options. A standard buttercream is just one part softened, unsalted butter to two parts confectioners' sugar: Beat the butter well, then slowly add the sugar, taking your time so you don't end up unleashing clouds of powdery sugar across your kitchen. Slacken with a little milk to make it a smoother consistency. For an 8 inch (20cm) cake, a rule of thumb is that you'll need about ¼ cup (55g) butter and 1 cup (100g) confectioners' sugar between each layer of cake. To flavor the buttercream, you could use a couple of teaspoons of vanilla, lemon or orange extract. A couple of tablespoons of cocoa powder will give you a smooth chocolate frosting that's easy to work with; for a slightly softer but shinier chocolate frosting, melt a little dark chocolate—about 1 ounce (25g or so) per ¼ cup (55g) butter—and stir it into the buttercream, adding a touch more confectioners' sugar if needed. Very strong black coffee (or instant espresso powder—not ground coffee or granules) can also be added, or a few drops of rose water or orange blossom extract. Orange, lemon or lime zest also work well, especially if you've filled the cake with curd. If, like me, you're a peanut butter nut, beat a tablespoon or two of peanut butter into the butter before you add the confectioners' sugar. A passion fruit buttercream can work nicely if you replace the milk with strained passion fruit juice, although in general I'd recommend dry rather than wet flavorings in a buttercream (if you overdo it with the liquid, you'll have to add a scary amount of confectioners' sugar to balance things out and make the buttercream stiff enough to spread).

If buttercream is too sweet for you, I can't relate but I can advise: A bittersweet chocolate ganache will help to balance the buttery sponge, and will work well on either a vanilla or a chocolate cake. Heat ⅔ cup (160ml) heavy cream over a low heat and very finely chop a scant 1 cup (150g chopped) dark chocolate. Once the cream is scalding hot, turn off the heat and add the chocolate, stirring until melted. Add honey (or golden syrup) and salt to taste, then let it cool slightly before using it to top and sandwich a two-layer 8 inch (20cm) round cake.

Another option, particularly if you've made a lemon or orange zest-flecked version of the sour cream cake, is a simple water frosting. Just slowly add lemon or orange juice to confectioners' sugar until a loose paste forms— do this carefully, as just a drop or two too much can make the frosting so runny that it slides clean off the cake.

And finally, grated chocolate, lemon zest, crystallized rose petals, chopped nuts, raspberries, strawberries and melted chocolate drizzle are all good decorations, depending on the flavor of your cake, filling and buttercream. But, of all the birthday cakes I've ever made, or had made for me, none are ever quite as fun as the ones encrusted with a rainbow of Smarties. (For the uninitiated, Smarties are a British alternative to M&M's—but better.)

SOUR CREAM VANILLA CAKE

I've made versions of this cake for years now, but I've finally nailed it here. This cake is as butter-rich as a Madeira cake, but with a lighter, more tender crumb and the gentle tang of sour cream to bring everything into focus.

It's up to you whether you make this as a loaf cake or as an 8 inch (20cm) round cake. The benefit of making a loaf cake is that the top has a chance to deepen to a rich sandstone color as it bakes (the "skin" of a Madeira cake has always been my favorite part). If you want to make this as a birthday cake, you may find a round shape more versatile. See page 198 for some inspiration for filling and frosting a birthday cake. Whatever cake pan you choose, I've included cooking times for both versions.

Serves: 6–8

Ready in: 1 hour 10 minutes in a loaf pan, but much less in a round cake pan; you'll need to let it cool before you slice and eat it though!

Make-ahead and storage tips: page 327

Vegetarian

⅔ cup (150g) unsalted butter, well softened

¾ cup (180g) superfine sugar

1½ teaspoons vanilla extract

1½ cups (180g) all-purpose flour

2 teaspoons baking powder

¼ teaspoon table salt

2 medium or large eggs, at room temperature

½ cup (120ml) sour cream

Special equipment: 8 inch (20cm) round springform pan, 2 × 8 inch (20cm) round cake pans or a 2 pound (900g) loaf pan (roughly 8½ x 4½ inches/ 11 x 22cm across its top)

1. Preheat the oven to 350°F (180°C). Line your pan(s) with parchment paper.

2. In a large mixing bowl, cream the butter with the sugar and vanilla extract for a good few minutes (with an electric whisk or mixer if you have one, or vigorously by hand), until lighter in color and fluffy. If you rub it between your fingers, you'll notice the sugar crystals have begun to break down or—if you beat the mixture really well—dissolved completely into the smooth, whipped butter.

3. In a separate bowl, combine the flour with the baking powder and salt. Into the butter mixture, add one of the eggs, beating together until the mixture is slippery and light but pretty much homogeneous, then add half of the flour mixture and mix briefly until smooth. Repeat with the remaining egg and the rest of the flour mixture, then gently fold in the sour cream until the batter feels satin-smooth.

4. Spoon the batter into the lined pan(s) and place in the preheated oven. In a loaf pan, the cake will take 45–55 minutes to bake. In a deep 8 inch (20cm) round springform pan, it will take 35–45 minutes. If the batter is divided between two 8 inch (20cm) round cake pans, the cakes should take about 20 minutes. No matter the size or shape of your pans, the cakes are ready when a small knife or skewer inserted into the middle of the loaf comes out clean.

Variations and substitutions:

If you have self-rising flour in the cupboard, you can use this in place of the all-purpose flour. In this case, leave out the baking powder. This cake can be made with a gluten-free flour blend in place of the all-purpose flour—just swap it directly.

Crème fraîche works well in place of the sour cream if that's what you have. Full-fat yogurt is also a good swap.

For a brighter flavor, use the zest of 2 lemons instead of the vanilla extract.

MARBLED CHOCOLATE AND ALMOND CAKE

"Something sweet?" is so often on the tip of my tongue. I know I'm not alone in this. It's a feeling that swells to a dissenting chorus after every lazy weekend lunch, sending everyone rifling through the kitchen cupboards for something to take the edge off. This yearning is a bit like peckishness, but certainly not so physical as hunger. It's more like a mouth hunger, a restless need to bookend your dinner with a sweet full stop. When you're in this kind of mood, even the most robust meal isn't really *done* until you've soothed your palate, whether with a hunk of cake, some chocolate from the corner store or a pint of ice cream that you hid in the depths of the freezer earlier in the week. When I was a kid, we'd routinely go to the bakery round the corner or the local store for that elusive something sweet on a Saturday afternoon. We might end up carrying home an apple-swirled bun or a bag of cheap doughnuts or some Bakewell tarts, but most often it'd be a half-moon marble cake rippled with chocolate and vanilla. It really wasn't vital nutritionally or functionally, but it fed our mouth hunger all the same, and sometimes that's enough. This recipe re-creates that cake.

When you cut it, each slice of this tender cake has whorls of pale gold and chocolate brown. The effect is beautiful, but the method couldn't be more simple: You make just an almond-scented batter, then mix a paste of cocoa powder and water into one half of it. As you ladle alternating spoonfuls of these mixes into the tin, you gently marble them together. This makes a beautiful base for a birthday cake—see page 198 for some tips.

Serves: 6–8
Ready in: 1 hour 15 minutes in a loaf pan, but much less in round pans; you'll need to set aside time to let it cool before eating though
Make-ahead and storage tips: page 327

Vegetarian

⅔ cup (150g) unsalted butter, well softened
¾ cup (175g) superfine sugar
1 teaspoon almond extract
2 medium or large eggs, at room temperature
1 cup (125g) all-purpose flour
¾ cup (75g) ground almonds
1½ teaspoons baking powder
¼ teaspoon table salt

3 tablespoons milk or water
2 tablespoons cocoa powder

Special equipment: 8 inch (20cm) round springform pan, 2 x 8 inch (20cm) round cake pans or a 2 pound (900g) loaf pan (roughly 8½ x 4½ inches/11 x 22cm across its top)

1. Preheat the oven to 350°F (180°C). Line the bottom of your cake pan(s) with parchment paper.

2. In a mixing bowl, beat the butter until soft and smooth, then briskly stir in the superfine sugar and almond extract. Once combined, continue to beat the mixture for a few minutes, until it's delicate and pale, and the heavy grittiness of butter and sugar has transformed into a smoother, more airy mix. Beat in the eggs, one at a time, then add the flour, ground almonds, baking powder and salt until you have a thick golden batter. Stir in 1 tablespoon of the milk or water.

3. Mix the cocoa powder with the remaining 2 tablespoons of milk or water in a separate mixing bowl to give a smooth paste. Add half of the cake batter to this bowl—no need to measure it, just eyeball it—and mix until evenly chocolaty.

4. Into your lined pan(s), dollop alternating tablespoonfuls of the light and dark cake batters so that the different colors are roughly jumbled. Drag a spoon in a weaving, winding pattern through the batter to help marble the batters together, but take care not to overmix it or you'll lose that definition.

5. Bake in the preheated oven for 50–55 minutes in a loaf pan, 35–45 minutes in an 8 inch (20cm) round springform pan or roughly 20 minutes if divided between two 8 inch (20cm) round cake pans. The cake is done when a small knife inserted into the middle comes out with no raw batter stuck to it.

Variations and substitutions:

If you have self-rising flour, use this in place of the all-purpose flour but decrease the amount of baking powder to ½ teaspoon. You could also make a gluten-free version of this cake by swapping the all-purpose flour for an all-purpose gluten-free flour blend.

If you're not keen on the marzipan-like flavor of bitter almond, swap the almond extract for 2 teaspoons vanilla extract. Alternatively, use 1 teaspoon orange extract for a chocolate orange kind of vibe, or try out 1 teaspoon or so of orange blossom water for a more grown-up variation.

MOLTEN CHOCOLATE, OLIVE OIL AND ROSEMARY COOKIE PIE

This cookie pie doesn't really know what it is. I love it. It's half crisp-edged, chewy cookie and half molten cookie dough. It's kind of grown-up—with the woody fragrance of rosemary and peppery olive oil and big sea salt flakes. In essence, it's just a big batch of cookie dough, baked until just cooked but gooey and oozing in the middle—ideal for when you need something more showy than a cookie, but just as crowd-pleasing.

You can make this either in a large sharing dish or in individual ramekins. I've given instructions for both. You can also use this dough as a template for actual cookies! Skip to the following recipe to see how.

Serves: 8
Ready in: 40 minutes (if you make a big one) or
   30 minutes if you make in ramekins
Make-ahead and storage tips: page 327

Vegan

¾ cup (150g) soft light brown sugar
scant ½ cup (100ml) olive oil
¼ cup (60ml) milk, dairy *or* non-dairy
1½ teaspoons vanilla extract
1⅔ cups (200g) all-purpose flour
1 teaspoon baking powder
½ teaspoon flaky sea salt or
  ¼ teaspoon table salt, plus extra
  to sprinkle on top
scant 1 cup (5 ounces/150g) dark
  chocolate, chopped into small chunks
Leaves from 2 fresh rosemary sprigs

Special equipment: 8 inch (20cm)
  round springform pan, 9 x 6 inch
  (15 x 22cm) roasting pan or 8 small
  ramekins

1. Preheat the oven to 350°F (180°C).

2. In a large mixing bowl, briskly stir together the sugar, olive oil, milk and vanilla extract until smooth. Add the flour, baking powder and salt, and mix to make a smooth, thick dough. Stir in the chocolate chunks and the rosemary leaves.

3. Spoon the mixture into your pan or ramekins and sprinkle with a little extra sea salt if you want. (If you're using table salt, don't sprinkle extra on top or the cookie pie will be too salty.) Bake a large one for 20–24 minutes in the preheated oven. Individual ramekins will take 12–14 minutes. Exactly how long you give it will depend on whether you want oozing, lava puddings or fudgy, semi-set cookie dough. I'll leave that judgment to you, but here's one thing you must do: let the dessert cool for at least 5 minutes before you eat it or you'll lose the skin off the roof of your mouth.

Variations and substitutions:

Superfine sugar can be used in place of the soft light brown sugar.

If you have self-rising flour, you can use this in place of the all-purpose flour, but leave out the baking powder.

White chocolate chunks also work well in this dough.

SALTED CHOCOLATE CHUNK COOKIES, THREE WAYS

Adapt this recipe however you see fit—this is just a basic (easily veganized) chocolate chunk cookie dough that can be respun to suit pretty much any craving. I give a few flavor ideas in the recipe to get you started. If you do want these to be vegan, make sure your dark chocolate doesn't contain dairy.

Makes: 16 cookies
Ready in: 30 minutes (set aside a few extra minutes
   to let them cool before eating)
Make-ahead and storage tips: page 328

Vegan

For the basic dough:
¾ cup (150g) soft light brown sugar
scant ½ cup (100ml) olive, almond or
   hazelnut oil
¼ cup (60ml) milk, dairy *or* non-dairy
1½ teaspoons vanilla extract
1⅔ cups (200g) all-purpose flour
1 teaspoon baking powder
½ teaspoon flaky sea salt or
   ¼ teaspoon table salt

For simple chocolate chunk cookies:
scant 1 cup (5 ounces/150g) dark
   chocolate, chopped into small chunks

**For rosemary, dark chocolate
and sea salt cookies:**
scant 1 cup (5 ounces/150g) dark
   chocolate, chopped into small chunks
Leaves from 2 fresh rosemary sprigs
Flaky sea salt, to sprinkle on top

**For dark chocolate, orange and
hazelnut cookies:**
⅔ cup (3½ ounces/100g) dark
   chocolate, chopped into small chunks
⅓ cup (50g) hazelnuts, roughly
   chopped
Zest of 1 orange

1. Preheat the oven to 350°F (180°C) and line a large baking sheet with parchment paper.

2. In a large mixing bowl, stir together the sugar, oil, milk and vanilla extract. Once the mixture is smooth, add the flour, baking powder and salt and mix until you have a cohesive dough. It won't be quite as firm as some cookie doughs, but it should be fudgy and thick.

3. Mix in whichever extras you want, following the suggestions I've given above or freestyling it with your own additions.

4. Spoon the cookie dough into 16 shaggy mounds on the baking tray, leaving space between each one (these will spread a bit). If you need to bake them in two or three batches, do that. Bake for 13–14 minutes in the preheated oven, until lightly browned, with firm edges but puffy centers. They'll sink and firm up as they cool, giving them a pleasing chewiness, so don't eat them straightaway.

Variations and substitutions:

Self-rising flour can be used in place of the all-purpose flour if that's all you've got, but I prefer the less vigorous lift that you get from using all-purpose flour and that small amount of baking powder. If you have to use self-rising flour, leave out the baking powder.

PEACH COBBLER WITH GOLDEN CORNMEAL CRUST

There's an episode of the sitcom *Black Books* when filthy, dyspeptic Bernard Black fantasizes about his summer girl—the girlfriend he'll take for summer, just like sickly Victorians would take the waters in Bath or the air in Bern, a perfect tonic for all the misery of the rest of the year. "I've got to get a girlfriend, just for the summer, until this wears off," Black exclaims. "She'll play tennis and wear dresses and have bare feet, and in the autumn, I'll ditch her, because she's my summer girl!" I know this is ridiculous, but that is how I feel about this cobbler. It is my summer treat, my golden, breezy, bountiful summer treat—something that feels special and very much *not* like it was made in a flat off a London inner-city highway. I make it repeatedly when I'm feeling flamboyant and fanciful, and then not at all for months on end. I'd encourage you to figure out what your summer-girl food is: that weird, perfect, in-the-moment concoction that you dream about and then ditch the moment the weather begins to turn.

A note on cobbler and cornmeal: In case you're not familiar with cobbler, it's similar to a crumble or a fruit pie, but is topped with islands of cakey, scone-like batter instead. This one uses fine cornmeal to make it particularly summer-girl special. It's vital that you use fine cornmeal and not coarse cornmeal, which would take far too long to cook. What you're looking for should be powdery and yellow, not visibly gritty or rough (like coarse cornmeal and some types of polenta), but also not superfine and white (like cornstarch).

Serves: 4
Ready in: roughly 1 hour, about half of which
   is hands-off while the cobbler bakes
Make-ahead and storage tips: page 328

Vegetarian   Vegan option

For the cobbler topping:
½ cup (60g) all-purpose flour
½ cup (60g) fine cornmeal
3 tablespoons superfine or
   granulated sugar
1 teaspoon baking powder
Generous pinch of salt
3 tablespoons salted or unsalted
   butter
scant ½ cup (100ml) buttermilk
   or whole milk

For the peaches:
4 large peaches (or more if you use smaller
   or doughnut peaches—you want roughly
   1–1⅓ pounds/500–600g)
1–4 tablespoons superfine or granulated sugar,
   to taste
1 tablespoon lemon juice (from roughly ½ lemon)

Serve with: heavy cream or ice cream
Special equipment: food processor, optional

1. First, make the cobbler topping. In a mixing bowl, combine the flour, fine cornmeal, sugar, baking powder and salt (use a little extra salt if your butter is unsalted). Combine the butter with the dry ingredients: rub the mixture between your fingers (or pulse it in a food processor, if you don't like getting your hands dirty) just until the butter pieces are about the size of split peas or red lentils. Add the buttermilk or milk and mix with a spoon until roughly combined. The batter will be thick and a little lumpy and that's fine. Let it sit while you prepare the peaches.

2. Next, preheat the oven to 350°F (180°C) and put a kettle full of water on to boil.

3. Make a small cross at the bottom of each peach using a small knife—just deep enough to slice a cross shape into the skin. Fill a large bowl or medium deep pan with the freshly boiled water, then carefully add the peaches. Let the peaches sit in the hot water for 45 seconds, then remove and run under a cold tap for a minute. Now you should be able to remove the peach skins using just your fingers. Start where you scored the skin at the bottom, and peel off the skin from there. If you have any trouble, just use a small sharp knife to help tease off the skin. (I'm not sure how to write about disrobing a plump peach without this whole recipe turning to smut, but please bear with me.)

4. Once the peaches are freed from their furry skins, cut each one into wedges, removing and discarding the pit once you can access it. Toss the peach wedges into an appropriately sized roasting dish—I used a 9 x 6 inch (15 x 22cm) dish, and it was ideal. You want the slices to be snug in the dish, but not heaped high. Sprinkle over the sugar and the lemon juice next: if your peaches are very sweet and ripe, you'll need only 1 tablespoon of sugar; if they're less enticing and maybe even a little sour, add extra sugar to taste. Toss everything together to combine.

5. Dollop the rested cornmeal batter over the top of the peaches in the roasting dish to create interconnected puddles with little spaces in between where the sunny peach juices can bubble through. The surface should be about 75–80 percent covered with cobbler mixture.

6. Place in the preheated oven for 30 minutes. When done, the cobbler topping should be risen and fluffy and the peaches bubbling underneath. Serve immediately or when warm.

Variations and substitutions:

To use canned peach slices, you'll need 2 x 14 ounce (400g) cans of peaches in juice or syrup—this will give about 1 pound 2 ounces (500g) of ready-to-use peach slices in total. Drain the cans and give the peach slices a little rinse if they came in syrup, then just follow the steps in the recipe. You should need to use only the minimum amount of added sugar with canned peaches, as they tend to be sweet.

This recipe also works really well with frozen cherries. Sometimes you can find Morello cherries, which have the sour cherry flavor you'll recognize from cherry soda—these are well worth getting if you can. But if the standard dark sweet cherries are all you can find, that's also fine. Just use 1 pound 2 ounces (500g) frozen cherries—no need to defrost or chop them. Toss the cherries with the sugar (use more sugar for sour cherries, and less for sweet ones), top with the cobbler and bake for slightly longer than specified prior—40–45 minutes is about right. Blueberries also work in this way.

Cornmeal is what really makes this dessert: it's a deep yellow color and has a slightly sweet, nutty flavor, creating a cobbler that's golden and flavorful. If you can't get it, you can use all-purpose flour instead, but it won't be quite the same.

If you don't have all-purpose flour, you can use self-rising flour instead. You'll still need to add ½ teaspoon baking powder though to help lift the cornmeal. Alternatively, if you want to make a gluten-free version of this dessert, swap the all-purpose flour for a gluten-free blend.

If you want to make a vegan version of this, swap the 3 tablespoons butter for 2–3 tablespoons coconut oil, and swap the buttermilk or whole milk for coconut milk.

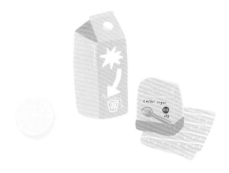

WILDFLOWER HONEY CHEESECAKE

Show me any cheesecake and I will eat it: cheesecakes in plastic supermarket containers, the god-tier frozen ones topped with mandarin slices in Jell-O, Basque cheesecake cooked until puffy and burnished, a barely defrosted slice in a seafront Italian restaurant, cheesecake ice cream (Nigella Lawson has a good recipe), sloppy cheesecake that got bashed around in its takeout container, the Honey & Co feta and honey cheesecake on kataifi pastry, cheesecakes from corner stores and delis and freezers. So, when I say this particular cheesecake is good—and not just good, but also beautiful, balanced and simple—you can trust that I've done my research. The wildflower honey sits perfectly alongside the tang of cream cheese and the fiery ginger base.

There are lots of ways to make a great cheesecake, from baking hot and fast (like in the aforementioned Basque cheesecake) to baking, as Nigella often does, in a water bath for the gentlest possible cook. I settled somewhere in the middle with this one: a low oven for a little over an hour seems to create a dense, custardy set.

Serves: 8–10
Ready in: 5 hours 40 minutes, but that includes 4 hours
   to let the cheesecake chill before serving
Make-ahead and storage tips: page 328

Vegetarian

---

5 ounces (150g) gingersnap cookies
⅓ cup (75g) salted or unsalted butter
1 pound 5 ounces (600g) full-fat cream
   cheese, at room temperature
½ cup plus 1½ tablespoons (200g)
   runny wildflower honey
⅔ cup (150g) sour cream or crème
   fraîche
4 tablespoons all-purpose flour
3 medium or large eggs
2 teaspoons vanilla extract
¼ teaspoon salt

Serve with: berries, compote,
   honey or **salted honeyscotch sauce**
   (page 259), all optional
Special equipment: 8 inch (20cm)
   round springform pan; food
   processor, optional

1. Start by making the ginger base: Preheat the oven to 350°F (180°C). Get out an 8 inch (20cm) round springform pan. Smash the gingersnap cookies into a very fine, powdery rubble: you can do this either by blitzing them in a food processor or by breaking them into a large bowl and bashing them with the end of a rolling pin. Melt the butter, either in a small pan or in the microwave, and add to the cookie crumbs, stirring together so that the mixture starts to clump. Tip into the pan and compact the crumbs really well under a spoon or, better still, under the flat bottom of a drinking glass. Bake in the preheated oven for 15 minutes.

2. When the base is cooked, remove it from the oven and decrease the oven temperature to 285°F (140°C). Let the base cool while you mix the cheesecake: In a large bowl, beat the cream cheese firmly, but not overzealously, until completely smooth. Lightly stir in the honey and the sour cream, then mix in the flour. One by one, stir in the eggs, then add the vanilla extract and salt. The batter should be smooth, satiny and thick.

3. Pour the cheesecake mixture over the prebaked base. Place in the middle of the oven and bake for 65–75 minutes, or until the cheesecake has just the gentlest wiggle in its middle when you shake it. If it's sloppy in the middle, it's not done yet, but don't wait until it's completely firm throughout or you risk overdoing it: you want it to be barely set, with a custard-like center.

4. As soon as it's done, run a small knife around the outside of the cheesecake to loosen it from its pan (this will minimize the risk of it cracking as it cools) and leave to cool to room temperature in the pan. Place in the fridge to chill for at least 4 hours before eating—the texture and flavor will massively benefit from this chilling time. When you're ready to eat it, unclip the pan, slice and serve.

Variations and substitutions:

In place of the wildflower honey, you can use orange blossom honey.

If you can't eat gluten, use gluten-free ginger cookies or graham crackers for the base, and swap the 4 tablespoons of all-purpose flour in the cheesecake batter for 3 tablespoons of cornstarch.

If you can't get hold of sour cream or crème fraîche, you can use heavy cream in the cheesecake mix instead. If you do this, I'd recommend stirring in 1 tablespoon lemon juice at the end with the vanilla extract and salt, to add a touch of acidity.

For a blank canvas cheesecake, you can use a scant 1 cup (7 ounces/ 200g) superfine sugar instead of the honey and swap the punchy gingersnaps for graham crackers.

MIDNIGHT CHOCOLATE TART WITH COCONUT AND SEA SALT

Made with dark chocolate and sea salt, this ganache tart has a bittersweet intensity that makes it seem a lot more sophisticated than it really is— nobody ever needs to know that it's basically a stir-together job, requiring no pastry skills and very little finesse. It is also vegan, if you want it to be, which means there's no excuse anymore for palming off your vegan friends with fruit for dessert. Just use a vegan dark chocolate and graham crackers (or similar) for the crust if necessary.

Make sure you use full-fat coconut milk—not a "light" version—for this, as the fat helps the ganache filling to set. Or, to make this with dairy instead of coconut, just skip to the variations and substitutions at the end.

Serves: 8–10

Ready in: 4 hours 30 minutes (only 30 minutes of this is prep time—the rest is time to allow the tart to cool and set)

Make-ahead and storage tips: page 328

Vegan

For the crust:

5 ounces (150g) graham crackers, crackers or crunchy salted pretzel bites*

⅓–½ cup (75–100g) coconut oil *or* butter

2 tablespoons soft light or dark brown sugar

1 tablespoon milk, dairy *or* non-dairy

Salt, to taste

For the chocolate ganache filling:

2½ cups (14 ounces/400g) dark chocolate, roughly chopped

1¼ cups (300ml) full-fat coconut milk

4–5 tablespoons (40–60g) soft light or dark brown sugar

2 tablespoons coconut oil *or* butter

2 teaspoons vanilla extract

1¼ teaspoons flaky sea salt

Serve with: heavy cream or sweetened coconut milk

Special equipment: 8 inch (20cm) round springform pan or 9 inch (23cm) round loose-bottomed tart pan; food processor, optional

---

*I've been vague here because there are so many options. Crunchy pretzel bites work well, with their mahogany sheen and salt crystals. Graham crackers or gingersnap cookies also work, as do matzo crackers. Use what you have.

1. Start off by making the crust: blitz the cookies, crackers or pretzel bites until they're reduced to a very fine rubble—you can do this either in a food processor or in a large bowl or freezer bag using a rolling pin as a kind of mallet.

2. Melt the coconut oil or butter either in the microwave or in a small pan. Start with the lower amount—around ⅓ cup (75g)—but bear in mind that you may need extra in a moment to bring the mixture together. In a large bowl (or in the food processor, if you used one to blitz the crunchy stuff), combine the crumbs with the melted oil or butter, the sugar and the milk, and mix briskly until the crumbs begin to clump together. If the mixture is still very dry and sandy, melt the remaining oil or butter and add it now. You may want to add salt if you used a sweet cookie, but hold off if you used salty pretzels.

3. Get out your pan, choosing a dish with a removable bottom so you can easily lift the tart from it. Cutting a circle of parchment paper to line the bottom of the pan will also help with this. Tip the crust mixture into the

pan and pack down as firmly as possible to create a dense, even layer over the base of the pan. Place in the freezer for 10 minutes (or the fridge for 30 minutes), to allow it to set.

4. When the crust is nearly set, prepare the filling: In a large bowl, combine the dark chocolate, coconut milk, sugar, coconut oil or butter, vanilla extract and 1 teaspoon of the salt. If you're using very dark, bitter chocolate, you'll need slightly more sugar; if you're using the cheaper supermarket-brand stuff, use less sugar. Microwave on full power in short bursts—no longer than 15 seconds or so each time—and stir well in between. Keep going until the chocolate has smoothly melted into the coconut milk. If you don't have a microwave, do this over a very, very low heat in a small saucepan on the stovetop.

5. When the ganache is smooth, pour it over your tart crust and set the pan in the fridge for 3–4 hours, to cool and set completely. During this time, the chocolate ganache should transform from molten and glossy to dense, fudgy and dark.

6. To unmold, run a small knife round the side of the pan to loosen the edges, then unclip the pan (if it's a springform one) and lift out the tart on its base. Sprinkle the remaining ¼ teaspoon of sea salt flakes on top before serving.

Variations and substitutions:

You could also use this ganache to make easy dessert pots if you can't be arsed to make and set the base. Just make the ganache as above, divide between eight small ramekins and set in the refrigerator. Top with crumbled cookies or whipped cream if you want.

Instead of flaky sea salt, you can use fine sea salt or table salt in the ganache filling. You'll need less in this case though—about ½ teaspoon should be fine, though add slowly and to your own tastes. Don't bother sprinkling these finer salts on top at the end.

You can use superfine or granulated sugar in place of the soft light or dark brown sugar in the crust and ganache, but you'll lose out on some of that toffee-like brown sugar depth.

Wild appetites

Normal perfect moments

HOW TO SNACK IN STYLE

Recipe list

Introduction

In this chapter, you'll find easy breakfasts, nourishing soups and countless snacks, from kimchi and Cheddar cornbread muffins to fried plantain with crunchy peanuts. I'll admit that these are the kind of recipes that I usually bypass in a cookbook: I'm guilty of falling into the go-big-or-go-home mentality, choosing either the biggest most elaborate cooking project or just resorting to grilled cheese. But, as I've tested and retested these recipes, I've found myself buoyed by them in ways that go beyond just their nutritional content: When I go to the effort of making these good, small things, I feel very clearly that I've cared for myself. That nurturing energy then reverberates through the rest of my day. Sometimes food is the one thing that can be counted on to bring some life into our humdrum daily routines. These are straightforward recipes to soothe and to energize you, illuminating even the dullest days with flashes of goodness.

Further reading

Grandbaby Cakes by Jocelyn Delk Adams

Original Flava by Craig and Shaun McAnuff

Indian-ish by Priya Krishna

If I Can Cook/You Know God Can by Ntozake Shange

Zoe's Ghana Kitchen by Zoe Adjonyoh

The Groundnut Cookbook by Duval Timothy, Jacob Fodio Todd and Folayemi Brown

La Grotta Ices by Kitty Travers

Hibiscus by Lopè Ariyo

Short and Sweet by Dan Lepard

Carbs by Laura Goodman

Normal perfect moments

GALAXY GRANOLA

sunflower
seeds

oats

salt

sesame
seeds

ripe banana

dark chocolate

Mmmm
honey!

flaked coconut

coffee granules

oil

I'm a sucker for a romantic recipe name, I know. But this granola holds up: it has everything in it—a whole galaxy of delicious stuff—from banana-laced sweet–salty oat clusters to pockets of bitter coffee and the crunch of toasted seeds. Make a double quantity if you're stocking up.

Makes: roughly 1¼ pounds/500g
Ready in: 1 hour 30 minutes, most of which is
   hands-off time while the granola bakes
Make-ahead and storage tips: page 328

Vegan

---

3 cups (250g) oats
⅓ cup (50g) sunflower seeds
¼ cup (30g) sesame seeds
2 teaspoons instant coffee granules
½ teaspoon salt
1 banana
4 tablespoons olive, vegetable
   or coconut oil

4 tablespoons honey
½ cup (30g) unsweetened shredded
   coconut or coconut flakes
1¾ ounces (50g) dark chocolate

Serve with: ice-cold milk or yogurt

1. Preheat the oven to 300°F (150°C). Get out a decent-sized roasting pan—no smaller than 13 x 9 inches (22 x 33cm) across its base: you want a pan big enough to comfortably accommodate the mix, but not so big that the granola is spread really thin; otherwise it's likely to burn.

2. In a large mixing bowl, combine the oats, sunflower and sesame seeds, coffee granules and salt. In a separate bowl, mash the banana really well, until pulpy. Add the mashed banana, oil and honey to the mixing bowl and combine until the oats are evenly coated and coming together in clumps.

3. Tip the oat mixture into your roasting pan and bake for 40 minutes, stirring well halfway through to make sure the granola browns and crisps evenly. Add the flaked or shredded coconut, stir to combine and return to the oven for a further 20 minutes. If the granola is getting a bit too dark or threatening to burn, just take it out early.

4. Let the granola sit for at least 20 minutes, or until cool to the touch. It will crisp more as it cools. Chop the dark chocolate into small chunks—no larger than ⅜ inch (1cm) cubes—and add to the granola. Serve with ice-cold milk or yogurt.

Normal perfect moments

CINNAMON APPLE OVEN PANCAKE

If I describe this pancake as both custardy and cloud-like, you're gonna think I'm overselling it, but it really is the best of all worlds. An oven pancake does what it says on the package: it cuts out the part of the morning where you stand in front of the hot stove, flipping pancake after pancake while sweating and maybe even swearing. Here, a pancake mix very similar to a Yorkshire pudding batter is poured over sugared, buttered apple slices, and stuck in the oven until golden and crisp. No more Sunday morning rows or frayed tempers—just perfect pancake.

Braeburn and Granny Smith apples both work really well here, but use whatever you have around. What's nice about this recipe is that you can toss in even the most well-traveled fruit (those battered, bruised apples that have been at the bottom of a school backpack for a week) and trust that it'll come out great.

Serves: 4

Ready in: 50 minutes, about half of which is zero-stress time while the pancake bakes

Make-ahead and storage tips: page 328

Vegetarian

---

4 medium apples (see note above on variety)

3 tablespoons salted or unsalted butter

¼ cup (50g) superfine, granulated or soft light brown sugar

1 cup (125g) all-purpose flour

1 teaspoon baking powder

½ teaspoon cinnamon

¼ teaspoon salt

3 medium or large eggs

1 cup (250ml) whole milk or buttermilk

1 teaspoon vanilla extract, optional

Serve with: yogurt or sour cream, optional

1. Preheat the oven to 400°F (200°C) and get out a large roasting pan, roughly 13 x 9 inches (22 x 33cm). While the oven heats, peel, core and thickly slice your apples.

2. Once the oven is hot, put the butter in your roasting pan and put it in the oven for 3–4 minutes, or until the butter is fully melted and sizzling.

3. Add the sliced apples to the butter in the roasting pan and sprinkle over the sugar. Stir the apples to coat evenly with the sugar, then return the dish to the oven for a further 10 minutes.

4. While the apples start cooking, prepare the batter. Mix the flour, baking powder, cinnamon and salt in a mixing bowl, then break in the eggs and whisk until you have a thick, smooth batter. Add the milk or buttermilk gradually while whisking, then stir in the vanilla extract if you're using it. Once all the liquid is incorporated, the batter should be smooth and pourable, with a consistency similar to heavy cream.

5. Once the apples have had their 10-minute head start in the oven, they should be beginning to soften, and the butter and sugar should be sizzling together in the pan. Pour the batter over all of this and return the roasting pan to the oven for a further 25 minutes.

6. If you're curious, you can watch through the oven door as it cooks: For the first few minutes, the batter will be flat and heavy. After a while, the batter will puff up around the apple slices, quivering as it's brought to life by the oven's heat. Towards the end of the cooking time, the crust will mottle a lightly bronzed color and the edges will begin to crisp. Once the cooking time is up, remove the pan from the oven and serve straightaway.

Normal perfect moments

223

CHEESY KIMCHI CORNBREAD MUFFINS

Despite both being bold flavors, kimchi and cheese go beautifully together. I think of them like Simon & Garfunkel: the soaring notes and the steady beats, and all the harmony in between. God, I love those guys.

In these cornbread muffins, these two old friends come together amid a tender cornmeal crumb. I've adapted the base from a cornbread recipe by Jocelyn Delk Adams, of *Grandbaby Cakes*, who has become a favorite whenever I wanna bake something new and need a gentle guide to see me through. Just halve the quantities below if you have only a 6-cup muffin pan.

Makes: 12 muffins
Ready in: less than 40 minutes
Make-ahead and storage tips: page 328

Vegetarian

⅔ cup (90g) fine yellow cornmeal
¾ cup (90g) all-purpose flour
2 teaspoons baking powder
1–2 teaspoons gochugaru (Korean red
   pepper flakes—see page 53), to taste
Generous pinch of salt
¾ cup (175g) cabbage kimchi
   (vegetarian if required)
6–7 tablespoons (100ml) kimchi juice*

4 scallions, thinly sliced
1 cup (120g) grated Cheddar
2 medium or large eggs, lightly beaten
¼ cup (60g) salted or unsalted butter,
   melted

Special equipment: 12-cup
   (or 2 × 6-cup) muffin pan(s)

*This is the bright red liquid that the kimchi is packed in. It's full of flavor. When you prepare the kimchi, you'll squeeze it from the leaves and collect some. Any extra you can pour from the jar or pouch. If you don't have 6–7 tablespoons (100ml), top up with water or milk if necessary.

1. Before you do anything else, preheat the oven to 400°F (200°C) and get out a 12-cup muffin pan. You don't need muffin or cupcake liners for these—the muffins tend to stick to paper but come out without any trouble at all from an unlined pan.

2. In a mixing bowl, stir together the fine cornmeal, flour, baking powder, gochugaru and salt. Squeeze out the kimchi cabbage leaves really well using your hands, until most of the liquid is drained—collect the kimchi juice in a small bowl though, as you'll need it in a moment. Chopped the squeezed kimchi into smallish chunks.

3. Add the squeezed and chopped kimchi, scallions and Cheddar to the flour mix in the bowl and stir to roughly combine. Add the kimchi juice, then add the egg and melted butter and stir together until you have a thick golden batter.

4. Divide the batter between the cups in the pan, being sure to fill each one no more than three-quarters full. Place in the preheated oven and bake for around 20 minutes, or until well risen and springy to the touch, with browned cheesy tops. Enjoy warm or cold.

Normal perfect moments

SIZZLING CHIPOTLE TUNA FRITTERS

These smoky chipotle-spiced fritters are an amazingly easy lunch or breakfast. Chipotle paste is made from blended chipotle chilies, so popular in Mexican cooking, and is available in any big supermarket, usually near the herbs and spices: it's smoky and spicy and a really quick way of making quick cooking taste great. Here, it takes pantry staples—tuna, sweet corn, onion and flour—to another level. I also use it in the **eden rice with black beans and plantain** on page 58, so you don't need to worry that it'll go to waste if you buy a jar. If you really can't be bothered, though, check out the variations and substitutions on the next page for an alternative.

These are very, very loosely based on Jamaican saltfish fritters, which combine salt cod with Scotch bonnet chili, scallions, flour and water. If you're curious about the real thing, Craig and Shaun McAnuff of *Original Flava* have a great recipe on their website and in their book.

Makes: 16 small fritters (serves 4–6)
Ready in: less than 30 minutes
Make-ahead and storage tips: page 328

---

7 ounces (200g) tuna (from roughly 2 small cans, drained)

1 cup (150g) sweet corn (and defrosted if frozen)

2 medium carrots (roughly 5–7 ounces/150–200g), peeled and coarsely grated

1¾ cups (200g) all-purpose flour

6 scallions, thinly sliced, or ½ medium red onion, finely chopped

1–2 tablespoons chipotle paste, to taste

2½ teaspoons baking powder

Pinch of salt

scant 1 cup (225ml) water

2–3 tablespoons olive or vegetable oil, for frying

Serve with: dressed green salad

1. In a large mixing bowl, combine the tuna, sweet corn, grated carrot, flour, scallions or red onion, chipotle paste, baking powder and salt. Pour in the water, stirring as you go, to create a thick but easily spoonable batter—the flour and water should stickily bind the tuna and veg together, rather than being a loose pancake-style batter.

2. Place a large frying pan over a medium-high heat, and add a tablespoon of the oil. Once the oil is hot, use a large spoon to dollop out spoonfuls of the mixture into the hot pan and pat them down so they're roughly ⅜ inch (1cm) thick—I cook these in three batches of 5–6 fritters. Fry for 3 minutes, turning down the heat if the bottom is browning very quickly, or turning up the heat if the fritters aren't vigorously sizzling. Once the first side is cooked, use a fork or fish spatula to carefully turn over the fritters and fry for a further 3 minutes on the other side.

3. Once cooked, keep the first batch of fritters warm under aluminum foil while you heat some more oil and fry the rest of the mixture in batches. Serve hot with a dressed green salad.

Variations and substitutions:

Instead of the chipotle paste, you could use 1–2 teaspoons chipotle chili flakes, or 1 teaspoon chili flakes and 1 teaspoon smoked paprika. If you happen to have gochujang—perhaps left over from the **mushroom and gochujang udon noodles** on page 87 or the **kimchi and potato hash** on page 164—you could also swap that in for the chipotle paste.

In place of the grated carrot, you could use an equivalent weight of grated zucchini, sweet potato, rutabaga or butternut squash.

Normal perfect moments

227

HERB-PACKED ZUCCHINI FARINATA

Farinata is an Italian chickpea pancake, popular along the Ligurian coast: the chickpea flour (also known as gram flour) gives it a rich nuttiness, and makes it much more robust than a wheat flour pancake. Here, the golden batter is mixed with an assortment of greens, from grated zucchini to fresh herbs and spinach, turning it into a (light) meal in itself.

You'll need to factor in at least 2 hours for the batter to rest, which gives the flour's bitterness a chance to subside. You can also rest the batter overnight if that's easier—check the recipe instructions for more details.

Chickpea flour is easy to find in South Asian grocery stores and in most large supermarkets. It's also good in kadhi—a chickpea flour and yogurt soup, for which Priya Krishna has a great recipe in her cookbook *Indian-ish*. I understand if you don't want to buy a big bag just for this recipe, though, so if you skip to the variations and substitutions you can find a non-farinata vessel for these same fresh, herby flavors: an omelet, a little like an Iranian kuku sabzi, made with beaten eggs.

Serves: 4 as a light meal
Ready in: 2 hours 25 minutes (2 hours of this is just letting the batter rest though—get this ready in the morning so it's ready when you're hungry later)
Make-ahead and storage tips: page 328

Vegan

1¾ cups (150g) chickpea flour
Generous pinch of salt
1 cup (250ml) water
1 medium zucchini (roughly 11 ounces/300g)
3.5 ounces (100g) spinach
2 cups (60g) fresh herbs—any mixture of basil, cilantro, dill, mint, parsley, tarragon or wild garlic
4 scallions
2 tablespoons olive or vegetable oil

Serve with: green salad

1. Start by preparing the batter: In a large bowl, combine the chickpea flour with some salt (I used ¼ teaspoon, but do this to your tastes), then gradually whisk in the water until you have a reasonably smooth, loose batter—it'll be roughly the consistency of thick cream. Cover the bowl with a plate or damp kitchen towel, then leave the batter to rest at room temperature for at least 2 hours, or up to 12 hours. During this time it'll become even smoother, and a light smattering of bubbles will appear at the top.

2. When the batter has rested and you're nearly ready to eat, prepare the greens. Start by coarsely grating the zucchini, then squeeze out any excess water: you can do this just over the sink using your hands, or you can wring it out inside a clean tea towel or piece of cheesecloth. You'll never get it completely dry: just squeeze until the water emerges drop by drop, not as a trickle. Place the grated, squeezed zucchini in a large bowl.

3. Wilt the spinach: Place it in a large bowl or pan and pour over a generous amount of boiling water to cover it. Let sit for 30 seconds, then drain through a sieve or colander and—just like you did with the zucchini—squeeze out any excess water. Once the leaves have been very well drained, roughly chop or tear them so they're slightly broken up. Add the spinach to the bowl with the zucchini.

4. Roughly chop or tear the herbs, discarding the stalks as you go. Thinly slice the scallions, greens and all. Add the herbs and the scallions to the bowl with the zucchini and spinach, then add the greens to the batter you prepared earlier and mix well to combine, so the batter is laced with green.

5. Heat the oil in a large frying pan over medium-high heat. Once the oil is hot, add half of the mixture and sauté for roughly 2 minutes, then use a spatula to flip the pancake and cook for a further 2–3 minutes. It's ready when it's nicely browned—not just lightly golden, but mottled a lovely walnut color. Tip the pancake onto a clean plate and cover with a tea towel to keep it warm while you cook the remaining mixture in the same way. Slice and serve warm with salad.

Variations and substitutions:

To make a quicker omelet version of this basic recipe, whisk 8 eggs together with a generous pinch of salt (I used about ¼ teaspoon) and use this instead of the chickpea flour batter. There's no need to rest the omelet mix, so just combine it immediately with the greens and cook as instructed above.

Normal perfect moments

LEMONY GREEN LENTIL SOUP

This is a restorative soup enhanced with the holy trinity of lemon, garlic and chili to drag you out of even the flattest mood.

Serves: 4
Ready in: less than 1 hour
Make-ahead and storage tips: page 328

Vegan

2 tablespoons olive oil, plus extra to serve
2 celery sticks, cut into ⅜ inch (1cm) slices
2 medium carrots, cut into ⅜ inch (1cm) slices
4 garlic cloves, crushed or finely grated
6 cups (1.5 liters) water
2 x 14 ounce (400g) cans green lentils, drained
3½ ounces (100g) Tuscan kale, spring greens or kale, cut into ½–¾ inch (1–2cm)-thick strips across each leaf
3 bay leaves
2 vegetable *or* chicken stock cubes, crumbled
½–1 teaspoon chili flakes, to taste
2 lemons
Salt, to taste

Serve with: thickly sliced bread

1. In a large, deep saucepan, warm the oil over a medium heat. Add the celery and carrots, put on a lid and let sweat for 10 minutes or so. Remove the lid, then add the garlic and sauté for a few minutes, until it no longer smells raw.

2. Add the water, lentils, sliced greens, bay leaves, stock cubes and chili flakes to the pot. Using a sharp knife, slice four long, thin strips of lemon peel (from roughly ½ a lemon), cutting as little of the bitter white pith as possible. (Some of you might find a potato peeler easier and safer for this job.) Add the lemon peel strips to the pot. Bring the soup to a simmer and stir it, then decrease the heat slightly and cook for 30 minutes, or until the vegetables are perfectly tender and the broth aromatic.

3. Squeeze the lemons and add lemon juice to the soup to taste—you'll probably want it all, but it's up to you. Add salt to taste, and then spoon it into deep bowls, drizzle with a little oil and serve with lots of bread.

Variations and substitutions:

In place of the hardy Tuscan kale, spring greens or kale, you can use chard or spinach if you prefer. If you make this swap, I'd recommend adding the greens later—about 5 minutes before the end of the cooking time—as they cook much faster.

I use canned green lentils for this, though any kind of precooked brown, French or beluga lentil—whether it comes in a can or a pouch—would be fine. If you have dried lentils, you can swap these for the canned lentils. Use green, brown or French lentils (not red lentils—these will become mushy) and cook exactly as specified in the recipe, just increase the amount of water to 2 quarts (1.8 liters) or so.

STUFFED FLATBREADS, THREE WAYS

These flatbreads, inspired by Turkish gözleme, Indian paratha and Afghan bolani, are a very easy way to perk up a weekend lunchtime. They're not a super-quick meal—you need to make a basic dough, let it rest for an hour, make the filling and then fill and fry the breads—but they're ideal for a slow day when you have some time on your hands. There are three recipes that follow from this base recipe, which guide you through a few filling ideas: spinach and feta, cumin-spiced potato and, finally, Mumbai chili cheese.

Makes: 4

Ready in: maximum 2 hours (an hour of which is fallow time while the dough rests), but much quicker if you get on a roll with rolling and filling the flatbreads

Make-ahead and storage tips: page 329

Vegetarian   Vegan option

For the dough:
2½ cups (300g) all-purpose flour, plus extra for dusting
1 teaspoon active dry yeast (about ½ of an 8g package)
½ teaspoon salt
2 tablespoons olive oil
scant ⅔ cup (150ml) water, at room temperature

To fill and cook the breads:
1 batch flatbread filling, according to the recipes on the following pages
1–2 tablespoons olive, coconut or vegetable oil, for cooking

Serve with: a crisp leaf salad

1. In a large bowl, mix together the flour, yeast and salt. Add the oil, then pour in the water and use a spoon to bring the mixture together into a shaggy ball of dough. Once roughly combined, tip the dough out onto a clean worktop and use your hands to gently knead it (there's a more in-depth description of kneading in the recipe for **rosemary baby buns** on page 296 if that's helpful) for around 5 minutes, or until smooth and supple. Return the dough to the mixing bowl, cover the bowl with plastic wrap or a plate and leave to rest for 1 hour: during this time, the yeast will get to work, making the dough expand to almost double its original size. Even if you're using baking powder instead of yeast (see the variations and substitutions below), this resting stage is still important: it's during this time that the dough relaxes, the texture changing from taut and bouncy to puffy and squidgy and, crucially, it becomes much easier to roll out.

2. While the dough is resting, skip forward to the filling recipes and prepare your chosen filling.

3. Once the dough has rested and your filling is ready, it's time to get on with assembling the flatbreads. Have some extra flour ready for dusting the worktop, along with a rolling pin, a flat spatula, a frying pan and a little bowl or ramekin with your oil for cooking the flatbreads. The more organized you can be here, the better: you'll be a one-person production line, rolling, filling, rolling, frying and flipping flatbreads like a well-oiled machine.

4. Divide the dough into four equal portions, using scales if you're anxious about making them even, but just eyeballing it if not. Lightly flour the worktop and place a portion of dough on it. Cover the remaining three portions of dough with the upturned mixing bowl to stop them drying out.

5. Dusting the dough with a little flour, pat it into a rough square shape (please don't lose sleep over this—it doesn't need to be perfect), then roll out to a 9–10 inch (23–25cm) square. If it's sticky, add a sprinkling more of flour but try not to overdo it, as it can toughen the dough.

6. Twist the square so that one corner is facing you: it'll now be skewed like a diamond. Spread a quarter of your prepared filling in a square in the middle of the diamond—it should cover only roughly a third of the area of the dough. If you have a couple of different elements to your filling, as in the chili cheese, just layer them up: spread the green chutney over the central part of the dough, then scatter the cheese mixture on top. (Remember, half of the green chutney is meant to be set aside as a dipping sauce, so don't use it all.)

7. Next, fold two opposite corners of the dough up towards the center, so that the two corners fold over the filling and touch in the middle. Then fold the two remaining corners in so they enclose the filling and slightly overlap. Gently press together to seal. You should be left with a little square(ish) dough parcel. Now roll the parcel out until it's roughly double as wide—roughly 8 x 8 inches (20 x 20cm). Don't worry if a little bit of the filling pops out or the dough tears: just patch it up as best you can.

8. It's up to you whether you start frying now and make the next flatbread while you're cooking this first one, or whether you make all the flatbreads first and then fry them after. If you're prone to losing track of timings in the kitchen, I'd recommend getting all the flatbreads made and filled first! But if you're feeling confident, the 6 minutes that each bread takes to cook should be more than enough time to crack on with making the next one.

9. To cook the flatbreads, rub both sides with oil, massaging it gently into the dough. Heat a large frying pan over a medium heat and lay the flatbread in the pan. Cook for 2½–3 minutes on one side, then flip over using a spatula and cook for a further 2½–3 minutes on the other side. The heat needs to be high enough to give the bread some brown spots, but not so high that those spots become ashy and burnt: adjust the temperature up or down accordingly. Enjoy these while they're still warm.

Variations and substitutions:

If you don't have yeast, baking powder also works here. The flavor won't be quite as good (yeast really unlocks the flavor in flour, with some of the big starch molecules broken down into sugars) but the flatbreads will work just fine. Just swap the yeast for 2 teaspoons baking powder, and follow the recipe exactly as written.

If you're a real bread-head and have fresh yeast in the house, swap the active dry yeast for ⅓ ounce (8–10g) fresh yeast, dissolving it in the water before adding it to the flour and salt mix.

Bread flour also works in this recipe, or you could swap half of the all-purpose flour for whole wheat flour. Either way, you'll want to add a splash more water—just enough to bring the dough together so that it's hydrated and kneadable, not tough, crumbly and dry.

Spinach and feta filling

This is just like the filling for spinach and feta gözleme, the Turkish flatbread that forms the basis for the dough recipe and folding technique on page 231.

Vegetarian

---

7 ounces (200g) fresh or frozen whole leaf spinach*
1¾ cups (7 ounces/200g) feta, crumbled
Lots of freshly ground black pepper

*Frozen chopped spinach, which is very finely ready-chopped, tends to release a lot of water and so will be too mushy for this recipe.

1. If you're using frozen spinach, defrost it in the microwave. If using fresh spinach, place in boiling water for 1 minute, then remove from the heat and immediately drain through a sieve or colander. Run cold water over the blanched leaves for a minute or two, until they're cool to the touch.

2. Whether you defrosted frozen spinach or blanched fresh spinach, you need to get rid of some of the water in the leaves. Just squeeze the spinach between your hands or use a spoon to press it in a sieve, squeezing until only the occasional droplet of water drips out.

3. Mix the spinach with the feta and black pepper until roughly combined, with small chunks of bright white feta mottling the deep green of the spinach.

Cumin-spiced potato filling

This is a riff on aloo paratha: beautiful buttery Indian flatbreads stuffed with spiced potato. The dough for these flatbreads is less rich than paratha dough, but these are still great for breakfast, especially if you have some kind of chutney on hand (you could make the chutney from the chili cheese flatbread filling following) to electrify this soothing carb-on-carb meal with herbs, acidity and spice.

Vegan

---

1 pound (450g) russet potatoes, peeled and cut into ¾ inch (2cm)-thick slices
Salt
2 tablespoons vegetable or coconut oil
2 teaspoons black or brown mustard seeds
1½ teaspoons cumin seeds
1½ teaspoons mild or medium curry powder
½–1 teaspoon chili flakes, to taste

½ teaspoon amchur, optional (see page 269 for more information)
Small handful of fresh cilantro leaves (roughly ¼–⅓ ounce/5–10g), roughly chopped, optional
1 tablespoon lemon juice (from roughly ½ lemon)
Freshly ground black pepper
Generous pinch of salt

1. For the potato mash, place the potato slices in well-salted cold water in a medium saucepan. Bring to a boil, then simmer for 13–15 minutes, or until the potato is tender enough that you can pierce it with a fork. Drain well and mash until smooth.

2. Once the mash is ready, you can start with the seasonings. In a small frying pan or saucepan, heat the oil over a medium heat until very hot. Add the mustard and cumin seeds and let sizzle for roughly 60 seconds, until the cumin is fragrant. Take the pan off the heat, then add the curry powder, chili flakes and amchur (if using), letting the spices softly sizzle as you stir. Add this mixture to the mash along with the cilantro leaves (if using), lemon juice, pepper and a generous pinch of salt, and combine well.

Variations and substitutions:

If you don't have cumin seeds, you can use ground cumin instead. Fry it very briefly in the oil. In place of the black or brown mustard seeds, you could use 1 tablespoon wholegrain mustard. Add it when you add the salt and pepper.

Mumbai chili cheese filling

A Mumbai chili toasted sandwich is a beautiful thing: soft white bread, filled with cheese, chilies and a zingy green chutney and toasted until crisp outside and molten within. This recipe translates those flavors into flatbread form.

Vegetarian

1⅓ cups (150g) finely grated Cheddar

2 scallions, thinly sliced

1 green finger chili, thinly sliced (seeded if you want less heat)

Special equipment: stick blender, food processor or blender or mortar and pestle, optional

For the green chutney:

2 cups (60g) cilantro, stalks and all, roughly chopped

2 scallions, thinly sliced

2 thin green chilies, roughly chopped (deseed them if you want less heat)

2 tablespoons lemon juice (from roughly 1 lemon)

1–2 tablespoons water

Pinch of salt

1. Combine the grated Cheddar, scallions and sliced chili in a bowl.

2. For the chutney, blitz all the ingredients in a blender or food processor (or in a small bowl or jug if you're using a stick blender) until it's fairly smooth (don't worry too much though—it's hard to get it really smooth unless you have a very good blender or food processor). If you don't have any kind of blender, you can either use a mortar and pestle or just chop everything as finely as possible, mix together in a small bowl and stir in the lemon juice, water and salt.

3. Divide the chutney into two bowls: half is for putting inside the flatbreads, and half is for serving on the side.

A few other flatbread filling ideas:

- grated Cheddar, diced quince paste and dried thyme
- finely chopped dark chocolate and flaky sea salt
- raspberry jam
- handfuls of chopped fresh parsley, mint and basil with a sprinkling of salt and olive oil
- unsweetened shredded coconut mixed with coconut cream, sugar and golden raisins
- anchovies, roughly chopped black olives, tomato paste and parsley
- salted butter, brown sugar and cinnamon, mixed to a paste
- ground lamb fried with garlic, cumin and coriander, with golden raisins and chopped parsley

KELEWELE
Fried plantain with chili and peanuts

Fried plantain belongs in the god tier of all snack foods. Good snack food dances across your tongue, refusing to commit to being purely sweet or savory, piquant or comfortingly bland. This is why sweet and salty popcorn is so moreish and why you just can't stop grazing on a platter of barbecue wings. When snack food is truly great, it hits a sweet spot that makes it nearly impossible to stop munching. I prescribe this crispy, salty, spicy, sweet plantain for those middle-of-the-afternoon peckish moments or that time after dinner but before bedtime when persistent cravings tend to strike.

If you grew up eating fried plantain, you won't need any convincing of its merits. But if you aren't familiar with it, all I can say to you is that you need to try it. When fried, plantain becomes caramelized and crisp on the outside while collapsing into fudgy sweetness within. It's perfect snack food no matter how you season it, but I'm particularly fond of this version spiked with ginger, nutmeg and a generous hit of chili. It's what is known in Ghana as kelewele (pronounced keh-leh-weh-ley)—served either streetside as a snack or made as a side dish. I've suggested scattering it with peanuts as is traditional, but you could freestyle it with some toasted sesame seeds or even a drizzle of cayenne-spiced honey if you like. If you want to learn more about Ghanaian cooking, check out *Zoe's Ghana Kitchen* by Zoe Adjonyoh or *The Groundnut Cookbook* by Duval Timothy, Jacob Fodio Todd and Folayemi Brown.

You'll want ripe plantain for this: fruits that are yellow, soft and covered with black spots, not the firmer, starchier green ones. You can get them in some large supermarkets, but you'll find them cheapest and most reliably at Asian, Latin, African and Caribbean grocery stores.

Serves: 4
Ready in: 50 minutes, over half of which is hands-
off time while the plantain marinates

Vegan

4 ripe plantain
½ medium or 1 small onion
2¼-inch (6cm) piece of ginger, peeled
4 garlic cloves
½–1 teaspoon chili powder, to taste
1 teaspoon freshly ground black
  pepper
½ teaspoon salt, plus extra to serve
¼ teaspoon ground nutmeg

4 cups (1 liter) sunflower or peanut oil,
  for deep-frying
⅓ cup (50g) salted roasted peanuts, to
  serve

Special equipment: food processor or
  blender, optional; candy thermometer
  or instant-read digital thermometer,
  optional

1. First, prepare the plantain. Some of you will be abundantly familiar with plantain and will need no guidance about how to prepare it. If this is you—go forth and prosper! If you're a plantain novice, here's what you'll need to do: Cut off the very top and bottom of each plantain then run the knife lengthwise down the fruit, piercing just deep enough to slit open the peel. It'll now be easy to take off the skin. This is easier than to try to peel it like a banana.

2. Cut the plantain into small to medium chunks. I like to cut each plantain along its length into two long halves. Next, cut each piece into ¾ inch (2cm) slices, but do it on a slant, like how you might cut a baguette if you were trying to be fancy. This way, you'll get tapered diamonds of plantain rather than dumpy little nuggets. Place the plantain pieces in a large bowl.

3. To prepare the marinade, the easiest way forward is to just stick the onion, ginger, garlic, chili powder, black pepper, salt and nutmeg in a food processor and blitz until you've got a rough paste. If you don't have a food processor (or don't want to risk imprinting it with such strong flavors) you can just finely grate the onion, ginger and garlic, then stir in the spices and seasonings. Mix the plantain with the paste, cover and leave to marinate for half an hour.

4. Heat the oil in a medium pan or deep frying pan. It's ready when it's 350°F (180°C), which you can measure using a candy thermometer or an instant-read digital thermometer. If you don't have a thermometer, no need to panic. The oil is hot enough when a ¾ inch (2cm) cube of bread browns all over in 60 seconds. If it becomes very dark during that time, the oil is too hot. If the oil barely bubbles when you lower the bread in, it's too cold.

5. Fry the plantain in batches (don't overcrowd the pan!) for 3–4 minutes, until it's browned and caramelized all over. Don't mess around with the plantain once it's frying or you'll dislodge all the seasoning clinging to the outside.

6. Drain the plantain on paper towel when it's done, then serve straightaway scattered with the peanuts.

Variations and substitutions:

You can swap the nutmeg for calabash nutmeg, or African nutmeg, if that's what you happen to have in the cupboard. Chili flakes are a fine swap for chili powder.

Salted cashews can be swapped in if you can't eat peanuts.

To the shops

Foodies love to talk about the state of food shopping today: about how depersonalized it is, how sterile and detached from the rituals of plow, season and soil. And maybe it is, in a way. I think it's fair to say that most of us aren't particularly in touch with where our food comes from. We probably shouldn't be able to live out our personal food fantasies so disconnected from the people (and places) that made them possible. Food should be affordable to buy, but should also provide a fair wage to whoever made it. It shouldn't ravage the environment. Profit shouldn't be hoarded in the hands of a fortunate few. Beyond the reach of our individual purchase power, there are governmental measures that need to be taken too, from animal welfare standards to ensuring access to food for all.

But sometimes conversations about food shopping seem to be about more than just ethics. When people with—let's be honest—plenty of money to spare talk about gaudy packaging, it feels pointed. People with full use of their hands and plenty of energy to spare will laugh about the grossness of frozen dinners, as though everyone has the luxury of being able to prepare food from scratch—a process that can involve peeling, slicing, stirring, standing, tasting, mashing, can-opening, washing and scrubbing for even the simplest meal. Shoppers who have time to saunter for hours around a farmer's market picking the finest produce from about a dozen different retailers will complain that online grocery shopping just gives people "too much choice." Suddenly it's less about who food nourishes (or harms) and more about our own petty anxieties: what the food that we eat says about our standing in the world, and our need to convince others to live, and eat, the same way as us.

The rituals of most of our food lives are, I guess, unromantic compared to digging up your own carrots or picking mangoes from a tree at the end of the garden. But the ways we shop (and there really are myriad ways) aren't all bad. There is the trek to the supermarket with a carefully crafted list, for those of us determined to stick to our best-laid plans (and our budgets). There is the corner store run for the Twix we desperately need to keep up our blood sugar. We might go to the Chinese grocery store for chili crisp sauce and the Halal butchers when we can't face boning the chicken ourselves. In a hunger rampage, we can pop to the nearest store for a pint of milk and come back with a chocolate milk and a bag of chips. For idle browsing, we look to expensive department store food halls or the fruitful chaos of the wholesale market. These food worlds are fragmented and diverse. Here in the UK, we have Londis for instant gravy and the giant international store on the fringes of town for a 25lb bag of rice. We can wander through Moor Market in Sheffield or London's Brixton Market or our local equivalent, darting from stall to stall in search of Maggi cubes and new-season strawberries. Your food store microcosm may look different from this, but it's likely to have a similar range: big and small sellers, inexpensive and artisanal, everyday and luxury, and from every food culture.

There are veg boxes, meal kits, massive superstores in retail parks, food banks, dollar stores that sell food as if by accident, community-owned stores, everyday supermarkets, the corner stores that routinely save our bacon, market vendors, bulk-buy stores, local greengrocers, the guy on the corner who makes and sells his own jam, fishmongers, farm stands down country lanes, meals on wheels, work cafeterias, vending machines and those little stores named things like "The Shop" or "Provisions Hut," as though they sell wartime rations and not, in fact, expensive cans of Portuguese sardines. There are as many ways to shop as there are to eat. Considering how wildly different our lives are—from night-shift workers reliant on frozen dinners, to country cooks making everything from scratch—this variety doesn't seem like such a bad thing.

YORKSHIRE PUDDINGS
FOR EVERY OCCASION

I used to live in Sheffield, just a short train journey away from maybe the best station cafe in the country. Grindleford Station Cafe, nestled on the eastern fringes of the Peak District, is a strange heaven: a steady stream of walkers and cyclists file through, drawn in by the promise of tea served by the pint (!) and huge servings of steaming, salted fries. One of the best things you can get there is a Yorkshire pudding filled with fries and gravy—a feast to warm the very core of you, whether you've been hiking all day or just got the train in from Hathersage.

What I learned from Grindleford is that Yorkshire puddings—similar to popovers, and made from an egg-rich batter that is baked, with hot fat, in a hot oven—really deserve better than being relegated to a wingman for a Sunday roast dinner. Here's a Yorkshire pudding recipe that I like, and a few suggestions for how to make it work for you at any time, in any mood and for whatever occasion you wish.

Makes: 1 large or 12–18 individual Yorkshire puddings, serving 6 people
Ready in: less than 45 minutes

Vegetarian

1⅓ cups (165g) all-purpose flour
¼ teaspoon salt
3 medium or large eggs
1 cup (250ml) whole or reduced-fat milk
4 tablespoons sunflower or vegetable oil *or* beef drippings

Special equipment: large roasting pan, roughly 13 x 9 inches (22 x 33cm), or a 12-cup nonstick muffin pan

1. In a large bowl, combine the flour and salt, then vigorously whisk in the eggs and about a third of the milk. Once you've beaten out any lumps, whisk in the remaining milk until the batter is smooth and loose. Let the batter rest while you heat the oven.

2. Preheat the oven to 425°F (220°C). Get out your large roasting pan and add the oil or beef drippings. If you want to make small puddings, divide the oil between the cups of a nonstick muffin pan: it'll make 18 muffin-sized Yorkshire puddings or 10–12 normal-sized ones, so cook in batches as required. Once the oven is hot, place the pan in the oven for a few minutes to heat the fat until it's shimmering hot.

3. When the fat is very hot, pour in the batter and return the pan to the oven. Roast for roughly 20 minutes for small puddings, or 20–25 minutes for a large roasting pan pudding. Whether you're making big or small ones, the Yorkshire pudding is ready when the edges are puffy, crisp and a deep croissant-brown color, while the center is tender and pudding-like.

Toad in the hole:

A British favorite: sausages in a Yorkshire pudding, but in a fully integrated kind of way, with the sausages baked into the very fabric of the pudding, rather than being added upon serving. First cook 8 sausages—meat or vegetarian—in a large roasting pan for 10 minutes in the preheated oven, as described in the main recipe. Add the oil or beef drippings to the pan with the sausages and return to the oven for a further few minutes, until the fat is hot. Add the batter as outlined in the main recipe, then bake for 30 minutes, until the sausages are well cooked and the batter is risen and crisp on top.

Dutch baby with maple syrup and blueberries:

For this sweet Yorkshire pudding, swap the sunflower oil or beef drippings for butter. Make the batter just as in the main recipe, but add 1 tablespoon superfine or confectioners' sugar along with the flour. Cook in a large roasting pan, or make a half batch in a cast-iron skillet. Once ready, serve with blueberries, a good glug of maple syrup and a snowy dusting of confectioners' sugar if you want to.

Jammy leftover puddings:

For breakfast, reheat any leftovers in the oven for a few minutes or the microwave for 20–30 seconds. Once hot, add a pat of unsalted butter and a spoonful of jam (golden syrup is another very good option, if you can find it). Fold the pudding over on itself and enjoy warm and buttery.

OVEN FRIES WITH SHITO MAYO

Ah, chips! Or, as you Americans insist, *fries*. Heavy bags that you cradle to your chest on the walk home; chicken shop fries glistening with salt; limp McDonald's fries; curly fries that are somehow both burnt and undercooked at the same time; the fat fries you get in a pub; fries that spill out of their cardboard carton into your handbag; fries imperiled by swooping gulls. I love them all.

This is a strangely British fixation, I think, despite the popularity of chips—or fries—across so much of the world. We've taken a good thing and worked it into some kind of national identity. I'm always curious about how this obsession must look from the outside, from elsewhere in the french fry universe.

Most of us need no convincing of the merits of fries, but online food magazine *Vittles* might be of service if you need new pairing ideas for this god-tier snack. In "the hyper-regional chippy traditions of Britain and Ireland," there was Wigan's pie barm (a pie in a bun, served with fries and gravy), imli chips (doused in tamarind chili sauce) from Rochdale and orange battered fries from deep in the Black Country. These are testament to the incredible diversity of chip tastes even on this tiny cluster of islands. Most of the time, I like them Dutch style—with Indonesian-inspired satesaus, or satay sauce (you can use the **charred Brussels sprouts with satay and crushed peanuts** recipe on page 141 as a template)—or with the shito-spiked mayo featured below.

Shito is a Ghanaian chili condiment, including dried fish or shrimp, garlic and oil, available in larger supermarkets, online or in any West African store. It's incredibly hot and deeply savory, at the other end of the chili sauce spectrum from sweeter, more fruity chili sauces. Partnered with mayonnaise, it makes a perfect fiery dip for fries, though if you wanna put hair on your chest you could of course just dip your fries in it as it is. If you want to try a from-scratch shito mayonnaise, Zoe Adjonyoh has a recipe that will guide you all the way through whisking the egg yolks with cider vinegar and oil. Her cookbook, *Zoe's Ghana Kitchen*, is amazing if you want to make more Ghanaian food.

Serves: 4–6
Ready in: about 45 minutes, most of which is
  downtime while the fries bake
Make-ahead and storage tips: page 329

Vegetarian   Vegan option

Salt, to taste
2.2 pounds (1kg) russet potatoes
2 tablespoons olive or vegetable oil

For the shito mayo:
⅔ cup (125g) mayonnaise, vegan if
  required
½–1½ teaspoons shito, to taste

1. Fill a large saucepan with water, salt it well and place over a high heat. Preheat the oven to 400°F (200°C).

2. While the water comes to a boil, prep your potatoes: wash them well, then slice into fries roughly ½ inch (1.5cm) thick (leaving the skin on).

3. Once the water is boiling, add the fries and boil for 4 minutes. They won't be completely cooked at this point—this stage is only to start softening them before they hit the oven. Drain the fries and let them steam dry for a couple of minutes, then tip out onto a large baking sheet (or two) and toss with the oil and plenty of salt.

4. Bake the fries in the preheated oven for 15 minutes, then toss them and return to the oven for a further 15 minutes. They're ready when they're crisp and golden brown at the edges and light and floury within.

5. When the fries are ready, stir together the mayonnaise with the shito for the sauce: different brands vary in their spice levels, so add the chili to taste. Serve right away, dipping the hot fries into the shito mayo.

> ### Variations and substitutions:
>
> It should go without saying that you can use this less as a from-scratch recipe than as a prompt, if you want, and just use frozen oven fries instead of making your own.

GREEN APPLE SALAD
WITH TOASTED SEEDS

Everyone knows that apples taste 100 percent better when cut into thin, crisp slices than just eaten as they are. This simple recipe takes that truth and builds on it. It also gives me enormous pleasure to confirm that this salad goes perfectly with a grilled cheese sandwich.

Vegan

Serves: 4
Ready in: less than 15 minutes

1 teaspoon coriander seeds
12 almonds, walnut halves or pecan halves
3 tablespoons pumpkin seeds, sunflower seeds or egusi
½ teaspoon black or brown mustard seeds

3 medium apples (I like a crisp, semisweet green apple, such as Granny Smiths)
2 teaspoons olive oil

Special equipment: mortar and pestle, optional

1. First, prepare the nuts and seeds. Crush the coriander seeds under the flat side of a knife blade or with a mortar and pestle just until the seeds are roughly broken open. Cut the almonds, walnuts or pecans into small chunks (I cut an almond into three, but there's really no point in being super fussy about this). The remaining seeds can be cooked whole.

2. Heat a small, dry frying pan over a medium heat, then add the prepared nuts and seeds. Gently toast the nuts and seeds, stirring almost constantly, until they are fragrant and very slightly browned. When they're ready, the pumpkin, sunflower or egusi seeds should be beginning to darken in spots, and the mustard seeds will be starting to crackle and pop. This should take no longer than 3–4 minutes. Turn off the heat and immediately tip the mixture out of the pan and into a bowl so the nuts and seeds don't continue to cook.

3. Wash the apples, then core them and cut into thin slices (I like to leave the skins on). Arrange the slices on a large plate or serving dish, drizzle with the olive oil and scatter over the toasted seeds and nuts. Eat straightaway.

Variations and substitutions:

This works well with coriander seeds, as they have a citrus edge that really lifts the fruit, so I'd advise not substituting them. You should be able to find them—and the mustard seeds—in any large supermarket or South Asian grocery store. However, the remaining nuts and seeds can be swapped however you please. I've given a few substitution ideas in the ingredients list, but it's really about just using what you have on hand. The idea is to have a couple of aromatic seeds and then a mix of different sizes and flavors of other nuts and seeds for crunch. For the aromatic seeds, cumin, fennel, nigella or caraway seeds can work as alternatives to the mustard seeds in a pinch. For texture, poppy, flax, sesame and chia seeds are all good, and macadamia or brazil nuts add a welcome bite.

You can swap the apple for pear if that's what you have. This also works with slightly firm, underripe mango, but add a squeeze of lime juice along with the olive oil.

(SUPER)MALT LOAF

I love malt. I think my obsession started with malted candies. As I got older, I graduated to occasional malty beers and a silky, soul-lifting black malt vanilla ice cream, the recipe for which I highly recommend you check out in Kitty Travers's *La Grotta Ices* book. I go wild for malted breakfast cereals too and for malted sodas, downed ice cold and tingling on a summer's day. Malted bread, with its slightly deeper color crumb and slight sweetness, is my favorite. Again and again, I come back to this flavor, and I'm always looking for new ways to bring it into the recipes I make.

Even if you're not entirely sure what malt is, odds are you know the taste if you've ever tried any of the foods and drinks I just mentioned. Malt extract is a dark syrup, extracted from barley grains that have germinated, with enzymes transforming the barley's starch into a kind of sugar called maltose. This syrup, or derivatives of it, is what adds a sweet, nutty, roasted kind of flavor to, for example, malt loaf. It has a depth a little like roasted coffee beans or chocolate, but without that same bitterness.

I've been making malt loaf for years now, but was always irked by having to trek to a health food store to get hold of malt extract, which is seldom sold in supermarkets. Then one day last summer, while I was guzzling a malt soda, it occurred to me that in malt drinks like this, that deep, full-bodied maltiness was already there for the taking—and way more accessible than the concentrated extract. You can get Supermalt, Mighty Malt, Malta Goya, Vitamalt and similar drinks in lots of Caribbean and African grocery stores, and in some larger supermarkets. The result is a dark, sweet loaf, perfect sliced, microwaved or toasted, then slathered with salted butter. (My tester-in-chief, Kaila, said this reminds her of Jamaican Easter bun, so she recommends you could alternatively have it with slices of cheese.)

Makes: 1 loaf cake, serving 6–8
Ready in: less than 1 hour 30 minutes, most of which is baking time (you'll want to set aside extra time to let this cool before eating it though)
Make-ahead and storage tips: page 329

Vegan

---

1 cup (250ml) Supermalt, Malta Goya or other full-sugar malt soda (not a low-sugar version!)
1½ tablespoons molasses, optional
⅔ cup (120g) raisins or golden raisins
1½ cups (180g) all-purpose flour
2 teaspoons baking powder
½ cup (100g) soft dark brown sugar
¼ teaspoon salt

Serve with: salted butter or (as Kaila recommends) Cheddar cheese
Special equipment: 2 pound (900g) loaf pan, roughly 8½ x 4½ inches (11 x 22cm) across its top

1. In a large microwavable bowl or jug, heat the malt drink, molasses (if using) and raisins in the microwave until the liquid is scalding hot. You can also do this in a small pan on the stovetop. Set the hot mixture aside for 15 minutes to let the fruit plump up and the malt drink cool slightly.

2. Preheat the oven to 350°F (400°C) and line your loaf pan with parchment paper.

3. While the oven heats, combine the flour with the baking powder, sugar and salt in a mixing bowl. Add the slightly cooled malt and fruit to the flour mixture, but save two teaspoons of the malty liquid for later. Stir just until you have a smooth batter—it should be a milky coffee color and have a beautiful malty smell.

4. Spoon the batter into the lined loaf pan and bake in the preheated oven for 35–40 minutes. Test the cake to see if it's done by inserting a small knife into the middle of the loaf: if the knife comes out with just a little moisture and a crumb or two stuck to it, the loaf is done. While it's still hot, brush over the reserved couple of teaspoons of malt drink.

5. Let cool slightly before slicing, toasting (or microwaving—it works just as well) and spreading with salted butter. If you can bear to wait, this malt loaf gets much better with age: it's at its best (and most squidgy) on day two or three.

Variations and substitutions:

If you have self-rising flour, you can use this in place of the all-purpose flour (leave out the baking powder too). This cake doesn't work so well with gluten-free flour.

PUFF-PUFF
Nutmeg-spiced doughnut bites

I should probably call these boflot, bofrot or togbei—the Ghanaian names for these tiny, feather-light doughnuts—but I just love the Nigerian name, puff-puff, so much. Puff-puff do exactly that: they expand majestically when they're fried, transforming from gloopy batter to cherubic bread clouds.

Even if you've never had West African food, there's a chance you'll have some degree of doughnut déjà vu here: puff-puff look a lot like French beignets, Middle Eastern lokma, Dutch oliebollen and Icelandic ástarpungar (which translates, funnily enough, as "love balls"). Compared to some of its cousins, puff-puff batter is restrained, usually made without butter, eggs or fruit.

I consulted lots of recipes to help me perfect my puff-puff. There is one in the excellent *Hibiscus*, by Lopè Ariyo, and many on blogs like *Chef Lola's Kitchen*. But in spite of the fact that I am very much a word person (I never choose to watch a video where an article would suffice!), I owe a massive debt of gratitude to the cooking stars of YouTube, on channels such as Sweet Adjeley or Original Mama Betty. It wasn't until I watched their videos that I really understood how thick the batter should be, how to gently turn the doughnuts in their oil and how long to fry them for a perfect, golden crust. If you're in need of extra help, I'd recommend venturing beyond this cookbook and supplementing my recipe with their extra guidance.

Makes: approximately 20 small puff-puff
Ready in: 1 hour 45 minutes, about an hour of
   which is downtime while the dough rises
Make-ahead and storage tips: page 329

Vegan

For the batter:

2 cups (250g) all-purpose flour

2 tablespoons superfine, confectioners'
   or soft light brown sugar

1 teaspoon active dry yeast
   (about ½ of an 8g package)

½ teaspoon salt

Generous pinch of ground nutmeg

scant ½ cup (100ml) water, freshly boiled

scant ⅔ cup (150ml) milk, dairy *or*
   non-dairy

To cook and serve:

6 cups (1.5 liters) sunflower or
   vegetable oil, for deep-frying

4–6 tablespoons confectioners' sugar

Special equipment: candy thermometer
   or instant-read digital thermometer;
   stand mixer with dough hook
   attachment, optional; deep fryer,
   optional

1. In a large mixing bowl, stir together the flour, sugar, yeast, salt and nutmeg. In a separate bowl or jug, combine the hot water with the cold milk. The milk mixture should now be lukewarm: if it isn't, let it cool a few minutes before moving ahead.

2. Have a wooden spoon or a spatula on hand, and start pouring the lukewarm liquid into the dry ingredients, stirring as you go. What you'll be left with is more like a batter than a stiff dough, but don't panic: when it hits the hot oil, this flowing, sticky batter-dough will puff to well over double its original size, cooking to perfect airy lightness.

3. Once combined, beat the loose dough with a spoon or spatula really vigorously while counting to one hundred—this will start to develop the gluten in the dough, helping it to hold the air bubbles that will be so vital for the puff-puff to rise. You could alternatively use a mixer with a dough hook attachment, if all the stirring isn't an option. Once you've done this, cover the bowl with a damp tea towel or plastic wrap and set aside for 45–55 minutes to let the dough rise—it should be very puffy, bubbly and risen.

4. When the dough is nearly ready, start heating the oil. Pour nearly all of it (reserving just a few tablespoons) into a medium, high-sided pot: choose a pot that allows the oil to be at least 2½–3 inches (6–7cm) deep and deep enough that the oil comes no higher than halfway up the sides. If you have a deep fryer, you can of course use this, but you'll need more oil than I've specified above. Heat the oil to a temperature of 310°–320°F

Normal perfect moments

(160°C), using a thermometer to check it as you go (surrendering to the judgment of a thermometer is by far the best way of doing this). This is slightly cooler than the temperature you might usually deep-fry at, but I promise it works: this will create crisp, golden doughnuts that are springy and cooked through.

5. Get out a couple of tablespoons and line a large plate with paper towel. Pour the reserved few tablespoons of oil into a small bowl, jar or mug: you'll use this to grease the spoons as you're spooning out the dough to stop it sticking. Have a slotted spoon or tongs on hand.

6. To fry the dough, first give it a gentle stir, enjoying the moment when it softly deflates. Next do a test puff-puff. Dip your spoons into the small oil bowl (or similar), then scoop a flat tablespoonful of the sticky batter with one spoon and push it into the hot oil with the other. This mound of dough won't be remotely spherical or even right now, but trust that it'll sort itself out in the pot. As the dough hits the oil, it will sink before promptly bobbing back to the surface, sizzling happily and puffing into a ball. If it gets stuck at the bottom of the pot for any more than a few moments, just stir with a long-handled spoon and the puff-puff should dislodge and rise up. Keep the oil as close to a constant 310°–320°F (160°C) as possible and fry the puff-puff for 8–10 minutes, turning often, until it's a deep golden brown all over. If it browns too quickly or deeply, turn the heat down. Once cooked, drain the puff-puff on the paper towel you laid out.

7. If the test puff-puff is good—golden, well-risen and crisp—proceed with the rest of the batter, frying them in batches of 6–8. Don't be tempted to overcrowd the pot, or the oil will cool down and the puff-puff won't cook as they should.

8. When the puff-puff are all cooked and once they've cooled slightly for 4–5 minutes, dust them liberally with the confectioners' sugar and serve. These are absolutely at their best when they're still crisp and warm, and they don't keep too well—you shouldn't have too much trouble getting through a fresh batch.

Variations and substitutions:

If you don't have confectioners' sugar, you can dust these with superfine sugar instead. Add a couple of teaspoons of vanilla extract to the dough if you want.

FRUIT JUMBLE CRUMBLE BARS

My favorite thing to do these days (you tend to redefine excitement as you leave your early twenties and march towards thirty) is something I call "using bits up." Whatever's loitering at the back of the cupboard or the fridge, I find a purpose for it in a makeshift recipe. These crumble bars—an oaty shortbread base, jammy fruit and buttery crumble on top—are perfect for this. They work really well with apples, pears or stone fruit such as apricots, peaches, cherries or plums. Blackberries, blueberries, strawberries or raspberries also work nicely. Bananas are particularly delicious, cooking down to a fudgy, sweet, banoffee pie vibe underneath the crumble.

Makes: 12

Ready in: 1 hour 10 minutes, most of which is hands-off baking time, but you'll want to leave extra time for these to cool before slicing and serving

Make-ahead and storage tips: page 329

Vegetarian   Vegan option

---

10 ounces (300g) prepared fruit (see note above and instructions below)

1¾ cups (200g) all-purpose flour

1 cup (100g) oats

½ cup (100g) soft light brown sugar

½ teaspoon cinnamon

½ teaspoon ground ginger

½ teaspoon ground coriander

¼ teaspoon salt

½ cup plus 1 tablespoon (125g) salted or unsalted butter, melted

⅓ cup (50g) golden raisins or currants, optional

Special equipment: 8 x 8 inch (20 x 20cm) square baking pan or similar or medium roasting pan, roughly 9 x 6 inches (15 x 23cm)

1. Preheat the oven to 350°F (180°C) and line your roasting pan with parchment paper.

2. Next, prepare the fruit. If you're using apples or pears, peel and core them before cutting into ⅜ inch (1cm) cubes. Apricots, peaches and plums can have their skins left on: just remove the pit before dicing. Cherries should be pitted and then halved or quartered. Strawberries, blackberries and raspberries can be left whole if very small, or halved or quartered if

they're a bit chunkier. Blueberries can be tossed on as they are—no need to cut. As for bananas, just peel and cut into slim slices.

3. Mix the flour, oats, sugar, spices and salt in a large bowl. Add the melted butter and stir everything together to create a crumbly mixture. Press two-thirds of the mixture into the lined dish or pan, pressing it down firmly under a spoon or with your hands.

4. Scatter the fruit on top of the base. It's up to you whether you want to jumble the fruit together (if you're using a mix of fruits) or arrange it in "stripes." You can add the raisins or golden raisins if you've got a particularly sweet tooth or if you're using a slightly less sweet kind of fruit. Scatter over the remaining crumble mixture, then bake for 45–50 minutes in the preheated oven. When it's ready, the crumble should be a tawny golden brown on top and smell toasty and sweet. You'll be able to hear the fruit gently singing. It'll be really tender and fragile at first, so leave to cool before cutting into bars.

Variations and substitutions:

To make a vegan version of this recipe, just swap the ½ cup plus 2 tablespoons (140g) butter for ½ cup (120g) coconut oil and 1½ tablespoons of non-dairy milk. You could also just do a straight swap from butter to a vegan butter alternative (not adding the milk) if that's what you have.

The ground coriander adds a sprightly zestiness to the spice mix in these bars, but you can leave it out if you don't happen to have it in the house.

If you don't have soft light brown sugar, you can use superfine sugar, demerara or granulated white sugar in its place. If you use white superfine or granulated sugar, you won't get the same toffee flavor, but the bars will still work well.

For those of you who can't eat gluten, gluten-free flour is a fine replacement for the all-purpose flour. Just make sure you get specially labeled gluten-free oats, as some brands may contain traces of gluten.

PEANUT COOKIE DOUGH BITES

These fudgy, salty–sweet peanut cookie dough bites are perfect if, like me, you often raid the fridge for sweet treats. They can be made with next-to-no effort, and store well in the fridge or freezer for whenever cravings strike.

Because these cookie dough bites are designed to be eaten raw, I've made them without eggs, and you can make them completely vegan. It's also best to pasteurize the flour in order to kill any bugs that might be lying dormant in it. This is pretty unlikely (I've been eating raw cake batter and cookie dough with abandon for years and have never suffered for it), but I'd recommend taking a few extra minutes to carry out this simple step just for your peace of mind. I've outlined a couple of methods for doing this here.

A final note: This cookie dough is especially designed to be eaten as it is—as cookie dough—rather than baked into cookies. It won't bake well at all, so don't waste your time (and peanut butter) trying. If you're after a peanut butter cookie recipe, I can recommend Dan Lepard's recipe, which can be found in his book, *Short and Sweet*.

Makes: roughly 25
Ready in: less than 30 minutes, or as little as 10 minutes
   if you pasteurize the flour in the microwave, but you'll
   need to let them chill for an hour before eating
Make-ahead and storage tips: page 329

Vegan

⅔ cup (75g) all-purpose flour
⅓ cup plus 1 tablespoon (100g) smooth
   peanut butter
⅓ cup (75g) soft light brown sugar
3 tablespoons coconut oil
   or butter, melted
1 tablespoon water

1 teaspoon vanilla extract
¼ cup (30g) salted peanuts, finely
   chopped

Special equipment: candy
   thermometer or instant-read digital
   thermometer, optional

1. To pasteurize the flour in the oven, just preheat the oven to 350°F/180°C, spread the flour out on a baking sheet and bake in the preheated oven for 5 minutes. To pasteurize it in the microwave, place the flour in a microwavable bowl and heat in 15-second bursts on full power, stirring really well in between, until the flour reaches 162°F (72°C) or is hot to the touch, but not toasted. How long this takes will depend on your microwave, so I'd recommend using a thermometer to check this. In my 700W microwave, it took 50 seconds. Don't leave the flour in the microwave unattended!

2. Once the flour's been pasteurized and cooled, making these cookie dough bites is ridiculously straightforward. Just combine all the ingredients in a mixing bowl and mix well until the dough is smooth and no streaks of dry flour are left.

3. Roll the dough into roughly 25 little bites, each about the size of a fat blackberry. They might be slightly crumbly at first, but should come together into fudgy bites as you work them between your palms. Place in the fridge for an hour to firm up slightly, then enjoy.

Variations and substitutions:

Swap the smooth peanut butter for crunchy peanut butter if that's what you've got in the cupboard. You might want to halve the amount of added chopped peanuts if you do this. If you can't eat peanuts, almond butter also works in place of the peanut butter, and chopped toasted almonds work in place of the chopped peanuts.

If you can't eat gluten, you can use a gluten-free flour mix in place of the all-purpose flour.

To make these more special, you can roll them in melted chocolate (7 ounces/200g should be enough for the quantities given). It's really your call: I find dark chocolate, while smugly grown-up, detracts from the peanut flavor a bit, and the gentle sweetness of milk or white chocolate is more to my taste here. If you want to do this, I'd recommend putting the cookie dough bites in the freezer for an hour or so before dipping them in the chocolate, so that the chocolate shell sets almost instantly. It's best to melt chocolate in short bursts in the microwave, stirring often, or in a heatproof bowl set over a pot of simmering water: whatever you do, don't try to heat chocolate with direct heat, like in a saucepan on the stovetop, or it'll burn and become grainy.

SALTED HONEYSCOTCH SAUCE

On ice cream, in between chocolate cake layers, stirred into rice pudding, even spread on toast: this salted honeyscotch—honey butterscotch—is a versatile friend. I like how it can make even the cheapest soft scoop ice cream feel special, making something extraordinary from normal pleasures. Put it into jars and it makes a good present too.

A perk of making a butterscotch with honey, instead of the usual sugar, is that you don't have to stress about caramel and all the countless ways it can go wrong. Honey is already liquid, so you don't have to be an alchemist, transforming crystalline sugar into liquid gold, to make this work. All you need to do is cook the honey for a few minutes to darken it and deepen its flavor, then mix with butter, cream and salt. If you make this with heavy cream, it'll be luxuriously rich. With crème fraîche, it'll have a more sprightly tang. You can easily double the quantities if you want to make a big batch.

Makes: ¾ cup (180ml)
Ready in: 15 minutes
Make-ahead and storage tips: page 329

Vegetarian

---

5 tablespoons (100g) honey (eucalyptus honey works well, but any dark, deeply flavored honey is good)
3 tablespoons salted or unsalted butter
⅓ cup (75ml) heavy cream or crème fraîche
Salt, to taste

1. Heat the honey in a small saucepan over a medium-high heat. Once the honey reaches a steady simmer, set a timer and cook it for roughly 3–4 minutes more, keeping a close eye on it and stirring often. You want it to darken a shade, but this can be difficult to see through all the bubbles. It can help to get out a small piece of parchment paper and to drop tiny drops of the honey on it at points during the cooking. Against the white, you'll be able to see how well your honey has darkened. Ideally, if you started with a reasonably dark, rich honey, you'll be aiming for an amber color. You can also cook it by timer and by nose—after 3–4 minutes, it should smell honeyed and fragrant and toffee-like, but you must whip it off the heat instantly if you smell any burning. Courage is your friend here, though, because the longer you cook the honey (without burning), the darker and richer the honeyscotch sauce will be.

2. When the honey is ready, add the butter and cream or crème fraîche to the hot saucepan and reduce the heat to low. Stir constantly while the butter melts into the sauce. Once the honeyscotch sauce is smooth, add a couple of generous pinches of salt, tasting as you go. A slight salty tang will really bring out the best in this sauce, so don't cut corners here. Serve warm, or pour the sauce into tubs or jars and store in the fridge.

CLEMENTINE HOT CHOCOLATE

This is my friend Leah's idea, and it's a great one. During the wintry cold when clementines are abundant, this is a good way to eke some of the fragrance from their beautiful peels, by infusing them in hot milk and mixing as hot chocolate. Make sure you use fresh, supple peels—not ones that have been sitting on the arm of the sofa all day. As a general rule, if you're not immediately smacked in the face by its fragrance when you scratch it with your nail, then the peel is not at its best and won't give the kick you're after.

Makes: 1 mug
Ready in: 6–8 minutes

Vegan

Peel from 2 clementines
1 cup (250ml) milk, dairy *or* non-dairy
1½ teaspoons cocoa powder
2 teaspoons superfine or granulated sugar

1. First up, I know this sounds weird, but you'll need to scratch the outside of the clementine peels. If you run your nails over the bright orange outer peel, you'll notice the smell of citrus immediately hits your nose—this is because you've unleashed the citrus oils in the peel. So, give the peels a good scratch, put them in a large mug and pour in 1 cup (250ml) milk. Heat the peel and milk in the microwave for as long as it takes for the milk to almost reach boiling point—this could take between 1 and 2 minutes depending on the strength of your microwave, but keep checking regularly to avoid the milk boiling over. Once the milk is just shy of a boil, remove from the microwave and let steep with the clementine peel for 5 minutes.

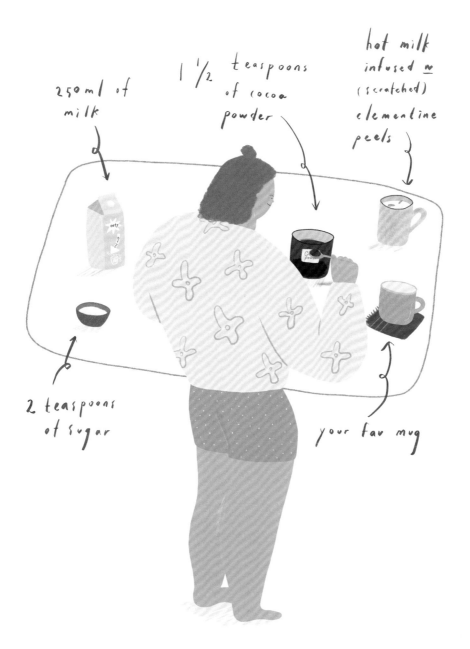

250 ml of
milk

1 1/2 teaspoons
of cocoa
powder

hot milk
infused ⌣
(scratched)
clementine
peels

2 teaspoons
of sugar

your fav mug

2. In a separate mug (you might as well pick out your favorite one), stir together the cocoa powder with the superfine or granulated sugar. Once the milk has infused with citrus scent, remove the clementine peel and pour the hot milk very slowly into the cocoa mixture, stirring all the time so that the cocoa first creates a thick paste, then a looser slurry, before easing into a velvety drinking chocolate. Blast for a few more seconds in the microwave if you want it piping hot. Enjoy straightaway.

FIERY GINGER CORDIAL

In the UK, we drink a lot of squash: fruit-flavored syrups, just like cordial, that we dilute with water. Maybe it speaks to the infantilization of our nation that we seem unable to drink water as water, but need the sweet hit of summer berry, or tropical fruit, or strawberry to help it go down. But maybe squash is just delicious. There are so many ways to squash. There's standard squash of course: a cup of blackcurrant-, orange- or summer fruit–flavored syrup diluted with tap water and, if you're after authenticity, served lukewarm in a musty community hall. You can also enjoy posh squash, which is exactly the same but with ice—perfect for drinking in the luxury of a steaming summer afternoon. Fizzy squash can be made with ice-cold carbonated water: when you do this, you can pass off Ribena as "sparkling blackcurrant cordial" at a dinner party and nobody will be any the wiser. And then of course there's homemade squash, which isn't something most of us ordinarily bother to make but which, if you do make it, will illuminate you with a wholesome domestic glow. When I make this fiery ginger cordial, I feel like someone who has a country kitchen and a pantry full of elderflower cordial, rhubarb syrup and sloe gin in glistening jewel colors, and not like someone sitting in a flat above a busy London bus stop. We all need to dream sometimes.

Makes: roughly 1½ cups (350ml)
Ready in: 35 minutes, but you'll need to then
   let the syrup cool before using
Make-ahead and storage tips: page 329

Vegan

3½-ounce (100g) piece of ginger
1 medium apple (roughly
   3½ ounces/100g), such as
   Granny Smith
¾ cup (175ml) water
6 tablespoons (75g) superfine or
   granulated sugar

6 tablespoons (75g) soft light brown
   sugar
3–4 tablespoons lemon juice (from
   roughly 1½ lemons)

To serve:
Sparkling water, well chilled

1. Peel and coarsely grate the ginger and place in a small saucepan. Grate the apple, skin and all, and add to the pan. Add the water, sugars and lemon juice.

2. Set the pan over medium heat and bring to a gentle simmer, then turn down the heat and cook over a low heat for 10 minutes. Take the pan off the heat and leave the fiery ginger syrup to steep for 10–15 minutes. Don't forget about it at this stage: if you leave it for too long, the syrup may start to taste grassy.

3. Strain the syrup through a mesh sieve, collecting the syrup in a jug or bowl. Make sure you squeeze as much liquid out of the apple and ginger as possible.

4. Decant the strained syrup into a mason jar or an airtight container and leave it to cool. When you're ready to drink this, dilute it in very cold sparkling water: 1 part cordial to 3 or 4 parts water seems about right, but I'll leave it to you to adjust the ratio depending on how sweet you like these things. Add ice cubes if you want.

Variations and substitutions:

I like the bright acidity of the Granny Smith apple here, but you can use a sweeter apple instead if that's what you've got.

This can be made with all soft light brown sugar instead of the 50:50 brown and white sugar mix. I wouldn't make it with just superfine or granulated sugar though, as the brown sugar adds a necessary caramel note.

Normal perfect moments

For the love of it

RECIPES TO LINGER OVER

Recipe list

Introduction

Most of the time we cook our way logistically towards an end point: the moment when the food passes our lips, settles in our stomach and finally fills us up. When we cook this way, the cooking itself is a means to an end, something to be endured but not necessarily enjoyed. And yet sometimes—on a long, lazy weekend, or if the kids have gone to Grandma's for the day—an opportunity arises for us to see cooking in a different light. The recipes in this final chapter are ones that center on the pleasure of cooking for cooking's sake. Meditatively chopping vegetables for a jewel-like salad, you'll notice details about smell, taste and texture that you might ordinarily miss. Making pesto from scratch is a feast for the senses, while making flaky roti canai is a soothingly tactile project for after a stressful week. Even when the recipes here are quick, they're designed to be enjoyed slowly, giving you a chance to anchor yourself—mind and body—in the fabric of your own life.

Further reading

How to Eat Your Feelings by Holly Haines

Fresh India by Meera Sodha

Salt, Fat, Acid, Heat by Samin Nosrat

Fresh From Poland by Michał Korkosz

Mamushka by Olia Hercules

Heart & Parcel Cookbook by Heart & Parcel

Flavor by Yotam Ottolenghi and Ixta Belfrage

Summer's Lease by Thom Eagle

Amazing Malaysian by Norman Musa

Malaysia by Ping Coombes

Brilliant Bread by James Morton

New World Sourdough by Bryan Ford

The Bread Book by Linda Collister

English Bread and Yeast Cookery by Elizabeth David

Rosetta by Elena Reygadas

7000 Islands by Yasmin Newman

The River Cottage Preserves Handbook by Pam Corbin

For the love of it

JEWEL SALAD

A lot of the recipes in this chapter are for "project foods"—the kind of recipe that you might learn a new technique from, or be able to spread over the course of an afternoon. This one is slightly different. This bright, crunchy salad—with so many tiny, jewel-colored cubes of veg—is something I enjoy making in moments when I need something that will keep my hands and mind busy. In her brilliant cookbook, *How to Eat Your Feelings*, Holly Haines divides recipes up by the kind of mood they're good for. Like pairing food with wine, Holly suggests fiddly tasks like making dumplings for when you're anxious, or slow, absorbing recipes like honey pandesal (a kind of Filipino bread) for when you're bored. Using a similar logic, I'd recommend this salad for whenever you want a task that will take you away from whatever slump you're in and into a more mindful space. The careful ordering of tasks, the attention to detail and the hand–eye coordination you'll need when chopping will all go some way towards planting you firmly back in your body with your senses. By the time it comes to eating this salad, you should be feeling reasonably relaxed, grounded and ready to tuck in with your whole appetite.

How many people this serves will depend on whether you're having it as a meal in its own right or as a side dish. I love this by itself, but I imagine it'd also be good with toasted pita, grilled meats or pretty much anything hot, starchy, salty or spicy. You could pair it with the **fries with chaat masala, pickled onions and pomegranate** on page 23 or the **roasted okra, green beans and paneer with green chutney and lime** on page 71.

Amchur, a South Asian ingredient, is basically dried, ground green mango, and it looks like a very pale, peachy colored powder. It's fruity and tongue-tinglingly sour, and perfect for whenever you want to give a salad dressing, curry or sauce a bit of tang without adding extra liquid. I use it here to add a fruity vibrancy to the salad, but it's optional, so don't sweat it if you don't have any. You can find it in Indian grocery stores and in some larger supermarkets.

Serves: 4–6
Ready in: less than 1 hour, but this is a recipe to take your time over
Make-ahead and storage tips: page 329

Vegan

---

7 ounces (200g) radishes
4 small or medium carrots
½ medium cucumber
3 peppers (I like to use 1 red, 1 yellow and 1 green)

For the dressing:
½ cup (125ml) yogurt, dairy *or* non-dairy
2 tablespoons lemon juice (from roughly 1 lemon)
1 tablespoon extra-virgin olive oil
1 teaspoon nigella seeds (also sold as black onion or kalonji seeds)
1 teaspoon amchur, optional
½–1 teaspoon chili flakes, to taste
Salt, to taste

1. Unless you're rushing to get this ready for a family picnic or something, I'd really recommend getting everything set up nicely for this recipe so that you can get stuck in as mindfully and as relaxed as possible. If you haven't already done so, start off by washing all the veg in plenty of cold water, paying attention to the weight, texture and color of the veg as you go, if you're in the mood. It's funny how much you notice when you actually use the full force of your attention like this: I hadn't realized till I started making this salad just how vividly pink radishes are, or noticed the pleasing knobbliness of carrots. If your carrots are anything other than the youngest, thinnest-skinned carrots imaginable, I'd recommend peeling them as well.

2. Organize the washed (and peeled) veg on a spacious work surface or table and pull up a chair or stool if you want to be comfortable as you do this. Working slowly and with care and pride, you're going to start off by trimming the veg: trim the roots and tops from the radishes, cut the tops and bottoms off the carrots, trim the end off the cucumber, cut out the seeds and stalks of the peppers. Then start cutting all of the veg into cubes no bigger than ⅜ inch (1cm) across. This takes a little while and it's fiddly work, but if you have the mobility in your hands and decent enough knife skills, it's a task you can really sink into. Just take your time, put on the radio if you want and spend a few minutes of your day immersed in this quiet, precise job. As you cut the veg, jumble it up in a big mixing or salad bowl.

3. Once the veg is all prepped, you can prepare the dressing: mix the yogurt, lemon juice, oil, nigella seeds, amchur (if using), chili flakes and salt, to taste. Remember this dressing needs to season all that veg, so it's not a problem if it's slightly over-salted. If you're eating the salad straightaway, toss the jewel-like vegetables with the dressing and serve. Otherwise, store the dressing separately until you're ready to toss and serve the salad.

Variations and substitutions:

This recipe really can be adapted any which way: just be sensible about the fruit and veg you choose. Something like avocado or apple will discolor quickly, so needs to be chopped and mixed as near to the serving time as possible. Meera Sodha has an excellent recipe for Hill Station Salad in *Fresh India*, which includes chopped fennel, chili and mint. Other options include celery, zucchini, red onion and pomegranate seeds.

BASIL AND EGUSI PESTO

It's always humbling when, after 8 hours spent testing complex, time-consuming recipes, all I can face eating is pesto pasta. Talking about this nursery food, food writer Laurie Colwin puts it like this: "A long time ago it occurred to me that when people are tired and hungry, which in adult life is much of the time, they do not want to be confronted by an intellectually challenging meal: they want to be consoled."

If you want to meet your hunger halfway, an easy pesto recipe is a fair bet. Although it only takes 10 minutes to pull together, I've put it in this chapter of the book because it's something that flies beyond the mere call of duty. If you wanted a truly no-hassle dinner, you'd just buy a jar of pesto from the corner store, so this recipe offers you familiar comfort while also giving you a chance to try something new. It's a pleasure, too, when the smell of basil and garlic fill the kitchen, and a chance to see humble egusi in a new light.

Egusi are little gourd seeds popular in West African cooking: they have a light nutty flavor and collapse into perfect creaminess when ground or blended, making them ideal for a homemade pesto. You can find them in West African grocery stores, if you don't already have a bag in the cupboard. Egusi can be pricey, but then so are pesto's traditional pine nuts, so it's really a case of what you have on hand and what your cultural reference points are. This recipe also works with pine nuts (of course) or walnuts or almonds.

Makes: about ½ pound/250g (serves 4 with pasta)
Ready in: 20–30 minutes, depending on whether you
  use a food processor or mortar and pestle
Make-ahead and storage tips: page 329

Vegetarian

½ cup (50g) egusi (pine nuts, walnuts
  or almonds will also work)
¾ cup (2 ounces/75g) grated Parmesan
  or vegetarian alternative
2 garlic cloves
2 cups (60g) fresh basil, stalks
  discarded
6 tablespoons (90ml) extra-virgin
  olive oil
1 tablespoon water, plus extra if needed
Salt, to taste

To serve: pasta (enough for 4 people);
  a squeeze of lemon juice, optional;
  alternatively, you could use this
  in the **one-pan smashed potatoes**
  with lemony sardines and pesto
  on page 110

Special equipment: food processor
  or mortar and pestle

For the love of it

1. Start by toasting the egusi (or whatever you're using) in a small frying pan over a medium-low heat; keep a close eye on them as they heat and begin to lightly brown, stirring them often. Once they're fragrant and gently toasted (the egusi will start to pop!), turn off the heat and tip them from the pan—it's important that they don't burn, or they'll become bitter. Pound the seeds or nuts until they're fine and rubbly using a mortar and pestle or pulse them in a food processor until they're coarsely crumbled. Set aside.

2. Very finely grate the Parmesan (or alternative vegetarian hard cheese). Finely grate or crush the garlic cloves. Set both to one side while you prepare the spiritual heart of this pesto: the basil.

3. Roughly chop the basil leaves. The traditional next step would be to pound the leaves with a little oil with a mortar and pestle, until they're pulpy and the oil is bright green. You're welcome to do it this way if you want, but it takes a lot of elbow grease. Instead, I've borrowed the method Samin Nosrat uses in her very helpful *Salt, Fat, Acid, Heat*: in a food processor blend the chopped basil leaves with most of the oil until you have an emerald green, highly fragrant, soupy mixture. There will still be small pieces of basil in the mix, and that's ideal: if you process the mixture for too long, the leaves will oxidize and lose their verdant luster.

4. Add the egusi, Parmesan, garlic and water to the food processor and pulse briefly to combine everything. Once combined, add a splash more water or oil to slacken the pesto, if you want to. Taste it now: if it needs a touch of salt, this is your chance.

TWARÓG
From-scratch farmer's cheese

This Polish farmer's cheese, known as twaróg or ser biały, is liberally adapted from a recipe in Michał Korkosz's excellent *Fresh From Poland*. It's a soft, exceptionally easy cottage cheese—not the kind of cheese that needs months in an Alpine cellar to mature, or for the westerly wind to blow across a harvest moon while the cows lactate. It's simple and it's delicious, especially because Michał cleverly suggests adding heavy cream to soften the cheese, enrich it and balance out the buttermilk's sourness.

I've suggested making a large batch because, frankly, if you're going to make homemade cheese then you might as well really make homemade cheese. Plus there are loads of ways that you can use this cheese once made, as described further along in the method. In a beautiful twist of fate, both the cheese and the leftover whey from the cheesemaking process can be used for the **pierogi ruskie**—dumplings with farmer's cheese, potato and caramelized onion—on page 275. The pierogi use the cheese in the filling, and the whey enriches the pierogi dough.

The instructions will look long at first glance, but the method is really simple: I've just given lots of background info, prompts and explanatory notes so that you can really immerse yourself in the process and in the sights, smells and tastes as you go along, and as the milk and thick cream transform.

Makes: 1¾ pounds/800g
Ready in: 2 hours 30 minutes, nearly all of which is quiet time while the milk sits and the curds form and drain
Make-ahead and storage tips: page 330

Vegetarian

---

5 cups (1.2 liters) whole milk
1¼ cups (300ml) heavy cream
2½ cups (600ml) buttermilk
Salt, to taste

Special equipment:
cheesecloth, or (brand-new!) tights

For the love of it

1. Heat the milk and cream in a large pot over a medium-low heat. I know what they say about a watched pot never boiling, but I love this stage: seeing the thick, yellowish cream marble with the bright white milk, and the whole mix come to life as it heats. Once the mixture is really steaming—shimmying and shivering at the surface and just about to boil—turn off the heat. If you have an electric stove where the burner stays warm for a while after you've turned it off, make sure you move the pot away from the heat.

2. Pour the buttermilk into the hot milk and cream mixture, stirring very gently. The acidic buttermilk will have an amazing effect on the luscious, creamy mixture: you should see the liquid begin to curdle almost instantly, with the milk proteins seizing up into bouncy little curds and swimming around in the pale yellow, misty whey. (Given enough time, milk can actually do this by itself. If you were to leave milk to sour at a warm temperature, it would naturally curdle as bacteria in the milk eat the natural sugars—the lactose—and create lactic acid as a by-product. This acid, just like the ready-soured buttermilk we're using in this recipe, causes the milk proteins to bundle up together in clumps.) As soon as the buttermilk is gently mixed in, stop messing around with the mixture. Cover the pot with a lid or aluminum foil and leave to sit at room temperature for an hour.

3. Once the hour is up, take a peek at the pot. The curds should be clearly visible amid the sea of translucent whey. Get out a large bowl or pot and set a sieve or colander over it, making sure there's plenty of room underneath the sieve or colander so that it doesn't end up sitting in the whey as it drains. Line the sieve or colander with cheesecloth or even cut-up tights. You want a material that's porous enough to let the whey drain through (if you're using cleaning cloths or tights, make sure they're brand-new and clean). Pour the curds into your cloth-lined sieve or colander, and notice as the whey starts to slowly trickle through, collecting in the pan or bowl below. Fold the cloth gently over the top of the curds so they don't dry out, then move the whole curd-sieve-bowl setup to the fridge. Leave to drain in the fridge for 1 hour. During this time, a lot of the whey will drain out, and the curds will be left behind in the cloth. Because this recipe uses heavy cream, the curds will be particularly rich and tender, and not too sour.

4. After the cheese has drained, remove it from the fridge and have a look at the texture. It should be slightly drier than ricotta, but still moist rather than dry and crumbly. If you used a cloth with a slightly tighter knit to

line your sieve or colander, gravity alone might not have been able to draw out enough of the whey. If the mixture is particularly soupy, gather up the cloth and gently squeeze the bundle to wring out some more of the liquid. Bear in mind that as the cheese continues to chill it will become firmer, so don't overdo this—it shouldn't be bone dry.

5. Once you're happy with the consistency of your cheese curds, you should pour the whey into a jug or tub and save it for later use. It's great in place of water or milk in bread dough (see the **rosemary baby buns** recipe on page 296), instead of water or stock in soups (see the **carrot, lemon and tahini soup** on page 25), or in smoothies and oatmeal. It's also great in the dough for the **pierogi ruskie** that follows.

6. Now, on to your finished cheese. The curds can be transferred to an airtight container and salted, if you wish. I tend to leave the cheese unsalted, as I usually cook with it and add salt later. But if you plan to eat it as a spread for bread or toast, or as an accompaniment to vegetable sticks, just sprinkle with 1 teaspoon of salt and gently mix in, then leave overnight for the salt to disperse and to evenly season the cheese. To cook with this cheese, have a go at the **pierogi ruskie** in the following recipe. You can also use your twaróg in place of ricotta in pasta sauces, lasagna and so on, like in the **harissa, spinach and ricotta cannelloni with toasted hazelnuts** on page 180.

PIEROGI RUSKIE

Dumplings with farmer's cheese, potato and caramelized onion

These beautiful Polish potato dumplings are a lot of work: I can't downplay that. But the pay-off—hearty, tender, cheesy, double-carbed, buttery little parcels—is so worth your time. Rather than getting hung up on getting from A to B really quickly, I think it pays to see this recipe as a wonderful process in itself. During the course of this recipe, you'll get to see dough as it transforms itself from a tough, resistant little mass to a silky, stretchy sheet. You'll have a chance to either be meditative, as you fill and seal countless little dumplings, or to throw yourself into social collaboration, making the pierogi with friends or family while you chat. You'll also have

For the love of it

the peculiar satisfaction of wrapping one carb in another, like a Russian doll of edible treasures, hearty enough to see you through even the most bitter winter. Set aside an afternoon and really enjoy the process. I promise it's almost (almost) as fun as eating the finished thing.

In case you're not familiar with pierogi, they're semi-circular dumplings, with a filling encased in a dough similar to an eggless pasta dough. There are such numerous and thriving Polish populations in the UK and in the US that it's ridiculous that pierogi are less known than the Italian ravioli or tortellini to which they bear a passing resemblance. If you want to learn more about Polish cooking—particularly Polish vegetarian cooking—I really recommend Michał Korkosz's *Fresh From Poland*. If you want to diversify your dumpling repertoire, *Mamushka* by Olia Hercules is great, as is *Heart & Parcel Cookbook*.

The quantities below make a large number of pierogi, because I figure that if you're gonna spend most of an afternoon working on a recipe, you might as well make a decent amount. You can freeze the pierogi before cooking, meaning you can save any you don't want to eat immediately for another day.

Finally, a note about twaróg: This is a soft, grainy white farmer's cheese, also known as ser biały. It's creamy and fatty and beautiful. I like it a lot. I've included a recipe on page 273 for how to make your own twaróg from scratch, so do check it out. You can also get it in larger supermarkets or in Polish stores and delis, though. Look in the dairy aisle, often in a triangular(ish) pack. Check the variations and substitutions below if you can't get hold of it.

For a vegan pierogi filling variation check out the recipe after this one, for sauerkraut, potato and black pepper pierogi filling.

Makes: 50–60 (serves 6)

Ready in: about 4 hours if you do everything together. You can
split up the stages though to spread this over a day or two:
the filling takes about 45 minutes to prepare and 2 hours to
cool and chill; the dough takes 10 minutes and then needs
to rest for an hour; filling the pierogi will take about an hour;
cooking the pierogi will take just 15 minutes or so.

Make-ahead and storage tips: page 330

Vegetarian

For the filling:

Salt, to taste

1⅔ pounds (750g) russet potatoes,
peeled and cut into ¾ inch (2cm)-thick
slices

3 tablespoons salted or unsalted butter

3 large (or 4 small-to-medium) onions,
finely diced

14 ounces (400g) twaróg (for a from-
scratch version, see page 273), also
sold as ser biały

Lots of freshly ground black pepper

For the dough:

4 cups (500g) all-purpose flour, plus extra
for dusting

½ teaspoon salt

¼ cup (60ml) olive oil

scant 1 cup (220ml) water (if you made
the twaróg for the filling from scratch,
use the leftover whey in place of the
water here)

To serve: 2 tablespoons salted
or unsalted butter

Caramelized onions, reserved
from the filling mixture

⅔ cup (160ml) sour cream

Special equipment: a pastry cutter,
mug or glass measuring 3–3¼ inches
(7.5–8cm) in diameter, optional

Making the filling:

1. Start off by preparing the filling, as it needs to be fridge-cold before you
   can fill the dumplings. Fill a large, deep pot with cold water, add plenty
   of salt, then add the potato slices. Bring to a simmer over a high heat,
   then cook for 13–15 minutes once the water is vigorously bubbling—the
   potatoes are ready when tender and when they can be pierced easily with
   a fork. Drain the potatoes well in a sieve or colander, then tip either back
   into the pot (if you want to save yourself an extra piece of washing-up)
   or into a large mixing bowl. Mash the potatoes until completely smooth.

2. If you don't mind multitasking, you can start this step while the potatoes
   are still cooking. If not, wait until you've mashed the potatoes to move
   on. Heat the butter in a large frying pan over a medium heat. Add the
   diced onions and a pinch of salt. Cook for roughly 20 minutes, stirring
   often. The onions are ready when they're translucent, softened and a
   caramel color.

For the love of it

3. Add three-quarters of the cooked onions to the mashed potato, reserving the rest to serve with the pierogi later. Add the twaróg to the mixture, stir really well to combine—the mash will be flecked with the palest specks of curd—and add lots of freshly ground black pepper and salt, to taste. Leave to cool to room temperature, then place in the fridge to chill for at least an hour.

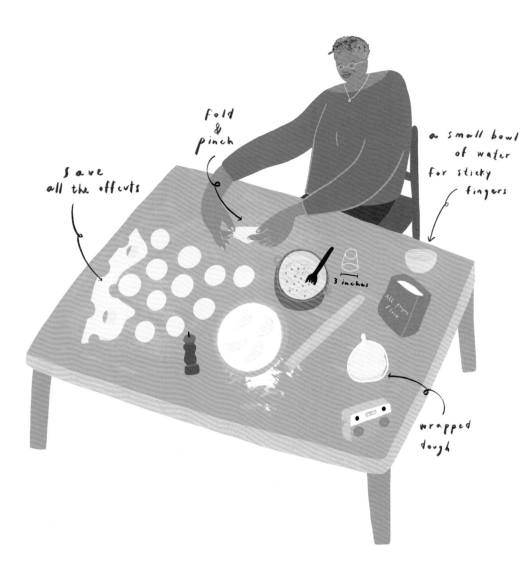

fold
&
pinch

a small bowl
of water
for sticky
fingers

save
all the offcuts

3 inches

ALL Purpose
Flour

wrapped
dough

Making the dough:

While the filling mixture cools and chills, prepare the dough: Combine the flour and salt in a large mixing bowl. Add the olive oil and water (if you made your own twaróg, you can use the leftover whey here instead), then use your hands to bring everything together to a rough, shaggy dough. Tip the dough onto a clean work surface, and lightly knead for just 2–3 minutes, until smooth. (You can find instructions for kneading on page 298, but beware that pierogi dough is much drier than a yeasted bread dough, so won't stretch very much during kneading!) Wrap the kneaded dough in plastic wrap or place in a bowl covered with a damp tea towel. Leave to rest for at least an hour—during this time, the tight, unyielding ball of dough will relax, loosen and become unrecognizably stretchy. If you rush this stage, you'll have a really hard time rolling out the dough!

Filling the pierogi:

1. Before you get started here, I'd recommend getting all your equipment set out. This is messy business and you don't wanna be digging through the cupboards with floury fingers. You'll need: a couple of baking sheets, each dusted lightly with flour; a rolling pin; a small glass or bowl of water; a ruler; a pastry cutter, mug or glass that measures 3–3¼ inches (7.5–8cm) in diameter across its mouth; a measuring tablespoon and some flour, for dusting. You'll also need to get out your dough and your chilled filling, obviously. I'd also recommend putting the radio on or, if you're lucky enough to have helpers around, pulling a few chairs around so you can work and chat together. It took me just over an hour to roll, fill and seal a batch of 50 pierogi, but I am very much an amateur, so if you have a) helpers and/or b) experience growing up making and eating pierogi, you'll likely be quicker than me!

2. Divide the dough into four portions. Rewrap or cover three of the portions to prevent them from drying out (this is really important). Roll out the quarter of the dough that you're working with on a lightly floured work surface to a square measuring roughly 10–11 inches (26–27cm) along each side (I've tested this out, and these dimensions will mean the dough is thin enough to delicately encase the filling, but not so thin that it'll rip). If you find the dough is sticking to the rolling pin or the work surface, you can add a tiny bit more flour, but I'd recommend keeping this to a minimum—otherwise it's hard to seal the pierogi.

3. Using your pastry cutter, glass or mug, stamp out as many rounds of dough as you can. Gather up the offcuts into a ball, wrap with plastic wrap or cover with a damp tea towel and set to one side. Place a level measuring tablespoon of the chilled potato filling into the middle of each of the circles you've stamped out, leaving a perimeter of fillingless dough around the edge of the circle. (A level measuring tablespoon is about as much as a generously heaped normal teaspoon—the kind you use to stir your tea—if you find that easier.) Once you've added a mound of filling to each circle, it's time to fold and seal the pierogi.

4. Take one potato-heaped circle of dough in one hand, cradling it between your thumb and fingers so that the dough scoops around the filling like a taco. Using a finger on your other hand, gently pat down the filling at the center so that it's smooshed deep into the middle of the "taco" parcel. Next, using the thumb and index finger of your free hand, pinch the two edges of the dough circle together at the fattest point, so that you're left with a bulging, semicircular dumpling. Now work outwards around the edge of the semicircle first towards one corner, then towards the other, until the filling is completely sealed in. Make sure that you gently press out any air as you go. If you're having trouble getting the dough to stick to itself, dip a finger in the water you set aside in a glass or bowl, and use this to very lightly dampen the edges before you start pinching them together. It's vital that you seal the dumplings well, so take your time here. If you find a different method works for you, that's absolutely fine. The end result you're aiming for is a fat, semicircular dumpling, well sealed at the edges. However you get there is fine by me.

5. Once each dumpling is filled and sealed, place on one of the trays you've floured and set aside. Don't let the pierogi touch each other, or they'll stick.

6. Continue this process, working through each quarter of the dough in turn. Once you've done that, gather up all the reserved offcuts, reroll to the same thickness and make as many more pierogi as you can. At this point you can freeze the pierogi if you want—see the instructions on page 330. If you're planning to cook the dumplings later the day you make them or the next day, place them in the fridge on their trays, lightly dusted with flour and covered with plastic wrap or a tea towel. Or, if you're ready to cook them straightaway, let's go.

Cooking the pierogi:

1. If you're cooking all 50 or so pierogi in one go, I'd suggest doing so in a few batches, and keeping the cooked pierogi warm on a well-greased baking sheet in an oven preheated to 325°F (160°C). If you're just cooking a couple of portions of pierogi, no need to worry about this.

2. Bring a large, deep pot of salted water to a boil (use the largest pot you have so that the pierogi have plenty of space to cook). Set a frying pan over a low heat and add the 2 tablespoons butter to serve, as well as the caramelized onions reserved from the filling mixture—the aim is just to keep these warm, so turn off the heat if they start to darken or dry out.

3. Add the pierogi to the boiling water in batches—I'd recommend cooking no more than 16 at a time, if you have a really big pot, or fewer if your pot is smaller. Keep the water at a lively simmer. Once the first pierogi rise to the surface, cook for a further 2 minutes (or 3 minutes if you've chilled your pierogi beforehand), then remove from the water using a slotted spoon. Place either on the greased baking sheet (if you need to keep them warm while cooking extra batches) or straight onto people's plates.

4. When you're ready to serve the pierogi, drizzle with some of the melted butter and caramelized onions, and place a hearty dollop of sour cream on each plate as well.

Another cooking option—fried pierogi:

You can also lightly fry the boiled pierogi if you want some browning and a slightly crisped exterior. Once they've boiled, just slip them straight into the frying pan with the melted butter and onions and fry over a medium-low heat for a couple of minutes, stirring gently to coat them with the buttery onions. They should be browned and crisped on one side. Serve as above, with a dollop of sour cream.

Variations and substitutions:

If you can't get hold of or make twaróg, you can use cottage cheese, quark or even ricotta (drained of a little of its liquid) as substitutes.

SAUERKRAUT, POTATO AND BLACK PEPPER PIEROGI FILLING

This is an easy vegan, but still Polish-inspired, variation on the previous pierogi recipe, using sauerkraut to add depth of flavor to a smooth potato and black pepper filling. Just make the filling using the recipe below, then refer back to the previous recipe to see how to make the dough and how to fill and cook the pierogi.

Makes: enough to fill 50–60 pierogi (serves 6)
Ready in: less than 1 hour 30 minutes, of which an
   hour is hands-off time while the mixture cools
Make-ahead and storage tips: page 330

Vegan

Salt, to taste
1⅔ pounds (750g) russet potatoes, peeled and cut
   into ¾ inch (2cm)-thick slices
3 tablespoons olive oil
3 medium onions, finely diced
1¾ cups (400g) sauerkraut, rinsed and drained
Lots of freshly ground black pepper
1 batch pierogi dough, see page 275

Serve with: sour cream (dairy *or* non-dairy), optional

1. Fill a large, deep pot with cold water, add plenty of salt and add the potato slices. Bring to a simmer over a high heat, then cook for 13–15 minutes, or until the potatoes are tender and can be pierced easily with a fork. Drain the potatoes well in a sieve or colander, then tip either back into the pan (if you want to save yourself an extra piece of washing-up) or into a large mixing bowl. Mash the potatoes until completely smooth.

2. If you don't mind multitasking, you can start this step while the potatoes are still cooking. If not, wait until you've mashed the potatoes to move on. Heat the olive oil in a large frying pan over a medium heat. Add the diced onions and the rinsed and drained sauerkraut (rinsing will decrease the saltiness). Cook for roughly 15 minutes over a medium heat, stirring often, until the onions are softened.

3. Add two-thirds of the cooked onions and sauerkraut mixture (save the rest for serving) to the mashed potato, mix well and add lots of black pepper. Check the seasoning, and add salt to taste. Leave to cool to room temperature then place in the fridge to chill for at least an hour.

4. Make the pierogi dough and fill and cook the pierogi following the instructions on pages 279–81 (if you want the dough to be vegan, do not use whey). Serve with the reserved fried onions and sauerkraut, and some (vegan) sour cream if you fancy it.

> ### Variations and substitutions:
>
> As it stands, this is a vegan recipe, but if you're not vegan you can add 1 cup (100g) grated Cheddar to the mashed potato mixture. You can also cook the onions and sauerkraut in butter instead of the olive oil.

HEARTY LENTIL RAGÙ

When you make a vegetarian or vegan ragù—this one is based *very* loosely on an Italian ragù alla bolognese—it's worth taking extra time to layer and deepen the flavors of the vegetables and seasonings you use. There's an ultimate traybake ragù in Yotam Ottolenghi and Ixta Belfrage's book, *Flavor*, which provided the inspiration for this recipe. It's slowly cooked in the oven, enriching the sauce as well as giving you more time away from the stove to get on with life. It takes a while, but it's a beautiful testament to the power of heat and time.

I've adapted the vegetables and flavorings here to suit my own tastes, but that should only serve as encouragement for you to tweak this recipe to make it work for you. If you want a stovetop version, check the end of the recipe: it's more hands on but slightly quicker.

Serves: 4–6

Ready in: 2 hours, only 15 minutes of which are active prep time, or 1 hour if cooked on the stovetop

Make-ahead and storage tips: page 330

Vegan

---

1 medium onion, finely diced

1 medium or large carrot, finely diced

1 celery stick, finely diced

4 garlic cloves, crushed or finely grated

2 bay leaves

2 tablespoons olive oil

1 teaspoon dried thyme or oregano

1½ teaspoons paprika

½ teaspoon fennel seeds

1¼ cups (250g) cooked French, beluga or green lentils

½ cup (125ml) water

½ cup (125ml) whole milk or coconut milk

5 tablespoons (75ml) red wine

1 x 14 ounce (400g) can chopped tomatoes

2 tablespoons white miso

Salt, to taste

Serve with: pasta (use roughly 3½ ounces/100g dry pasta per person)

1. Start by preheating your oven to 450°F (220°C). Combine the vegetables, bay leaves, oil, thyme or oregano, paprika and fennel seeds in a medium casserole dish or roasting pan—roughly 8 x 8 inches (20 x 20cm) should be about right. Place in the preheated oven for 30 minutes to soften the veg.

2. Once the veg is slightly softened, add the lentils, water, milk or coconut milk, red wine, chopped tomatoes and miso to the oven dish, and stir well. Reduce the oven temperature to 400°F (200°C). Cover the dish or pan with a tight lid, aluminum foil or a suitably sized baking sheet and bake for a further 45 minutes.

3. By now, the ragù should be flavorful and the vegetables tender, but it'll be slightly too wet. To reduce the sauce, you now need to remove the aluminum foil (or oven tray) lid and cook the ragù for a further 30 minutes uncovered. Check the seasoning and add salt to taste, then serve with pasta or put in a lasagna.

A stovetop version:

To make this on the stovetop, prepare the veg as outlined prior, then get out a large, deep saucepan. Heat the oil in the pan, then add the veg and sweat over a medium heat for 10 minutes, stirring often. Add the garlic, bay, thyme or oregano, paprika and fennel seeds, and cook for a further 2–3 minutes, until the garlic is fragrant. Add the lentils, water, milk or coconut milk, chopped tomatoes and miso, stir well, then bring to a simmer. Once bubbling, lower the heat and cook very slowly for 45–50 minutes, stirring regularly. You may want to adjust the temperature or add a splash more water if it's drying out. Season to taste once the cooking time is nearly up.

Variations and substitutions:

You can make this with dried lentils if that's what you've got. Add ½–⅔ cup (100–125g) dried green or brown lentils to the dish as outlined in the main recipe, but increase the amount of water from ½ cup (125ml) to 1½–1¾ cups (350–450ml) (start with 1½ cups/350ml and add more if the ragù looks too dry). Alternatively, just precook the lentils according to the instructions on the package, then add to the ragù exactly as specified in the recipe.

Instead of the fennel seeds, you could use cumin seeds or just leave them out altogether—I like the aniseed flavor the fennel seeds add though. I'm pretty sure I have my school friend Emily to thank for this idea.

If you have any celery root—maybe left over from the **yaji-spiced celery root with garlic greens and bulgur wheat** on page 120—you can use this instead of the celery. Finely dice ¾ cup (100g) or so of it.

SLOW-SIMMERED HERBY LIMA BEANS

The tempo of cooking—the mood of the recipe, and the rhythms we fall into when making it—is something we don't pay enough attention to. Too often, I'll feel a familiar tension set around my jaw or my shoulders while cooking, my brain will start to skip wildly around the recipe instructions and I start to feel harried. This is the point at which I realize I've been rushing for no good reason, hurtling through the recipe steps and losing all pleasure in the process. Fast cooking can be a lifesaver day to day, but it doesn't always need to be this way.

These Italian-ish beans are to be cooked adagio, slowly and steadily. You'll combine the beans with herbs, garlic and water, then cook gently for about 1½ hours, until the beans are perfectly tender and swimming in a garlicky pool of broth. You'll have to pay attention to the beans as they cook—they may need a splash more water as all that steam rises in a tall plume from the pan—but this is the entire point. Of course, you could just buy canned, precooked beans, saving you time and effort, but that's not really the point here: this is a calm kind of cooking, letting the kitchen windows fog up while you tend to a slow, simple dinner.

Serves: 4 as a main with bread, or 8 as a side dish
Ready in: 1 hour 30 minutes (you'll need to be present
to tend to the beans as they cook)
Make-ahead and storage tips: page 330

Vegan

---

2 cups (400g) dried lima beans (cannellini beans would also work)
1 teaspoon chili flakes
2 rosemary, thyme or sage sprigs
6 garlic cloves
½ cup (125ml) extra-virgin olive oil
Salt, to taste
2–4 tablespoons lemon juice (from roughly 1–2 lemons), to taste

Serve with: toast or crusty bread

1. In a large saucepan, combine the beans, chili flakes and whole herb sprigs. Peel the garlic cloves and smash them under the flat side of a large knife—they don't need to be pulpy and crushed, just roughly split open. Add the smashed garlic to the pan, then pour in enough water to cover the beans by about 1½–2 inches (4–5cm). Add half of the olive oil and a few generous pinches of salt.

2. Set the pan over a medium-high heat and bring to a simmer. Once it's happily bubbling, turn the heat down to keep the beans at a gentle simmer. Cook for roughly 1¼–1½ hours, or until the beans are tender and almost collapsing. You'll need to top up the water every so often to make sure the beans stay covered. It's worth taking your time to appreciate this process: At first the beans will wrinkle and pucker, then they'll slowly begin to swell. After about an hour, they should be soft at the edges but still chalky within, but as you approach the end of the cooking time they'll be bloated and cloudlike. Some beans will have split their skins, leaking starch into the cooking liquid to create a slightly thickened broth. If they need slightly more or less time than I've specified, that's fine: just tend to them regularly and use your judgment.

3. Once the beans are cooked, see if there's enough broth for your liking and either add or boil off a little liquid as necessary: I like a thick, almost pulpy mixture, but that's just me. If the smashed garlic cloves haven't completely broken down, crush them against the side of the pan using a spoon. Pluck out any herb stalks, then add salt and lemon juice to taste.

4. These beans are best eaten lukewarm, drizzled with the remaining ¼ cup (60ml) olive oil. If you made thicker, soupier beans they work well on toast. A brothier mixture is good served from the bowl, with crusty bread on the side for dipping.

PICKLED WATERMELON RIND

Watermelon doesn't do normal. It is a precious, portly prince of the world of fruit: never knowingly understated, always ready to be admired. It seems a shame to waste even an ounce of it. This easy pickle uses the white or pale green rind of the fruit, pickling it in a rosy-pink liquor made with vinegar, sugar and a little of the watermelon's deep red flesh. These pickled rinds go really well with anything carby or fried: grilled cheese sandwiches, fried chicken or even burgers. They're also good as part of a mezze spread with other vegetables, dips and breads.

The idea with these rinds is to minimize any food waste, so you might want to make them as a sister recipe to the **watermelon with peanuts, sumac and lime** on page 173, which uses the pink watermelon flesh.

Makes: 1 pound 2 ounces/500g
Ready in: 25 minutes, but you'll then need
   to let it cool for at least 1 hour
Make-ahead and storage tips: page 330

Vegan

---

12 ounces (350g) watermelon rind, with
   a sliver of pink flesh still attached
7 ounces (200g) pink watermelon flesh
scant ½ cup (100ml) white wine vinegar,
   rice wine vinegar or cane vinegar (I like
   to use the Filipino cane vinegar Datu
   Puti)
¼ cup (60g) superfine or granulated
   sugar
¾ teaspoon salt
30 black or pink peppercorns

Special equipment: stick blender,
   food processor or blender

1. Peel off the tough dark green peel from the rind and discard. (This can be tricky if your peeler isn't really sharp, so an alternative method is to first cut the rind into strips, as described next, and then use a small knife to individually cut the dark green peel from each strip.) Trim the rind into tiles about as wide and long as the top two sections of your little finger. Place the peeled rind pieces in a large jar or airtight container.

2. Blitz the watermelon flesh with a stick blender or in a food processor or blender. Combine this pulpy juice with the vinegar, sugar, salt and peppercorns in a small pan. Bring the mixture to a simmer over a medium heat, let it boil for 1 minute, then pour over the rind pieces in their container, making sure all the fruit is covered by the liquor. Put a tight lid on the container and leave to cool before using.

DILL-PICKLED CHERRY TOMATOES

These comparatively quick pickled tomatoes are a joy: sharp, sweet and herbal but without the worry of committing to a full ferment. If you want to learn about slow fermentation—like what you'd do to make kimchi or sauerkraut, taking many days or even weeks—I'd recommend Thom Eagle's amazing book *Summer's Lease*, which goes into the many magic ways that humans have learned to cook without heat. These are great with cheese and bread.

Makes: roughly 9 ounces/250g
Ready in: 2 days, but only about 45 minutes
   of active cooking time is needed
Make-ahead and storage tips: page 330

Vegan

½ cup (120ml) light-colored vinegar*
½ cup (120ml) water
3 tablespoons granulated or superfine sugar
¾ teaspoon fine sea salt or 1½ teaspoons flaky sea salt
½ teaspoon black peppercorns
2 bay leaves
9 ounces (250g) cherry tomatoes
1 garlic clove
6–8 fresh dill fronds (roughly ½ ounce/15–20g)

Special equipment: 2 cup (500ml) jar

*Apple cider vinegar, rice vinegar and white wine vinegar all work well here. Best not to use dark vinegars like malt or balsamic vinegar.

1. In a small saucepan, heat the vinegar, water, sugar, salt, peppercorns and bay leaves over medium heat. Once the mixture reaches a boil, turn off the heat and let cool to room temperature.

2. While the brine cools, prepare the tomatoes. Wash them well, then pierce each tomato a couple of times with a small sharp knife (to help the brine penetrate the tomatoes). Peel and halve the garlic clove. Layer the tomatoes, garlic and dill in your jar so that everything's well mixed—you should be able to see the dill swirling around the contours of the jar from the outside.

3. Pour the brine, including the peppercorns and bay leaves, into the jar (depending on the exact size of your jar, you may not need all of it). Add a lid and refrigerate for at least 48 hours before eating.

ROTI CANAI

These layered, flaky, pillowy roti are my favorite kind of flatbread. Roti canai is a Malaysian bread, closely related to paratha. Brushed with oil or ghee, the dough is stretched impossibly thin before being rolled, crumpled or folded into a flat round. The stretching process can be remarkable in the hands of a pro: street vendors twirl and throw the dough so that it stretches under its own spinning weight. In amateur hands, the process is less extraordinary (you slowly stretch and tease the dough out to size on an oiled work surface), but it's still a beautiful feat. There are lots of ways to shape the dough once it's stretched, but the simplest is a folding method and so that's what I've recommended here. If you're interested in other methods, YouTube is your friend. If you'd like to know more about Malaysian food, I can recommend both Norman Musa's *Amazing Malaysian* and Ping Coombes's *Malaysia*, both of which I found invaluable in putting together this recipe.

These go well with the **coconut, plantain and spinach curry with toasted cashews** on page 18, the **red lentil dal with lime** on page 43 and the **roasted okra, green beans and paneer with green chutney and lime** on page 71. You could also spread them with kaya (coconut jam) or jam.

Serves: 8
Ready in: 5 hours, but only 1 hour of this is hands-on prep time
Make-ahead and storage tips: page 330

Vegan

3–3¼ cups (375g) flour
2 tablespoons superfine or granulated sugar
1 teaspoon salt
scant 1 cup (200ml) water
3–4 tablespoons vegetable oil or ghee, melted

Special equipment: stand mixer with dough hook attachment, optional

1. In a mixing bowl, combine the flour, superfine sugar and salt. Add the water and use your hands to bring the mixture together to a cohesive dough—it should be slightly tacky to the touch, so add a splash more water if necessary. Tip onto a clean work surface and knead for about 8 minutes (check page 298 if you need some pointers on how to knead), until the dough is smoother and springier. Alternatively, knead briefly in a stand mixer with a dough hook attachment. Cut the dough into eight equal pieces, then shape into balls.

get ready your dough balls

they should be well oiled.

gently lift one side of the dough

then stretch as far as you can

2. Measure out a couple of tablespoons of the oil or ghee and rub each dough ball with a generous amount of the fat. Arrange the greased dough balls in a large covered container—if they touch each other, that's fine, but they need to be well oiled to make sure they don't stick together. Leave to rest, either in the fridge or in a cool room, for *at least* 4 hours, or ideally overnight.

3. Once your dough has rested, you'll notice how much more pliable and stretchy it is: rather than being tightly knitted together, the gluten will be relaxed and elastic, allowing you to tease the dough into ultra-thin layers. Get ready the remaining oil or ghee (if using ghee, melt it in a frying pan or in the microwave). Using a little of the oil or melted ghee, grease your work surface well, rubbing the oil over a 20 x 20 inch (50 x 50cm) area under your palms.

smear the dough across the surface to make it flat

For the love of it

4. Now, grab one of the dough balls and rub your hands with some more of the oil or ghee. Set the dough on the oiled work surface and press it under your hands until it's about 12 inches (30cm) across, smearing it across the surface as though you were trying to smooth a shirt on the ironing board. Once it's flat, gently lift one side and stretch it out as far as you can before it starts to rip—work gently and try not to pierce the dough with your fingers. Then lift and stretch another side of the dough, and repeat, working your way around the dough until it's roughly square and so thin that you could just about read through *it could look like this!* it. This process can take some getting used to, but you'll get there if you're patient. Don't stress out if you tear a few holes in the dough— the roti will be just fine regardless. When the dough is translucent and 16–18 inches (40–45cm) across, sprinkle it with a few more drops of oil or ghee and tenderly rub this over the dough's surface.

5. Next, fold the dough. Start by gently folding the top quarter of the dough square down and the bottom quarter of the dough up, so that the folded pieces meet in the middle. Don't do this too neatly—if there are air bubbles and creases and folds in the dough, all the better. If you compact the layers too much at this stage, the roti won't flake as well as they should. Next, fold the left-hand quarter of the dough in towards the middle, then fold in the right-hand quarter of the dough, so that they also meet in the middle. You'll be left with a smaller square of dough now—if you want, you can fold over the corners and turn the square into a rough circle, but this isn't vital. Set the finished roti to one side while you prepare the others. Once you're done, pour any leftover oil or ghee into a small jar and reuse it some other time.

fold the top ¼
↓
bottom ¼
↓
left ¼
↓
right ¼ of the dough

Tada!
nice square

6. It's now time to fry your roti. Heat a large frying pan over medium heat. Fry each roti for 1–2 minutes on each side (most pans won't need any oil due to the fat in the breads), until flaky with a few brown spots. (If you need to, turn the heat up or down slightly—these take me about twice as long on my electric stovetop at home compared to on my friend's gas one.) As soon as each roti is cooked, there is one crucial final stage: lay it down flat on a clean work surface and, putting your hands on either side so the roti is at 90° to your palms, clap your hands together to "smash" the roti and separate its layers. In case you're at all confused by this, just remember you want to clap the roti so that your hands meet its edges, not its flat faces. If you do this properly, the roti will crumple and become voluminous, layered and pillowy. Serve straightaway.

As soon as it's cooked, lay it on the work surface. Then _clap_ your hands to _smash_ the roti!

Variations and substitutions:

To enrich the dough, you could add a medium egg when you add the water (decrease the amount of water to a scant ⅔ cup/150ml though). If you have small or large eggs instead of the specified medium egg, just use slightly more or less water accordingly.

How bread works

If you've never made bread before, it can help to know a bit about what it's made of and how it works. Some breads, such as soda bread, use chemical raising agents (things like baking powder or bicarbonate of soda). Other breads, like flatbreads, are unleavened, which is to say that there's nothing in the mix to give them any "lift" as they cook. But most of the time when we talk about bread, we are talking about yeasted bread, which gets its "lift" from yeast.

Yeasts are single-celled organisms from the fungus kingdom. When added to malted grains, yeast will ferment, turning sugars into carbon dioxide and alcohol to form the building blocks of beer. In bread, enzymes in the yeast help to break the complex starch molecules into smaller molecules of sugar. These sugars are then fermented by the yeast, changing into alcohol (in very small quantities) and carbon dioxide. The carbon dioxide forms tiny bubbles in the dough, causing the dough to expand. When the dough is cooked, these gas bubbles get bigger again, so the bread rises even more in the oven.

Whatever kind of yeasted bread you make—whether it's a giant French boule or a batch of featherweight doughnuts—the four main ingredients remain the same: flour, water, yeast and salt. (There are some exceptions: in sourdough breads, wild yeasts in the flour and in the air are slowly and carefully nurtured, rather than yeast directly being added to the mix; some breads, such as Italian pane toscano, are made without salt.) Wheat flour contains proteins, including the much-maligned gluten, which develop into a strong, elastic "web" as you knead the dough. This "web" catches those bubbles of carbon dioxide produced by the yeast: you can see evidence of this in a bread's holey crumb, with little areas of dough surrounding bubbles of air. Water is crucial for hydrating the flour, which allows this gluten network to develop and the yeast to start fermenting. Yeast, as I've mentioned, provides lift, but also adds loads of flavor by breaking larger, tasteless molecules into smaller, more flavorful ones like sugars and amino acids. And salt, as well as enhancing flavor, helps to strengthen the gluten network, giving your bread some bounce. Just bear in mind those four cornerstones of breadmaking—flour, water, yeast and salt—and you'll be well on the way to being a confident bread baker.

In terms of the steps involved in breadmaking, I think the whole thing is best seen as a kind of dance—faster sections, slow parts and moments when you (and the dough) both rest. After you've mixed the ingredients, you knead the dough: a vigorous way of building up the dough's strength and elasticity. After that, you set it aside to rest and rise. Once the dough has risen, you return to it and shape it, gently coaxing it into its final form—whether that's a baguette or a bun. Then the dough rises some more, changing from compact and elastic to larger, airier and more fragile. At this point, it's time for it to go in the oven—a sudden ramping up of tempo and energy that will see the bread rapidly expand, cause the yeast to die and transform the soft dough into an airy crumb. If you want to learn more about bread, I'd really recommend James Morton's *Brilliant Bread*, *New World Sourdough* by Bryan Ford and the classic *The Bread Book* by Linda Collister.

ROSEMARY BABY BUNS

My friend came back from Mexico last year with two little buns wrapped inside a sandwich bag, inside a plastic bag, tucked into a corner of her backpack. From Panadería Rosetta in Mexico City, the buns were flavored with rosemary and sugar with sticky, salty, caramelized edges. My friend, knowing me as well as she does, knew I'd lose my head for these bollos de romero—rosemary buns—and so smuggled them a full 5,500 miles back to dreary England for me to try. Everyone should have a friend like this.

Luckily, you don't have to wait until someone happens to be coming back from Mexico City with room in their carry-on luggage: you can very easily make a version of these buns at home. The ones I tasted were made with lard mixed with the sugar and rosemary, which gave them a perfect semi-savory richness. If you want to replicate this exactly, check out the variations and substitutions section at the end of the recipe. But it's my guess that most of us are more likely to have a block of butter than of lard in the fridge, so with convenience and vegetarians in mind I have developed a butter-based version for you to try out.

If you can make these tiny "baby" swirls, as soft as a baby's bottom and sweet with rosemary, you can make any bread.

Makes: 24

Ready in: about 4 hours, but much of this is quiet time while the dough rises, so you can fit life into the gaps. There's a take-your-time method below in case you want more flexibility.

Make-ahead and storage tips: page 330

Vegetarian   Vegan option

For the dough:

4 cups (500g) bread flour, plus extra for dusting

1 teaspoon salt

2 teaspoons (8g package) active dry yeast or ½ ounce (15g) fresh yeast

1⅓ cups (315ml) lukewarm water

For the filling:

½ cup (110g) salted or unsalted butter, softened, plus a little extra to grease the tin

¾ cup (175g) superfine granulated or soft light brown sugar

Pinch of salt, optional

Leaves from 8 fresh rosemary sprigs, finely chopped

Special equipment: stand mixer with dough hook attachment, optional

1. In a large mixing bowl, mix together the flour and salt. In a measuring jug, mix the yeast with the water until dissolved. Make sure the water is barely lukewarm: if it's too hot, the yeast will die. Pour the yeasted water into the flour and salt mixture, and bring together using a wooden spoon until a shaggy dough forms and there are no more big patches of dry flour. At this point, it's time to ditch the utensils and get your hands dirty. There's nothing so effective for kneading dough as a human hand, so unless you have mobility problems or sensory aversions that might make it difficult to hand-knead the dough (in which case you can use a food processor with a dough hook attachment), you should get in there yourself.

2. It's much, much easier to see how to knead dough by watching the process rather than reading about it. There are lots of different techniques, but they all achieve roughly the same thing: stretching, building and reinforcing the gluten network in the dough. With this in mind, it might help you to have a look on YouTube at examples and to find a method that works for you. Here's a simple method that I use: Tip the rough dough onto a clean work surface. (Don't worry if the dough's a bit sticky. Stickier dough means lighter bread, and it'll become less glue-like the more you knead it.) Holding the nearest edge of the dough under the heel of one hand, stretch the far side out under the heel of your other hand, dragging the dough out into an oblong or oval shape along the surface. Then fold the far end back over to meet the near end, so the dough is folded in half. Give the dough a quarter turn, so another side is now nearest to you. Repeat: stretching, folding and then turning the dough again and again for 5–8 minutes, or until the dough is elastic and smoother, rather than shaggy, torn and very dimpled. (Realistically, you can't over-knead it if you're kneading by hand—no matter your optimistic googling of "can you over-knead dough" around the 2-minute mark. Just be patient, put a podcast on and let the dough come alive in your hands.)

3. Wash out your mixing bowl and dry it, then return the kneaded dough to it. Cover with a plate, plastic wrap or a damp tea towel. Leave to rest and rise at room temperature—around 65–75°F (18–24°C). If your house is slightly warmer or cooler than this, don't worry! Just remember that you're working with a living organism—yeast—and this organism works faster when it's slightly warmer, and slower when it's cold. At very cold temperatures, around freezing point or below, the yeast will stop working altogether. The dough is ready when it has almost doubled in size, which should take anywhere between 1 and 2 hours depending on the ambient temperature.

4. While the dough rises, mix the butter and sugar to a paste. If you're using unsalted butter, add a pinch of salt.

5. Once the dough is risen and ready, tip it out from its bowl onto a work surface lightly dusted with flour. Use your hands to tease the dough into a rectangle shape around ¾ inch (2cm) thick. Dust the top of the dough rectangle with a little flour. Now take a large rolling pin and roll the dough out to a very large, long rectangle, around 12 inches (30cm) long and 27–31 inches (70–80cm) wide. (If your kitchen space is limited, you might want to divide the dough in half and create two 12 x 16 inch/30 x 40cm rectangles instead of the one large one.) It might spring back as you roll it out, but if you're patient with it you'll eventually manage to coax it to the right size.

6. Using a small knife or spatula, thinly spread the butter and sugar mixture all over the dough. Sprinkle over the chopped rosemary leaves. Now, starting at the very long bottom edge of the dough rectangle, roll it away from you like a Swiss roll. You should end up with a very long, slim log of swirled dough. Cut this log into 24 slices (each 1–1¼ inches/2.5–3cm wide)—you'll be able to see the pale spiral streak of butter and specks of rosemary.

7. Grease a large roasting pan—roughly 13 x 9 inches (22 x 33cm)—with plenty of butter (the size matters here, because you want the buns to be close enough that they begin to touch as they rise and bake). Arrange the buns in the pan, cut side up so that you can see the swirls, like a tray of cinnamon buns. Leave to rise, uncovered, for about an hour—or until they're about 1½ times their original size and noticeably puffy and soft. While they rise, preheat the oven to 425°F (220°C).

8. Once the buns are risen, bake them in the preheated oven for 15–18 minutes, until they're well-risen, their tops are beginning to brown and crisp and the butter is sizzling up through the swirls. Leave to cool for just a few minutes, then transfer out of the pan and to a wire rack while they're still warm—otherwise the caramelized sugar might stick them to the pan. These buns are best served warm.

The take-your-time method:

If you've got a busy day ahead, you can mix and knead the dough in the morning, using cold rather than lukewarm water. Put the dough in a bowl, cover the bowl tightly with plastic wrap (the dough will dry out otherwise) and place in the fridge until the evening. That evening, take the dough out of the fridge, shape into buns and leave to rise at room temperature for 3–4 hours, or until roughly 1½ times their original size. Bake as above. If you prefer to bake these in the morning, make the dough the evening before, leave to rise in the fridge overnight, then shape first thing in the morning and let rise at room temperature for 3–4 hours.

Variations and substitutions:

To make a version with lard instead of the butter, just like they make at Panadería Rosetta, swap the ½ cup (110g) butter in the filling for 3 ounces (80g) or ⅓ cup plus 1 tablespoon lard. To make a vegan version, swap the butter for 3 ounces (80g) or ⅓ cup plus 1 tablespoon coconut oil and a good pinch of salt.

I wouldn't recommend swapping the rosemary for any other herb: rosemary is intensely aromatic, woody and strong as a flavor, and it's not really something that any other herb could approximate. But feel welcome to use the dough and technique as a starting point for making cinnamon buns (swap the rosemary for 2 teaspoons ground cinnamon), cardamom-scented swirls (swap the herb for the ground seeds of 10 cardamom pods) or even a zesty orange variation (replacing the rosemary with the finely grated zest of 3 oranges).

If you want to give these some gloss, you can add an orange glaze—1⅓ cups (150g) confectioners' sugar mixed with orange juice until it's the consistency of thick heavy cream—brushed over the tops of the buns while they're still warm.

PRETZEL SANDWICH LOAF

There is nothing more lovely than the deep pecan-brown shine of a pretzel. It's as whole-body soothing to me as the first sip of Coke, or catching the microwave just before it beeps. Some things are just good, and we owe it to ourselves to re-create that goodness at every possible opportunity.

I decided to add some of that pretzel gloss to this sandwich loaf—a fluffy, delicate milk bread, designed to be cut into slices for sandwiches or toast. Pretzels are traditionally boiled in lye water, an alkaline solution, to nudge along the Maillard reaction, which makes them darken in the oven. The last thing anybody needs is a boiled sandwich loaf, so I've simplified things here by just brushing the top of the bread with egg yolk, milk and bicarbonate of soda: the bicarb makes the glaze alkaline and so helps with the browning, while the egg adds luster. The result is a milky white loaf with a rich, burnished—but not crusty—top. Consider it a kind of anti-sourdough, perfectly soft for everyday eating. I like to eat it toasted and well buttered, sometimes with **rosy rhubarb jam** (page 318) or **salted passion fruit, pineapple and coconut curd** (page 320).

A quick note: the **spiced apple pudding with brown sugar crisp** on page 154 uses breadcrumbs, so if you don't get through the whole loaf you can always use up the stale crumbs in that.

Makes: 1 medium sandwich loaf
Ready in: about 3 hours 30 minutes, most of which is idle time while the dough rises, rises again and then bakes. You can also adapt the method to work better with your schedule by splitting up the different stages: check out the take-your-time method on page 303.
Make-ahead and storage tips: page 331

Vegetarian   Vegan option

3½ cups (425g) bread flour
2 teaspoons (8g package) active dry yeast
1 tablespoon superfine or granulated sugar
1 teaspoon salt
1 cup plus 3 tablespoons (275ml) whole or reduced-fat milk, lukewarm
2 tablespoons melted butter, plus extra for greasing the loaf pan

To glaze:
1 egg yolk
1 tablespoon whole or reduced-fat milk
½ teaspoon bicarbonate of soda

Special equipment: 2 pound (900g) loaf pan, roughly 4½ x 8½ inches (11 x 22cm) across its top; stand mixer with dough hook attachment, optional

For the love of it

1. In a large mixing bowl, stir together the flour and yeast, then add the sugar and salt and mix until well combined. Add the lukewarm milk (it should feel just warm to the touch, but no warmer than this, or it may kill the yeast! If it's as warm as your evening bath, let it cool a bit before adding it). As soon as the milk has been poured in, add the melted butter. Time to get your hands dirty: use your hands to mix the wet and dry ingredients together until they form a rough, shaggy dough. Let the dough sit in its bowl, covered with plastic wrap or a large plate, for 10 minutes. During this time, the flour will absorb some of the liquid and the dough will become easier to handle.

2. After 10 minutes, tip the rested dough onto a clean work surface and start kneading it. Check out the recipe for **rosemary baby buns** on page 296 if you need any guidance on how to knead by hand. Alternatively, use a stand mixer with a dough hook attachment, kneading slowly. Knead for roughly 5 minutes, during which time the dough should become less sticky and more elastic. Don't worry if it's still slightly tacky: The wetter the dough, the more airy it'll be when it rises. This stickiness might be a problem if we wanted to elaborately shape the dough, but it's going to be guided by the loaf pan here so it'll be fine.

3. Return the kneaded dough to the mixing bowl, cover the bowl with a large plate or plastic wrap and leave to rise at room temperature for 1–1½ hours. After this time, the dough should be pretty much doubled in size. If it's slow to rise, just give it slightly more time.

4. Once the dough is risen, grease the loaf pan with a little butter. Tip the risen dough from its bowl onto a clean work surface and notice how it softly deflates as you remove it from its sanctuary—I relate hard to this sunken, deflated kind of feeling. Tease the dough into a fat oval shape roughly as long as your loaf pan.

5. Next, you're going to create some surface tension, which means stretching the top surface of the dough to make it taut and elastic— this will help the bread to rise evenly, rather than flabbily, as it bakes. Use your hands to firmly roll the dough into a fat log, folding it along its length and tucking away any flabby bits, so that the outside is smooth and stretched. Turn it over so that the seam is underneath and the taut side faces up, and place the dough in the loaf pan. Cover loosely with plastic wrap or a tea towel and leave to rise for a further 45–60 minutes. As it rises, the loaf will swell up and become puffy and delicate, growing to at least 1½ times its original size. While the bread rises, preheat the oven to 350°F (180°C).

6. Once your dough is ready, whisk together the egg yolk, milk and bicarbonate of soda for the glaze. Use a pastry brush or clean paintbrush (or your fingers if you must) to brush this all over the top of the dough, taking care not to let too much run down the edges and into the pan. Bake the loaf in the preheated oven for 45 minutes, until majestically risen, firm to the touch and a rich mahogany brown. Cover the bread with a tea towel while it cools—this helps to keep the crust soft. Wait until completely cool before slicing and serving.

The take-your-time method:

It sounds weird to give a slower version of this recipe for busy people, but it really works. If you lengthen the breadmaking process, you can let it rise overnight or while you're at work during the day, fitting the "active" parts of the process into those moments when you actually have time to spare. Mix and knead the dough as above, but use room temperature—not lukewarm—milk. Place the kneaded dough in its mixing bowl and cover the bowl tightly with plastic wrap to stop the dough drying out. Place in the fridge for 8–10 hours: the dough will rise more slowly in cooler temperatures as the yeast will be less active. Once you're ready, remove the dough from the fridge and shape it as described above. Let it have its second rise at room temperature this time, for 2–3 hours, or until the dough is at least 1½ times its original size. Bake as above.

Variations and substitutions:

To make a vegan version of this loaf, use a non-dairy milk (I used soy milk and found it worked well) and use melted coconut oil in place of the butter. For the glaze, combine 1 tablespoon non-dairy milk, ½ teaspoon bicarbonate of soda and ½ teaspoon superfine or granulated sugar. It won't be as shiny as the egg yolk glaze, but it'll still add a deep brown color to the loaf.

FRANZBRÖTCHEN

Swirled cinnamon butter pastries

The lovechild of a croissant and a cinnamon bun, these German cinnamon butter franzbrötchen are perfect pastries: shatteringly crisp and flaky on top, with a honeycomb-light crumb inside. They're made with a laminated dough—just like Danish pastries or croissants—which combines the lift of yeast with the richness of a frankly incredible amount of butter. I have to warn you, to incorporate the butter into the dough is a long process: you make and rest a yeasted dough, then wrap it around a whole slab of butter before repeatedly rolling and folding the dough over the course of several hours. The result is amazing though, with flour and fat layered on an almost geological scale.

I've given modest quantities below, because rolling out the dough can be daunting if this is your first time making laminated dough. If you're feeling confident, you can of course double the amounts given. You can also check out the pain au chocolat and croissant variations listed at the end of this recipe: once you've mastered the basic dough, the world of breakfast pastries is your oyster.

Makes: 9

Ready in: 24 hours, including 8–12 hours of overnight resting, 4–6 hours of intermittent rolling and folding the dough, 3–4 hours of rising time and a 20-minute bake.

Make-ahead and storage tips: page 331

Vegetarian

For the dough:

2 cups (250g) bread flour, plus a little extra for dusting

2 tablespoons superfine or granulated sugar

1 teaspoon active dry yeast (about ½ of an 8g package)

¾ teaspoon salt

5 tablespoons (75ml) ice water

5 tablespoons (75ml) reduced-fat or whole milk

2 tablespoons unsalted butter, well softened

For the lamination:

⅔ cup (150g) unsalted butter, chilled

1 tablespoon all-purpose or bread flour

For the filling:

2 tablespoons superfine sugar

2 tablespoons (30g) unsalted butter, well softened

1½ teaspoons cinnamon

For the glaze:

1 egg, any size

1 teaspoon water or milk

Special equipment: stand mixer with dough hook attachment, optional

1. First up, consider timings: The dough will need to chill for 8–12 hours once made, so it's best to make the dough in the evening for an overnight rest. When you shape and bake the pastries the following day, you'll need 7–10 hours. Most of this is hands-off time while the dough rests, but you'll need to be available—so don't make too many other plans.

2. In a large mixing bowl, combine the flour, superfine sugar, yeast and salt, and stir to combine. Add the water, milk and butter and stir everything until a shaggy, slightly sticky dough comes together. Tip the dough onto a clean work surface, and knead for 6–8 minutes, checking the kneading guidance on page 298 if you need to. Use a stand mixer with a dough hook attachment (set it to a low speed) if that helps. Once kneaded, the dough will be smoother, less sticky and more elastic.

3. Pat the dough into a flattish square, wrap it tightly in plastic wrap (it's important that the dough isn't exposed to the air, or it'll dry out) and place in the freezer for 15 minutes. This short spell in the freezer will counterbalance the warmth imparted to the dough by your warm hands during the kneading—we want to delay the dough rising until after the pastries are shaped. After 15 minutes, transfer the dough to the fridge—best to put it in the coldest part—and let rest for 8–12 hours.

4. When the dough is nearly rested, start preparing the butter for the lamination. The butter should be a solid rectangular block, not cut into pieces. Sprinkle the butter block with the tablespoon of flour, then place it between two sheets of parchment paper. Use a rolling pin to firmly press the butter down, gradually working your way up and down the block until the butter is pliable and bendy. You're aiming to flatten it to a rectangle measuring roughly 10 x 7 inches (25 x 17cm), and less than ¼ inch (.5cm) thick. Set it in the fridge for a moment while you prepare the dough.

5. Unwrap the dough and very lightly dust a work surface with flour (too much flour will toughen the dough). Roll the dough to roughly 11 x 11 inches (28 x 28cm). Place your butter rectangle on top of the dough, aligning one of the long (10 inch/25cm) sides of the butter with the edge of the dough square nearest to you. The top third of the dough should be "naked": fold this third down and over the butter so that it covers roughly half the butter. Now fold the bottom third of dough and butter up and over the middle, to create a slim rectangle of dough roughly 11 x 3½ inches (28 x 9cm). (If you're struggling to visualize this, it's just like doing a letter fold: one third over towards the middle, then another third.) Pat the edges shut to enclose the butter. This is your dough-butter parcel.

6. The next step is an important one: the roll, fold and chill. First, roll out your dough-butter parcel to roughly 8 x 16 inches (20 x 40cm), and less than ⅜ inch (1cm) thick. Then do another letter fold: fold the top third of the dough down towards the middle, then fold the bottom third up and over. You should be left with a rectangle roughly 8 x 5 inches (20 x 13cm). Wrap this in plastic wrap or parchment paper and place in the fridge to chill and rest for 1–2 hours—whatever's convenient for you. This chilling time lets the dough relax between rolls—otherwise it'd be too tough to stretch out.

7. You need to repeat this roll, fold and chill process two more times. Each time you reroll the dough, give it a 90° turn first so the short end of the rectangle is towards you. This is so that you're not overworking the dough along one axis. Once you've done this, the dough-butter parcel will have been rolled, folded and chilled three times.

8. When the dough is done chilling after its final roll, fold and chill, it's time to shape and fill the pastries. If you're interested in making pains au chocolat or croissants, check the instructions on the next page, otherwise here's the drill for franzbrötchen. In a small bowl, beat together the sugar, butter and cinnamon for the filling. Roll the dough to roughly 8 x 16 inches (20 x 40cm) and smear with the filling mixture. Roll up from long edge to long edge, like a Swiss roll, to form a plump roll roughly 16 inches (40cm) long. Cut into 9 slices. Lightly flour the round handle of a wooden spoon (or a pen or pencil) and press firmly down into the middle of each slice, almost as if you were cutting each piece in half again into even thinner slices. The aim is to almost bisect (but not actually cut) the dough, causing the swirls to splay out on each side.

9. Arrange the pastries on a couple of baking sheets lined with parchment paper, setting them with the wooden spoon indentation facing up. Cover with plastic wrap or parchment paper. Leave to rise for 3–4 hours at room temperature, or until pretty much doubled in size and tender to the touch. How long this takes will really depend on the temperature of your house and the tenacity of the yeast: don't rush it though, as this slow step is vital for crispy, flaking pastries.

10. When the franzbrötchen are nearly risen, preheat the oven to 425°F (220°C). Mix the egg with the water or milk for the glaze, whisking until smooth. Very gently brush the top of the pastries with the glaze, taking care not to bruise them and making sure that the glaze covers only the tops of the pastries. If you let the glaze run onto the cut edges (where you can faintly see the cross-section layers of butter lamination) you'll effectively glue the layers together.

11. Place the pastries in the preheated oven and bake for 10 minutes, then turn the heat down to 400°F (200°C) and bake for a further 10 minutes. The franzbrötchen are ready when they're crisp and a deep orange-brown color on top. They should have expanded magnificently in the oven. Let cool for at least 5 minutes before eating.

Pains au chocolat:

Roll the prepared dough to a square measuring roughly 12 x 12 inches (30 x 30cm), then cut into thirds lengthwise and widthwise, to make 9 small squares each measuring roughly 4 x 4 inches (10 x 10cm). Have 5½–7 ounces (150–200g) dark chocolate on hand, broken into chunks. Lay 3–4 chunks of chocolate along one half of each square, then fold over the other half and pinch tightly shut to seal. Check the instructions in the main recipe to see how to let these rise, then glaze and bake them.

Croissants:

Roll the prepared dough to roughly 20 x 8 inches (50 x 20cm)—it will spring back as you roll it, but you'll get there eventually. Cut the dough into triangles: each will be 4 inches (10cm) wide across its base, and 8 inches (20cm) tall, which means there will be a row of 5 triangles with their bases on one long edge of the dough, and then 4 upside-down triangles tessellated between them. The triangles will each be as tall as the height (8 inches/20cm) of the dough. Cut a small—¾–1¼ inch (2–3cm)—slit into the middle of the base of each triangle, as if you were starting to cut the triangle in half. Pull the dough on either side of this cut apart slightly to create a couple of "feet": the triangle will start looking like a mini Eiffel Tower. Now, starting with the "feet," roll up the croissants to create tapered rolls. Once rolled up, lay with the tip of the triangle on the bottom, to stop the croissants unfurling. Leave to rise, then glaze and bake according to the instructions in the main recipe.

FRIED APPLE PIE BITES

These are like something from a sweet-toothed fever dream: apple slices rolled in butter, cinnamon and brown sugar, then enrobed in spring roll wrappers and deep-fried. When cooked, they're shatteringly crisp on the outside, jammy and sweet within. They're inspired by two very different culinary masterpieces: Filipino turon—sweet plantain dipped in sugar, wrapped in spring roll pastry and fried—and the McDonald's apple pie. If you're curious about the original Filipino turon, a recipe for that follows this one.

You can get spring roll wrappers from lots of larger supermarkets and pretty much any East or Southeast Asian grocery store. Look for square ones roughly 8 x 8 inches/20 x 20cm (you should find them in the freezers).

Makes: 16 mini apple pies
Ready in: roughly 1 hour 30 minutes, or less if you're
  speedy when rolling the little spring rolls
Make-ahead and storage tips: page 331

Vegetarian   Vegan option

---

16 spring roll wrappers (roughly
  9 ounces/250g)
2 tablespoons unsalted butter
⅓ cup (75g) soft light brown sugar
1 teaspoon cinnamon
4 medium apples* (roughly
  14 ounces/400g)

6 cups (1.5 liters) sunflower or
  vegetable oil, or more if using a deep
  fryer

Serve with: ice cream, optional
Special equipment: candy
  thermometer or instant-read digital
  thermometer; deep fryer, optional

*I used tart, crisp apples, as these hold their shape best when cooked. A bigger apple will need to be cut into eighths or even sixteenths, depending on its size.

1. Start by getting the spring roll wrappers out of the freezer if you haven't already done so: they'll need 30–60 minutes, in the package, to defrost.

preparation part

a bowl for melted butter

another bowl for sugar + cinnamon mix

2. Once the spring roll wrappers are defrosted, you can prepare the filling. Melt the butter and put into a small bowl. Into a separate bowl, add the sugar and stir in the cinnamon. Once everything is in order, peel and core the apples and slice each one into quarters. Have a damp tea towel on hand: this will stop the spring roll wrappers from drying out once you start working. Get out a small bowl or glass of water, to help to seal the pastry shut.

slice each apple into quarters

damp teatowel to cover the remaining slack of wrappers

a little glass of water for sealing

3. To assemble each apple pie bite, take one spring roll wrapper (replace your damp tea towel over the remaining stack) and lay it on the work surface in front of you. Take one apple piece and dip it in the melted butter, rolling it over to coat it. Now roll the buttered apple in the cinnamon sugar mixture until well coated. Lay the sugared apple slice near the bottom edge of the spring roll wrapper, in the center. Roll the wrapper up over it so that it's cradled near the bottom, then fold in the left and right sides of the wrapper so the apple is tightly enclosed, and your roll is as wide as the piece of apple. Roll up from the bottom to create a fat parcel of apple and pastry. Once you're nearly done rolling, dip your finger in the water that you got ready earlier and smear across the top edge of the wrapper: this will seal the pastry shut as you give the apple a final turn and encase it in its wrapper. You should be left with a neat(ish) tightly packed spring roll.

rolling part

1

2

rolllll!

3

4

cosy little parcel
ready to be fried!

4. Repeat this process until you've buttered, sugared and wrapped all 16 pieces of apple. When you're nearly done, heat the oil in a medium to large saucepan, making sure it's at least 1¼ inches (3cm) deep, but comes no higher than halfway up the sides of the pot. Monitor the oil temperature with a candy thermometer or digital thermometer. Once the oil is 350°F (180°C), adjust the temperature to keep it around that point. If you have a deep fryer, you'll need more oil to fill it, but it will keep the oil a steady temperature for you.

5. When the oil is hot and the spring rolls are ready, you can start frying. Add the spring rolls to the hot oil in batches of no more than 8. Let them fry for 10 minutes, turning them regularly. They'll sizzle and spit as they cook, and a few beads of sugar may leak out into the oil: all this is absolutely fine, just watch over them and keep an eye on the oil temperature. Once they're done, they should be a deep gold color and will rattle crisply when you move them with a slotted spoon.

6. Remove from the oil with your slotted spoon and transfer to a plate or board. Your instinct might be to blot these with paper towels to remove excess oil, but I'd caution against it: the paper can stick to any caramelized flecks of sugar on the outside of the rolls. Let cool slightly before enjoying either by themselves or with ice cream.

Variations and substitutions:

For a vegan version, swap the butter for 2 tablespoons coconut oil.

Superfine sugar will work in place of the soft light brown sugar, but won't give the same toffee flavor.

TURON
Caramelized plantain lumpia or spring rolls

I was introduced to turon by a Filipino friend a couple of years ago. When she made me these crisp, deep-fried lumpia (spring rolls) filled with caramelized, toffee-like plantain, I was instantly smitten. In a blissed-out haze, we ate our way through the whole batch in one glorious sitting.

Saba bananas—a short, fat cultivar usually used for cooking—are the usual choice for turon, but they can be difficult to find. Very ripe plantain makes a good substitute. In her book *7000 Islands*, Yasmin Newman suggests you could use Cavendish bananas (the type we're most used to seeing in the UK) if that's all you can get hold of, but it's worth noting that they'll need slightly less sugar and will cook to a much softer texture.

Makes: 16
Ready in: roughly 1 hour 30 minutes, or less if you're speedy
   when rolling the little spring rolls
Make-ahead and storage tips: page 331

Vegan

---

16 spring roll wrappers
2 large, very ripe plantain*
½ cup plus 2 tablespoons (125g) soft light brown sugar
6 cups (1.5 liters) sunflower or vegetable oil,
   or more if using a deep fryer

Serve with: ice cream, optional
Special equipment: candy thermometer
   or instant-read digital thermometer; deep fryer, optional

*Look for plantain that are black nearly
all over—not yellow and certainly not starchy and crisp green.

1. For the most part, you'll be following the same method as described in the previous recipe for **fried apple pie bites**, so refer back to that as you go.

2. First, defrost your spring roll wrappers for 30–60 minutes.

3. Next, cut the fruit: Large plantain need to be peeled and cut into eight fat batons. Halve the plantain to create two shorter pieces, then cut each of

these pieces in half lengthwise once, and then again, to yield eight slim batons from each plantain.

4. Set up your lumpia (spring roll) assembling station as described in the previous recipe for **fried apple pie bites**, including getting a damp tea towel ready to cover the spring roll wrappers, and having a small bowl or glass of water on hand to seal the pastries.

5. Roll each plantain piece in the sugar, making sure you encrust the fruit generously. For super-sweet cavendish bananas, you won't need as much sugar. One by one, start wrapping and sealing the lumpia. You'll need to follow exactly the same method as in the previous recipe.

6. Once you've assembled the turon, you can fry them as per the previous recipe. One final note: Yasmin Newman cooks her turon for 4 minutes for a light golden color, but many recipes specify 8–10 minutes for a deep golden-brown shattering crust. With this in mind, it's up to you how long to fry them, but I do roughly 8 minutes. Serve warm.

Variations and substitutions:

In place of the plantain, you can use 8 saba bananas or 4 Cavendish bananas. When preparing the fruit, little saba bananas should be peeled and cut in half along their length to give two long pieces. For Cavendish bananas, peel and cut into two shorter halves, then cut each of these in half lengthwise to create batons.

NKATE BRITTLE, CARDAMOM AND SALTED MILK ICE CREAM

Nkate cake is Ghanaian peanut brittle—roasted peanuts set in hard caramel like the *Jurassic Park* mosquito in its amber. In this ice cream, the salty nkate brittle is smashed and rippled through a cardamom ice cream.

If you prefer, you can just buy peanut brittle from the store: It'll save you the hassle of making a caramel from scratch. You'll just need 3–4 ounces (80–100g). But I figure that if you're already in the mood to make ice cream from scratch, the nkate cake probably won't be enough to push you over the edge. Unlike the **salted, malted, magic ice cream** on page 102 this is a "real" ice cream, which is to say it's made with a custard rather than the quick-fix condensed milk and cream mixture. This proper ice cream needs to be churned as it freezes—otherwise it'll set in a solid lump. So, to make this recipe you'll either need an ice cream maker (which stirs the mixture while freezing it) or a few spare hours (to stir the mixture at regular intervals as it freezes).

Makes: about 3–3½ cups/800ml
Ready in: 16 hours, only 40 minutes of which is active cooking time
   (the rest is overnight chilling and freezing)
Make-ahead and storage tips: page 331

Vegetarian

For the ice cream:	For the nkate brittle:
6 cardamom pods	Vegetable oil, for greasing
1¼ cups (300ml) whole milk	3 tablespoons superfine sugar
1¼ cups (300ml) heavy cream	3 tablespoons water
3 egg yolks	½ cup (60g) roasted salted peanuts
½ cup (100g) superfine sugar	
1 tablespoon cornstarch	**Special equipment:** food processor, optional;
2 teaspoons vanilla extract	stick blender, optional; ice cream machine,
Generous pinch of salt	very useful but not essential

1. Start off by making the ice cream. Crack the dusty green cardamom pods under the flat edge of a knife. Add the cracked cardamom pods to the milk and heavy cream in a medium saucepan and set the pan over a low heat. Heat the mixture until it's steaming hot and just about to simmer.

2. While the milk and cream mixture heats, whisk together the egg yolks, sugar, cornstarch and vanilla extract in a mixing bowl. When the milk and cream mixture is hot, very slowly pour it into the bowl, whisking constantly as you go. It's important to do this slowly to avoid shocking the eggs, which may curdle if suddenly drowned in the hot milk. Once you've combined everything, pour it back into the saucepan and set back over a low heat. Cook it slowly, stirring nonstop, for a few minutes—you don't want it to boil, but you'll need to give it long enough for the custard to thicken slightly. By the time it's done, the custard should coat the back of a spoon in a light layer, and steam should be rising in a steady plume from the saucepan.

3. Turn off the heat and add the salt to taste, stopping once there's the gentlest salty tang. Pluck out the cardamom pods and discard them.

Pour the ice cream mix into a decently sized container, let cool, then cover and place in the fridge overnight: this is called tempering, and it gives the custard a chance to settle before freezing, making for a smoother, denser ice cream.

4. The next day, make the peanut brittle. Start off by generously greasing a large plate or baking sheet with oil. In a small saucepan, combine the superfine sugar and water and set over a medium-high heat. Bring the mixture to a simmer, swirling the pan gently but resisting the temptation to stir it, as this could make the sugar crystallize.* Once the sugar has all melted, stop fiddling with it but keep an eye on it as it darkens in color from clear, to light straw, to honey, to a deep caramel brown. As soon as it's dark, turn off the heat, then add the peanuts and stir together. Quickly pour this mixture onto your greased plate or baking sheet and leave to cool—as it cools, it'll set hard. Once it's completely set, use a rolling pin to bash it until it's broken, or pulse it very briefly in a food processor.

5. It's now time to freeze the ice cream. If you have an ice cream maker, just decant the chilled custard into the machine and follow the manufacturer's instructions. Once the ice cream is very thick, stir in the crushed peanut brittle and place in a tub in the freezer to freeze completely. If you don't have an ice cream maker, you can churn the ice cream yourself. Place the custard in its tub in the freezer for an hour, then blitz briefly with a stick blender or, if that's not an option, whisk vigorously with a fork. This will break up any ice crystals, keeping the ice cream smooth and dense. Return to the freezer for another hour, then whisk again. Repeat every hour for 4–5 hours, until the ice cream is very thick and creamy, then stir in the smashed peanut brittle. Return to the freezer to finish freezing, undisturbed, for 3–4 hours.

*If you have any trouble with crystallizing sugar—where the caramel becomes grainy and gritty instead of molten—try again but with the addition of a tablespoon or two of golden syrup, if you can find it, in addition to the sugar and water. The syrup is a good influence on the sugar, and should nudge it towards a liquid state.

Variations and substitutions:

Instead of the cardamom, you could make this with a couple of pinches of cinnamon or leave out the spice altogether, though I think the floral cardamom balances the nutty heft of the brittle well.

You can use hazelnuts or almonds for the brittle if you can't use peanuts—just toast and salt them before using.

On jam

The idea of preserving fruit—because ultimately that is what jam does—might seem incongruous with (many) modern lives. When we can buy exactly the amount of fruit we want and need—whether that's from a supermarket or a greenmarket stand—there's no need to make good with "excess." We know we can get strawberries from polytunnels in far-flung places, so we don't have to trouble ourselves with the idea that we won't taste another strawberry for 9 months. We can buy jam from even the most unreliably stocked corner store. This makes jam-making kind of unnecessary, I guess, but maybe that's no bad thing. These days, if you set a heavy pan on the stovetop with fruit and sugar and watch as it slowly simmers and sputters, you can do it for no reason other than the sheer joy of the process. And it really is a joy. Just keep your windows shut if it's wasp season, or the whole meditative aspect goes south pretty quick.

Until recently, I was never confident about jam. I've made runny jams, jams that looked like fruit blobs in plasma, jams that tasted like caramel and muddy-looking jams so solid they needed to be cut out of their jars. When people described jams as preserving the essence of fruit—quivering, spritely flavorful jams as bright as jewels—I was skeptical. On good days, I blamed my fruit or the candy thermometer for my trouble. In a less generous mood, I thought everyone was just kidding themselves: people too caught up with the romance of country living. Well, as is so often the case, I was wrong.

Considering that jam only has two vital ingredients—fruit and sugar, in pretty much equal amounts—it's wild how many variables there are on the path to a good jar. But if you've never made jam before, I have to reassure you that it's not all that difficult if you actually take the time to consult the experts rather than (like I did) rushing in recklessly. *The River Cottage Preserves Handbook* by Pam Corbin is a vital book if you're interested in the art of preserving and its many idiosyncrasies, but for now there are just a few basics you should probably know.

First, whether you're making a Seville orange marmalade or a midsummer strawberry jam, fruit and sugar are the two integral components of a jam. These are cooked together until the mixture reaches its "setting point," the temperature—roughly 220°F (105°C)—at which enough water has evaporated, so that once the jam cools it sets to a loosely jammy consistency. If you cook jam too long, it'll set firm; if you don't cook it enough, the jam will be liquid. The easiest way to test this is with a jam or candy thermometer or a digital thermometer. If that fails, Pam Corbin recommends the crinkle test: Put a small plate in the freezer when you start the jam-making process, then once the jam has boiled for 6–9 minutes, drop a small dollop of jam on the cold plate. Let it cool for a minute or two, then nudge it with your finger. If the jam crinkles, it's ready; if it flows around your finger, it needs more time.

Another factor that helps jam to set is pectin: a naturally occurring substance in fruit flesh, skin, pith and seeds that helps to set the syrup into a jelly-like quiver. (For reference, pectin is what they use in a lot of vegetarian candies in place of the usual pork or beef gelatin.) Some fruits, like cooking apples and citrus fruits, are high in pectin. Other fruits, like strawberries and rhubarb, have very little, and need the addition of a little lemon juice or liquid pectin to help the jam to firm up.

Corbin recommends using fruit that's slightly underripe (it has more pectin this way). She also specifies that fruit must be dry: if you have to wash it, pat it dry before making your jam. And—importantly—dissolve the sugar gently with the fruit *before* allowing the mixture to boil. This helps the fruit to hold together. Only then should you turn up the heat, boiling the mixture rapidly to preserve the flavor and color of the fruit. If you go low and slow with jam, it'll lose that vibrancy and you'll end up with a sludgy mess, like I used to.

For the love of it

ROSY RHUBARB JAM

The rhubarb jam recipe here is rosy in both flavor and hue, with a teaspoon of rose water added to the bright pink mixture after cooking. It's best, by far, to make this with early-season rhubarb—the thin, bright pink stalks that appear in the stores between January and March in the UK and a little later in North America—so this is essentially a winter/early spring jam. You can make this with the later, greener, more fibrous rhubarb if you have to, but it won't be half as cute and blushing. The recipe below follows Pam Corbin's lead in using some extra pectin to help the set, but this is optional: if you don't use it, your jam will be slightly looser but still delicious.

Makes: 2 cups/500ml
Ready in: roughly 45 minutes, but you'll need to let it cool before eating
Make-ahead and storage tips: page 331

Vegan

---

14 ounces (400g) young pink rhubarb
1¾ cups (360g) superfine or granulated
   sugar
¾ teaspoon pectin powder or
   2 tablespoons liquid pectin
   (such as Certo), optional
1½ tablespoons lemon juice

(from roughly ½–1 lemon)
1 tablespoon butter *or* margarine
1 teaspoon rose water, or to taste

Special equipment: candy
   thermometer or instant-read digital
   thermometer, optional

1. Start off by trimming the ends of the rhubarb and cutting the stalks into 1¼ inch (3cm) chunks. Combine the rhubarb with the sugar in a large, heavy saucepan. If using pectin powder, stir in it now; if using liquid pectin, wait to add it later. Add the lemon juice to the pan and mix well. Let the fruit macerate in the sugar for 30–60 minutes: during this time, the pink will transform from snowy and dry to stickier and a light blush pink color, as the rhubarb's juices are drawn out.

2. While the fruit sits, prepare your mason jar. Heat the oven to 325°F (160°C). Get out a 2 cup (500ml) preserving or mason jar (if a 1¾ cup/450ml mason jar is the closest you can find, that's fine—you'll just have a couple of spoonfuls of jam leftover to eat on the fly). Fill the jar to the rim with freshly boiled water and leave to sit for 5 minutes. Pour the boiling water over the lid as well. After 5 minutes, drain the jar and its lid and place both upside down in the preheated oven while you get on with the jam-making.

If you don't have a jam or candy thermometer or a digital thermometer, put a small plate in the freezer now so that you can do the crinkle test (described on page 317) to judge when the jam is set.

3. Once the fruit has sat with the sugar for at least 30 minutes, you can start cooking. Set the pan over a low heat. As the fruit warms, it'll release its juices and the sugar will transform from dry and grainy to soupy and molten. Stir occasionally while this happens to prevent the sugar from browning, but do so gently: if you stir too much, the rhubarb will break apart.

4. When the sugar is pretty much entirely molten, add the butter or margarine (this will stop a big head of foam forming on top of the jam when it boils) and, if using, the liquid pectin. Turn the heat up to medium-high and bring the mixture to a rapid boil, so that a constant stream of bubbles sputters across the jam's surface. Once it's boiling, cook the jam for 6–9 minutes, or until it reaches 220°F (105°C). You can test this either with a thermometer or by doing the crinkle test.

5. Let the jam sit for a couple of minutes to settle, then stir in the rose water to taste—some brands are more perfumed than others. The jam may look slightly runny at the moment, but it'll set more as it cools. Decant the jam into the sterilized jar, filling it to within ¼ inch (.5cm) or so of the rim. Put the lid on straightaway and seal tightly.

Variations and substitutions:

Leave out the rose water if you don't like that floral note, or swap for vanilla extract, a vanilla pod (slit along its length and simmered with the fruit and sugar) or a 2-inch (5cm) piece of ginger (peeled and finely grated and added to the saucepan with the rhubarb).

If you want to experiment with other jam flavors, go ahead, but be aware of the different pectin contents of different fruits—it's not always as simple as swapping one for another. At the risk of repeating myself, I really can't recommend *The River Cottage Preserves Handbook* highly enough if you want to learn more, but as a rough guide I'll say this: low-pectin fruits like strawberries will need a little added pectin like in this recipe, the fruit needs to be cut into sensibly sized pieces and you'll need roughly equal weights of fruit and sugar.

For the love of it

SALTED PASSION FRUIT, PINEAPPLE AND COCONUT CURD

Not all cooking projects need to be taxing, hone your technical skills or fill an entire afternoon. This easy, breezy curd recipe is one that even the kids could make, if they wanted to. You just need to blitz some fruit, strain it and cook briefly with sugar and coconut milk. A traditional curd recipe would use eggs, but this is a vegan version with cornstarch to thicken, so no need to worry about scrambling it. So much of the pleasure of this recipe is in the process of making it, with the sunny sweetness of pineapple pulp and passion fruit and the murmur of simmering curd. Put some tunes on the radio and relax into it.

This is ideal in cakes (see the birthday cake suggestions on page 198), with ice cream or granola, in yogurt or on heavily buttered toast.

Makes: 2–2½ cups/500–600ml
Ready in: less than 40 minutes
Make-ahead and storage tips: page 331

Vegan

---

1 x 8 ounce (220g) can pineapple pieces in juice
3 passion fruits
⅔ cup (160ml) full-fat coconut milk
¾ cup (150g) superfine or granulated sugar
3–4 tablespoons lemon juice (from roughly 1½ lemons)
½ teaspoon flaky sea salt or ¼ teaspoon table salt, plus extra to taste
3 tablespoons cornstarch
¼ cup (60g) coconut oil

Special equipment: stick blender, food processor or blender

1. Into a food processor or blender (or using a stick blender if that's what you've got), blitz the pineapple with all its juice until smooth. Strain the pineapple pulp through a sieve into a medium saucepan, stirring it briskly and pressing it against the mesh until as much juice as possible has been squeezed from it. Scoop the fibrous pineapple remains out of the sieve and into the compost bin.

2. Now cut the passion fruits in half and scoop the fleshy, orange, seeded pulp into your sieve. Strain this mixture into the pan with the pineapple juice. Make sure you beat the passion fruit pulp really well, scraping the seeds up against the sieve again and again, until as much juice as possible has been extracted. At this point, you can scoop a couple of teaspoons of the black passion fruit seeds into the saucepan if you want: they look great in the curd, but they're not vital. Discard all remaining seeds.

3. Add the coconut milk, sugar, lemon juice and salt to the saucepan, and mix with the pineapple and passion fruit juice. Set the pan over a medium-low heat and bring to a simmer. While it heats, measure the cornstarch into a small bowl and have it nearby.

4. Once the mixture in the pan is just starting to simmer, spoon a couple of tablespoons of it into the bowl with the cornstarch and mix until you have a smooth, starchy slurry. Add this slurry to the saucepan and stir really well. Keep cooking, stirring constantly now, while the cornstarch gets to work. Within a couple of minutes, you'll notice the curd become custard-like and thick. Turn off the heat and add the coconut oil, beating until glossily smooth. Taste it and add a touch more salt if you think it needs it. Cool in the fridge.

Variations and substitutions:

In place of the coconut oil, you can use ⅓ cup (75g) unsalted butter.

MAKE-AHEAD/FREEZE/STORAGE INSTRUCTIONS

Coconut, plantain and spinach curry with toasted cashews

Store in an airtight container in the fridge for up to 3 days, or in the freezer for up to 3 months. Defrost overnight in the fridge before reheating in the microwave or on the stovetop. To keep the veg at its best, you could alternatively make and freeze just the sauce, then add the plantain and spinach when you reheat it.

Earthy, smoky lentil and beet stew

Store in an airtight container in the fridge for up to 3 days, or in the freezer for up to 3 months. Defrost overnight in the fridge before reheating in the microwave or on the stovetop. You may want to add a splash of water when reheating.

Carrot, lemon and tahini soup

Store in an airtight container in the fridge for up to 3 days, or in the freezer for up to 3 months. Defrost overnight in the fridge before reheating in the microwave or on the stovetop.

Tinolang manok

This will keep in the fridge in an airtight container for up to 3 days. Reheat really well—either on the stovetop or in the microwave—before serving, making sure the chicken is very hot. It can also be frozen: as soon as it's cool, pour into an airtight tub and freeze. It will keep this way for up to 2 months. Defrost overnight in the fridge, then reheat thoroughly within 24 hours of defrosting.

Silky, smoky eggplant stew

Store in an airtight container in the fridge for up to 5 days, or in the freezer for up to 3 months. Defrost overnight in the fridge before reheating in the microwave or on the stovetop.

Red lentil dal with lime

Store in an airtight container in the fridge for up to 5 days. This also freezes really well: store in an airtight container and freeze for up to 3 months. Defrost in the fridge overnight, then reheat in the microwave or on the stovetop, adding a splash more water if necessary, until piping hot.

Tofu and greens with hot and sour chili sauce

This keeps well in the fridge: just put in an airtight container and refrigerate for up to 3 days. It doesn't freeze well.

Spicy soft tofu and mushroom stew

This is best eaten immediately after cooking. To prepare it in advance, make the stew but stop before adding the tofu. Store in an airtight container in the fridge for up to 3 days, or in the freezer for up to 3 months. Defrost overnight in the fridge. Reheat the stew on the stovetop until bubbling, then turn down the heat and add the tofu as described on page 54.

Eden rice with black beans and plantain

The rice and beans can be made in advance and stored in the fridge in airtight containers for up to 3 days. Reheat in the microwave until steaming hot—take particular care with the rice. The plantain is best served fresh.

In-the-oven tomatoes and lima beans in a spiced coconut broth

Store in an airtight container in the fridge for up to 3 days, or in the freezer for up to 1 month. Defrost overnight in the fridge before reheating in the microwave or on the stovetop until piping hot.

Roasted okra, green beans and paneer with green chutney and lime

The veg and paneer can be roasted a day in advance and stored in an airtight container in the fridge, but I'd recommend waiting until just before serving to make the green chutney. This dish doesn't freeze well.

Weeknight tomato and sardine pasta

Once cooked, the sauce can be stored in an airtight container in the fridge for up to 3 days. Cook the pasta separately when you're ready to eat.

Effortless cod in red lentil, tomato and lemongrass broth

To make this ahead of time, cook the lentil broth as described in the recipe, but stop short of adding the fish. This soupy mixture can be cooled in its pan, then covered and stored in the fridge for up to 3 days. When you're ready to finish cooking, add more water until the lentils are soupy rather than thick (they will have absorbed a lot of liquid in storage), then heat in the oven until piping hot. At this point, you can add the fish and proceed according to the recipe.

Roast chicken thighs with spiced cauliflower, cranberries and herbs

This dish will keep in an airtight container in the fridge for up to 2 days, though I find it is best eaten on the same day as making. Either reheat until piping hot in the oven or microwave, or serve cold as a salad.

Summer zucchini with halloumi and mint

Leftovers can be stored in an airtight container in the fridge for up to 3 days, though I find this dish is best eaten on the same day as making.

Mushroom and gochujang udon noodles

The ingredients for the sauce can be stirred together in advance to make assembly quicker when you're ready to eat this dish. Mix and store in an airtight container in the fridge for up to 1 week. I wouldn't recommend cooking the mushrooms or noodles ahead of time. Leftovers can be stored, covered, in the fridge for up to 2 days, but you'll want to add a splash of water as you reheat them.

15-minute cream of tomato soup
Store in an airtight container in the fridge for up to 3 days, or in the freezer for up to 3 months. Defrost overnight in the fridge before reheating it gently in the microwave or on the stovetop, until piping hot but not bubbling.

Potato, caraway and sauerkraut soup
Store in an airtight container in the fridge for up to 3 days, or in the freezer for up to 3 months. Defrost overnight in the fridge before reheating in the microwave or on the stovetop.

Pea green soup
Store in an airtight container in the fridge for up to 3 days, or in the freezer for up to 3 months. Defrost overnight in the fridge before reheating in the microwave or on the stovetop.

Roasted five-spice carrots with brown butter and sesame
Store in an airtight container in the fridge for up to 3 days. It's best not to freeze it.

Bok choy with ginger and clementine
Stored in an airtight container in the fridge for up to 3 days. It's best not to freeze it.

Cloud mash
Store in an airtight container in the fridge for up to 3 days. This reheats particularly well in the microwave. If reheating on the stovetop, add an extra splash of milk.

10-minute zesty lemon and thyme pudding cake
Store in the fridge in an airtight container for up to 3 days. I'd recommend rewarming leftovers in the microwave before eating, as the texture of microwaved cakes can be heavy if they're served cold.

Salted, malted, magic ice cream
This will keep well in a sealed container in the freezer for up to 1 month, but it's at its best within a couple of weeks of making.

Goes-with-everything groundnut soup
Store in an airtight container in the fridge for up to 5 days, or in the freezer for up to 3 months. Defrost overnight in the fridge before reheating in the microwave or on the stovetop until piping hot.

Chili-stewed greens with black-eyed peas
This keeps very well in an airtight container in the fridge for up to 3 days, or in the freezer for up to 3 months. Defrost overnight in the fridge before reheating in the microwave or on the stovetop.

Yaji-spiced celery root with garlic greens and bulgur wheat
The roasted celery root and the greens will keep in an airtight container in the fridge for up to 3 days. The bulgur wheat is best served immediately after cooking.

No-waste whole cauliflower and macaroni cheese

Once assembled, this dish needs to be eaten straightaway, as the pasta absorbs the sauce and becomes gummy when it cools. However, you can prepare the dairy version of the sauce up to 2 days in advance, storing it in an airtight container in the fridge until you're ready to use it. The vegan version of the sauce is best made on the day.

Beets with lentils, halloumi and clementine

This is best served immediately, but can be stored in the fridge in an airtight container for up to 2 days. Serve cool as a salad, or reheat in the microwave or on the stovetop.

Fish sticks with Japanese curry and rice

The curry sauce will keep well in an airtight container in the fridge for up to 5 days. Add a splash of water when reheating. It's always best to cook the fish sticks just before serving.

Homemade curry roux

Store in a sealed container in the fridge for up to 1 month.

Roasted carrots with chickpeas, garlic yogurt and herbs

The carrots and chickpeas can be stored in an airtight container in the fridge for up to 5 days. When you're ready to eat the dish, heat them in the microwave before stirring through the herbs. The garlic yogurt will keep in the fridge for up to 2 days.

Buttered miso linguine with leeks

The leeks can be cooked ahead of time and stored in an airtight container in the fridge for up to 5 days, or the freezer for up to 1 month. Defrost overnight in the fridge before cooking. Warm the leeks in a pan—with a splash of water if needed—before mixing with the pasta and remaining ingredients.

Charred Brussels sprouts with satay and crushed peanuts

The Brussels sprouts are best when fresh from the oven, but can be stored in an airtight container in the fridge for up to 2 days if necessary—they'll start to smell sulfurous after a while though! The satay sauce can be made up in advance. It will keep in an airtight container in the fridge for up to 5 days.

Pea, mint and chili toast with crispy paneer

As you can probably guess, toast isn't something you can make in advance. You can however make the pea mixture ahead of time and store in an airtight container in the fridge for up to 3 days. The crispy paneer can be made up to 24 hours in advance, and stored in a covered tub in the fridge.

Seeded rye cake with demerara crust

This cake will keep well in an airtight container in a cool, dark place for up to 5 days. To freeze, leave the cooked cake to cool completely, then place in a freezer bag or airtight container and freeze for up to 1 month. Defrost overnight at room temperature before serving.

Orange, olive oil and black pepper cake

This cake will keep well in an airtight container in a cool, dark place for up to 5 days. To freeze, leave the cooked cake to cool completely, then place in a freezer bag or airtight container and freeze for up to 1 month. Defrost overnight at room temperature before serving.

Pantry brownies

These will keep well in an airtight container in a cool, dark place for up to 5 days. To freeze, let the cooked brownies cool, then place in a freezer bag or airtight container and freeze for up to 1 month. Defrost overnight at room temperature before serving.

Lemon mochi squares

Store in an airtight container in the fridge for up to 5 days. Allow to warm slightly at room temperature before you eat it. It's best not to freeze these.

Spiced apple pudding with brown sugar crisp

Store in the fridge in an airtight container for up to 3 days. Reheat in the oven until piping hot (the breadcrumb topping will lose its crispness if heated in the microwave).

Creamy mango and ginger pudding pots

This pudding will keep in the fridge for up to 3 days. It doesn't freeze well.

Kimchi and potato hash

The cooked hash can be stored in an airtight container in the fridge for up to 3 days, but I'd recommend removing any egg as that won't store or reheat so well. Reheat in the microwave or in an oven.

Potato latkes

Store in an airtight container in the fridge for up to 2 days, or in the freezer for up to 2 weeks. Reheat—from chilled or frozen—in an oven until crisp.

Green plantain, coconut and chili rösti

Store in an airtight container in the fridge for up to 2 days, or in the freezer for up to 2 weeks. Reheat—from chilled or frozen—in an oven until crisp.

Smoky chicken, okra and chorizo casserole

This will keep, in an airtight container in the fridge for up to 3 days, or in the freezer for up to 3 months. Defrost overnight in the fridge before cooking and reheat in the microwave or on the stovetop—with an extra splash of water if necessary—until piping hot.

Jollof rice

Cool as quickly as possible at room temperature, in a wide, uncovered dish. As soon as it's cool, decant into an airtight container and refrigerate for up to 3 days. Reheat very thoroughly in the microwave, until piping hot throughout.

Harissa, spinach and ricotta cannelloni with toasted hazelnuts

If you're making this for a special occasion and want to save yourself the stress of filling cannelloni when there are guests to entertain, I'd recommend assembling the whole thing beforehand and letting it rest in the fridge until you're ready to bake it. If you do this, make sure your tomato sauce is on the wetter side, because the pasta will absorb some of that liquid as the dish sits. To bake it straight from the fridge, add 10–15 minutes to the baking time given in the recipe. Any leftovers can be stored in an airtight container in the fridge for up to 3 days. Reheat in the oven or the microwave until hot. This dish doesn't freeze well.

Chicken, brown butter and mushroom pie

You can make both the pastry and the filling up to 48 hours in advance, but I find it works best to keep them separate until you're ready to cook and serve the pie. Prepare the filling exactly as per the recipe, then cool and store in the fridge until you're ready to make the pie. Make the pastry, then wrap it up and chill in the fridge. The only thing you may need to do is let the pastry soften for 10–15 minutes at room temperature before rolling it out (it can be difficult to roll when very cold). Leftovers can also be stored, covered, in the fridge, for up to 3 days, but don't freeze very well.

Aligot

Store in the fridge, covered, for up to 3 days. It's easiest to reheat in the microwave, but it can also be done in a pan on the stovetop if you add a splash of water.

Sausage and potato stew with rosemary dumplings

If you have leftovers, I'd recommend storing the stew and dumplings in separate containers—otherwise the dumplings will absorb all the liquid and bloat like nothing you've ever seen. Both can be stored in the fridge for up to 3 days. The stew freezes well in an airtight container for up to 3 months. Defrost in the fridge overnight before heating really well either in the oven or on the stovetop. You'll want to make the dumplings fresh for whenever you reheat the stew.

Cacio e pepe lasagna

Leftovers can be stored in an airtight container in the fridge for up to 3 days, then reheated in the oven or microwave. The lasagna will set firmer once stored and won't be as saucy upon reheating, but it'll still be very good.

Crêpes with mushroom, ricotta and thyme

The crêpes and the mushroom mixture can be made ahead and stored in the fridge for up to 3 days. The crêpes should be wrapped in parchment paper or plastic wrap, whereas the mushrooms should be kept in an airtight container. Once assembled, this dish is best cooked and eaten straight away.

Sour cream vanilla cake

Store in an airtight container in a cool, dark place for up to 5 days. To freeze, let the cooked cake cool, then place in a freezer bag or airtight container and freeze for up to 1 month. Defrost overnight at room temperature before serving.

Marbled chocolate and almond cake

Store in an airtight container in a cool, dark place for up to 5 days. To freeze, let the cooked cake cool, then place in a freezer bag or airtight container and freeze for up to 1 month. Defrost overnight at room temperature before serving.

Molten chocolate, olive oil and rosemary cookie pie

If covered with foil or plastic wrap, the uncooked individual ramekins keep in the fridge for up to 5 days, and freeze really well for up to 1 month. When it's time to bake them, remove the foil or plastic wrap and cook for 14–16 minutes (from chilled) or 17–19 minutes (from frozen).

Salted chocolate chunk cookies, three ways

Store the cookies in an airtight container at room temperature for up to 5 days. You can also freeze the baked cookies in individual freezer bags once cooled for up to 1 month. Defrost at room temperature, then warm in the microwave or oven before serving. To freeze the cookie dough, scoop it onto the baking sheet as instructed above, then put the whole tray in the freezer. Once frozen, transfer the cookie discs to a freezer bag. To bake from frozen, add a couple of minutes to the cooking time.

Peach cobbler with golden cornmeal crust

Store in an airtight container in the fridge for up to 3 days. Reheat in either the oven or the microwave before serving.

Wildflower honey cheesecake

Store in the fridge for up to 3 days, or in the freezer in an airtight container for up to 1 month. Defrost overnight in the fridge, then eat within 24 hours.

Midnight chocolate tart with coconut and sea salt

Store in an airtight container in the fridge for up to 5 days. This can't be frozen.

Galaxy granola

Store in an airtight container in a cool, dark place for up to 1 month.

Cinnamon apple oven pancake

Store in an airtight container in the fridge for 2–3 days. Reheat for a few minutes in the oven or a few seconds in the microwave before serving—the edges won't be crisp if you store and reheat it, but it'll still be good.

Cheesy kimchi cornbread muffins

These are at their best when fresh, but will keep in an airtight container in the fridge for 2–3 days, or in the freezer for up to 1 month. Defrost overnight in the fridge, then reheat in an oven for 5 minutes or so to freshen them up.

Sizzling chipotle tuna fritters

These are at their best when fresh, but can be stored in an airtight container in the fridge for 2–3 days. Reheat in a frying pan to serve.

Herb-packed zucchini farinata

These are at their best when fresh, but can be stored in an airtight container in the fridge for 2–3 days. Reheat in a frying pan to serve.

Lemony green lentil soup

Store in an airtight container in the fridge for up to 5 days, or in the freezer for up to 3 months. Defrost overnight in the fridge before reheating in the microwave or on the stovetop, adding a splash of water if necessary.

Stuffed flatbreads, three ways

Store in an airtight container in the fridge for up to 3 days. Reheat in a frying pan or in the microwave. They don't freeze very well.

Oven fries with shito mayo

Fries have a notoriously short shelf life so are best eaten straightaway. The shito mayo will keep for up to 2 weeks in a sealed container in the fridge though.

(Super)malt loaf

By some kind of weird alchemy, the flavor will be best on the second or third day after you make this. Store in an airtight container at room temperature for up to a week. To freeze, cut into slices then put in a freezer bag or airtight container and freeze for up to 1 month. Defrost at room temperature before toasting.

Puff-puff

If you really don't think you can finish these all in one sitting, hold off from dusting them with confectioners' sugar, let them cool, then store in an airtight container for up to 48 hours. When you're ready to eat them, warm them for 4–5 minutes in the oven and then dust with the sugar. They won't be quite the same, but they're still a class above pretty much any store-bought cookie if you're in need of an easy snack.

Fruit jumble crumble bars

These keep well in an airtight container in the fridge for up to 3 days. (You can store them for a couple of days at room temperature if you have to, but the base will become soggy over time.)

Peanut cookie dough bites

These will keep in an airtight container in the fridge for about a week (not that they'll go uneaten for that long), or in the freezer for up to 2 months if you want to make a big batch to dip into whenever you fancy. Defrost in the fridge before eating.

Salted honeyscotch sauce

This will keep well in a jar or an airtight container in the fridge for up to 2 weeks. It isn't freezable.

Fiery ginger cordial

The undiluted cordial will keep in a jar or an airtight container in the fridge for a week, or in the freezer for up to 3 months. If freezing, leave a couple of centimeters empty at the top of the jar to allow the liquid room to expand.

Jewel salad

If you make this ahead, I'd recommend storing the veg and the dressing in separate airtight containers in the fridge until you're ready to eat (if you mix them too soon, the salad will become watery as the salt in the dressing draws out the water in the veg). Both will keep for up to 2 days. This isn't freezable.

Basil and egusi pesto

Store in a jar in the fridge for up to 5 days, or in the freezer for up to 1 month. Defrost it in the fridge overnight before mixing it with pasta or cooking with it.

Twaróg

Store your finished cheese in an airtight container in the fridge—it will keep well for 2–3 days. I wouldn't recommend freezing it.

Pierogi ruskie

These only keep for a maximum of 8 hours or so in the fridge before the dough begins to suffer, so freeze them if you want to make them in advance—they'll keep for up to 2 months. To freeze the prepared, but uncooked, pierogi, set them well apart on a couple of lightly floured baking sheets. Put in the freezer like this until completely frozen—it should take 2–3 hours. Once frozen, you can take them off the baking sheet and transfer to an airtight container, which will take up less space. To cook the pierogi from frozen, boil in lots of well salted water. (It's important to use a lot of water so that the water temperature doesn't drop too much when you add the frozen dumplings. Cook them in batches if you must.) Once the first pierogi rises to the surface of the water, continue to boil for 4–5 minutes, or until all pierogi are risen and piping hot throughout. You can also finish the pierogi off in the frying pan as outlined on page 281.

Sauerkraut, potato and black pepper pierogi filling

You can store the prepared filling mixture in an airtight container in the fridge for up to 3 days before using it to make the pierogi. Once the pierogi make been made, you can freeze them following the instructions above for the pierogi ruskie.

Hearty lentil ragù

Once cooled, this'll keep in a sealed container in the fridge for 3–4 days, or in the freezer for up to 3 months. Defrost overnight in the fridge before reheating on the stovetop or in the microwave.

Slow-simmered herby lima beans

Store in an airtight container in the fridge for up to 5 days. Reheat on the stovetop or in the microwave until piping hot, adding a splash of water if necessary.

Pickled watermelon rind

This will keep in an airtight container for 2 weeks in the fridge.

Dill-pickled cherry tomatoes

Store in the fridge for up to a week. Because these tomatoes are only vinegar-pickled—and because the jar isn't sterilized—these aren't suitable for storing for longer periods or at room temperature.

Roti canai

Store in an airtight container at room temperature for up to 2 days. To reheat them, just blast them in the microwave or in a frying pan.

Rosemary baby buns

Store in an airtight container in a cool, dry place for a couple of days, but I'd recommend giving them a few minutes in the oven to refresh them before you eat. They can be frozen too: separate the buns, then store in sealed freezer bags for up to 1 month. Defrost overnight at room temperature and warm in the oven to serve.

Pretzel sandwich loaf

This loaf will keep in a bread bin or airtight container at room temperature for 2 days, or in the freezer for up to 1 month. If you want to freeze this, slice the bread first, then place in a sealed freezer bag. Defrost at room temperature in its freezer bag.

Franzbrötchen

To prepare these in advance, shape the dough into your pastry of choice, arrange on a baking sheet lined with parchment paper and then freeze immediately. Once frozen, transfer the pastries to a freezer bag or an airtight container for up to 1 month. Let rise (and defrost) overnight at room temperature, or for 4–5 hours in a slightly warmer room. Glaze and bake them as instructed once they're nearly doubled in size. Once your pastries have been baked and cooled, they'll keep well in an airtight container for 2–3 days, but benefit from being revived for 5 minutes in the oven before eating.

Fried apple pie bites

Because they're fried until very crisp, these will keep well in an airtight container at room temperature for a day, or in the fridge for 2–3 days. Reheat them in the oven at 350°F (180°C) for a few minutes to refresh them.

Turon

Because they're fried until very crisp, these will keep well in an airtight container at room temperature for a day, or in the fridge for 2–3 days. Reheat them in the oven at 350°F (180°C) for a few minutes to refresh them.

Nkate brittle, cardamom and salted milk ice cream

This will keep well in a sealed container in the freezer for up to 3 months, though it's always at its best when fresh.

Rosy rhubarb jam

This will keep for about a year if unopened and stored in a cool, dry place—it will sit so pretty on your cupboard shelves. Once opened, it'll need to be refrigerated and consumed within a month or so.

Salted passion fruit, pineapple and coconut curd

Because this curd has coconut milk in it and isn't quite as acidic as a lemon curd, I wouldn't jar it and keep it in the cupboard long term. Instead, spoon it into a couple of scrupulously clean Mason jars and store in the fridge: it'll be good for a couple of weeks. I don't think you'll have much trouble getting through it.

REFERENCE CHARTS

You'll notice that vegetarian and vegan recipes are clearly signposted throughout this book: just check out the key at the start of each recipe. For any other dietary requirements, accessibility needs or time or money constraints, these reference charts should help to guide you towards the recipes that will work for you.

These recipes involve less chopping and hands-on prep, making them useful if you have reduced mobility or energy. Check out the tips on page 5 as well as the variations and substitutions after the recipe itself to help you adapt these recipes if needed.

Low-prep

- **16** Pearl couscous with anchovies, tomatoes and olives
- **25** Carrot, lemon and tahini soup
- **27** Pasta with sauerkraut, caramelized onions and sour cream
- **29** Meatballs with basil, cream and mustard
- **35** Soba noodles with fermented black soybeans and broccoli
- **40** Zucchini pearl barley bowls with sour cream and dill
- **45** Back-of-the-net pasta
- **55** Gnocchi with harissa butter and broccoli
- **66** In-the-oven tomatoes and lima beans in a spiced coconut broth
- **68** Gnocchi with chili crisp sauce, capers and Parmesan
- **73** Weeknight tomato and sardine pasta
- **74** Roasting-pan orzo with broccoli and mozzarella
- **78** Effortless cod in red lentil, tomato and lemongrass broth

- **87** Mushroom and gochujang udon noodles
- **89** 15-minute cream of tomato soup
- **91** Potato, caraway and sauerkraut soup
- **92** Pea green soup
- **97** Cloud mash
- **102** Salted, malted, magic ice cream
- **110** One-pan smashed potatoes with lemony sardines and pesto
- **112** Goes-with-everything groundnut soup
- **117** Chili-stewed greens with black-eyed peas
- **126** Beets with lentils, halloumi and clementine
- **134** Buttered miso linguine with leeks
- **136** Baked semolina with mushroom and mozzarella
- **138** Whatever-you've-got fried rice
- **145** Pea, mint and chili toast with crispy paneer
- **151** Pantry brownies
- **154** Spiced apple pudding with brown sugar crisp

- **157** Creamy mango and ginger pudding pots
- **205** Molten chocolate, olive oil and rosemary cookie pie
- **206** Salted chocolate chunk cookies, three ways
- **208** Peach cobbler with golden cornmeal crust
- **211** Wildflower honey cheesecake
- **220** Galaxy granola
- **222** Cinnamon apple oven pancake
- **238** Kelewele
- **243** Yorkshire puddings for every occasion
- **247** Green apple salad with toasted seeds
- **249** (Super)malt loaf
- **260** Clementine hot chocolate
- **286** Slow-simmered herby lima beans
- **289** Dill-pickled cherry tomatoes
- **301** Pretzel sandwich loaf
- **320** Salted passion fruit, pineapple and coconut curd

These recipes can be made in less than 30 minutes. The timings I've given here are generous—including all the measuring and chopping, bringing cooking water to a boil and preheating the oven—so you may find recipes much faster than described if you do prep and organize beforehand.

Super speedy

- **16** Pearl couscous with anchovies, tomatoes and olives
- **27** Pasta with sauerkraut, caramelized onions and sour cream
- **33** Crisp brown butter lima beans with garlic yogurt and spiced tomato sauce
- **35** Soba noodles with fermented black soybeans and broccoli
- **45** Back-of-the-net pasta
- **55** Gnocchi with harissa butter and broccoli
- **68** Gnocchi with chili crisp sauce, capers and Parmesan
- **73** Weeknight tomato and sardine pasta

- **85** Lightning-quick asparagus and chili linguine
- **87** Mushroom and gochujang udon noodles
- **89** 15-minute cream of tomato soup
- **92** Pea green soup
- **95** Bok choy with ginger and clementine
- **97** Cloud mash
- **99** 10-minute zesty lemon and thyme pudding cake
- **116** Omo tuo
- **126** Beets with lentils, halloumi and clementine
- **138** Whatever-you've-got fried rice

- **145** Pea, mint and chili toast with crispy paneer
- **173** Watermelon with peanuts, sumac and lime
- **206** Salted chocolate chunk cookies, three ways
- **226** Sizzling chipotle tuna fritters
- **247** Green apple salad with toasted seeds
- **257** Peanut cookie dough bites
- **259** Salted honeyscotch sauce
- **260** Clementine hot chocolate
- **271** Basil and egusi pesto

These recipes involve a little prep and then plenty of hands-off time while the food roasts, chills or freezes, ideal for if you need to multitask. Many of them are roasting-pan dinners or no-fuss bakes.

Hands-off

- **55** Gnocchi with harissa butter and broccoli
- **66** In-the-oven tomatoes and lima beans in a spiced coconut broth
- **71** Roasted okra, green beans and paneer with green chutney and lime
- **74** Roasting-pan orzo with broccoli and mozzarella
- **78** Effortless cod in red lentil, tomato and lemongrass broth
- **80** Roast chicken thighs with spiced cauliflower, cranberries and herbs
- **82** Summer zucchini with halloumi and mint
- **91** Potato, caraway and sauerkraut soup
- **94** Roasted five-spice carrots with brown butter and sesame

- **102** Salted, malted, magic ice cream
- **110** One-pan smashed potatoes with lemony sardines and pesto
- **136** Baked semolina with mushroom and mozzarella
- **147** Seeded rye cake with demerara crust
- **149** Orange, olive oil and black pepper cake
- **151** Pantry brownies
- **153** Lemon mochi squares
- **154** Spiced apple pudding with brown sugar crisp
- **157** Creamy mango and ginger pudding pots
- **200** Sour cream vanilla cake
- **203** Marbled chocolate and almond cake
- **208** Peach cobbler with golden cornmeal crust

- **211** Wildflower honey cheesecake
- **213** Midnight chocolate tart with coconut and sea salt
- **243** Yorkshire puddings for every occasion
- **245** Oven fries with shito mayo
- **249** (Super)malt loaf
- **273** Twaróg
- **283** Hearty lentil ragù
- **286** Slow-simmered herby lima beans
- **287** Pickled watermelon rind
- **289** Dill-pickled cherry tomatoes
- **296** Rosemary baby buns
- **301** Pretzel sandwich loaf

These recipes rely on pantry and freezer staples and keep more expensive ingredients—including meat, fish, alcohol, nuts, fresh herbs and specialty produce—to a minimum. Prices can vary depending on where you live and which stores you use, however, so this list isn't definitive.

Cheaper

20 Earthy, smoky lentil and beet stew

25 Carrot, lemon and tahini soup

27 Pasta with sauerkraut, caramelized onions and sour cream

30 Tinolang manok

33 Crisp brown butter lima beans with garlic yogurt and spiced tomato sauce

41 Silky, smoky eggplant stew

43 Red lentil dal with lime

49 Tofu and greens with hot and sour chili sauce

58 Eden rice with black beans and plantain

66 In-the-oven tomatoes and lima beans in a spiced coconut broth

73 Weeknight tomato and sardine pasta

74 Roasting-pan orzo with broccoli and mozzarella

87 Mushroom and gochujang udon noodles

89 15-minute cream of tomato soup

91 Potato, caraway and sauerkraut soup

92 Pea green soup

94 Roasted five-spice carrots with brown butter and sesame

97 Cloud mash

102 Salted, malted, magic ice cream

110 One-pan smashed potatoes with lemony sardines and pesto

112 Goes-with-everything groundnut soup

116 Omo tuo

117 Chili-stewed greens with black-eyed peas

120 Yaji-spiced celery root with garlic greens and bulgur wheat

128 Fish sticks with Japanese curry and rice

134 Buttered miso linguine with leeks

136 Baked semolina with mushroom and mozzarella

138 Whatever-you've-got fried rice

141 Charred Brussels sprouts with satay and crushed peanuts

151 Pantry brownies

154 Spiced apple pudding with brown sugar crisp

157 Creamy mango and ginger pudding pots

167 Potato latkes

169 Green plantain, coconut and chili rösti

178 Jollof rice

188 Aligot

190 Sausage and potato stew with rosemary dumplings

208 Peach cobbler with golden cornmeal crust

222 Cinnamon apple oven pancake

226 Sizzling chipotle tuna fritters

228 Herb-packed zucchini farinata

230 Lemony green lentil soup

231 Stuffed flatbreads, three ways

238 Kelewele

243 Yorkshire puddings for every occasion

245 Oven fries with shito mayo

249 (Super)malt loaf

252 Puff-puff

260 Clementine hot chocolate

262 Fiery ginger cordial

286 Slow-simmered herby lima beans

287 Pickled watermelon rind

290 Roti canai

301 Pretzel sandwich loaf

ACKNOWLEDGMENTS

Like any cookbook, this has been a team effort from the start. I've been joined in the kitchen by cooks from many times and places, whether through YouTube, in the pages of books or sent direct to my phone in a frantic stream of WhatsApp messages. Every author, chef, blogger, vlogger, family member and friend referenced in these recipes has had a vital hand in the creation of this book, not to mention the many people whose normal daily cooking has slowly but surely forged the food cultures that I now live in and take inspiration from. Thank you all.

A few more specific words of gratitude: to Kaila Stone, for testing these recipes with so much care and generosity, and for bringing punk to the often staid world of cookbooks; and to Odhran O'Donoghue, for casting an eagle eye over this text and lovingly copyediting it into shape. Thank you to my editor, Cecily Gayford, for your unwavering trust. I owe so much to the entire team at Serpent's Tail for bringing this book into the world, and to Clare Sayer, Tasha Onwuemezi and Christine Bell for fine-tuning its message. Thanks also to Molly Friedrich, Hannah Brattesani and Stuart Cooper for having faith in this project. Thanks to Marin Toscano for helping to accurately and sensitively contextualize these recipes. A huge and heartfelt thank you to Tom Pold, Rita Madrigal, Lorraine Hyland, Amy Hagedorn, Morgan Fenton and Linda Huang for your care and dedication in publishing *Cook As You Are* in the United States. Kendra McKnight expertly translated the recipes here from British to American conventions—thank you so much for your eye for detail.

This book wouldn't exist if not for the vision, skill and patience of Evelin Kasikov, whose designs make these recipes a dream to follow. And I am always grateful for, and in awe of, the skill of Sinae Park, whose beautiful illustrations are at the spiritual heart of this book.

Thank you to my friends and family who have dutifully tested these recipes, given their advice or just provided a haven where I can bitch freely.

INDEX